TIME

A N N U A L

The Year in Review 1996

TIME
ANNUAL
1996
The Year in Review
By the Editors of TIME

TIME ANNUAL 1996

**DOWN UNDER: Olympic
swimmer Allison Wagner**

TIME ANNUAL 1996

EDITOR
Edward L. Jamieson

MANAGING EDITOR
Kelly Knauer

ART DIRECTOR
Gigi Fava

RESEARCH DIRECTOR
Leah Shanks Gordon

PICTURE EDITOR
Rose Quinn Keyser

PRODUCTION EDITOR
Michael Skinner

ASSOCIATE ART DIRECTOR
Sumo

RESEARCH ASSOCIATE
Anne Hopkins

COPY EDITORS
Bob Braine, Bruce Christopher Carr,
Ellin Martens, Peter McGullam

TIME INC. HOME ENTERTAINMENT

MANAGING DIRECTOR
David Gitow

DIRECTOR, CONTINUITY
David Arfine

**DIRECTOR,
NEW BUSINESS DEVELOPMENT**
Stuart Hotchkiss

FULFILLMENT MANAGER
Michelle Gudema

PRODUCT MANAGERS
Robert Fox, Michael Holahan, Jennifer McLyman,
John Sandklev, Alicia Wilcox

EDITORIAL OPERATIONS MANAGER
John Calvano

PRODUCTION MANAGER
Donna Miano-Ferrara

ASSISTANT PRODUCTION MANAGER
Jessica McGrath

PRODUCTION CONSULTANT
Joseph Napolitano

FINANCIAL MANAGER
Tricia Griffin

ASSISTANT FINANCIAL MANAGER
Heather Lynds

ASSOCIATE PRODUCT MANAGERS
Ken Katzman, Daniel Melore, Allison Weiss, Dawn Weland

ASSISTANT PRODUCT MANAGERS
Alyse Daberko, Charlotte Siddiqui

MARKETING ASSISTANT
Lyndsay Jenks

THE WORK OF THE FOLLOWING TIME STAFFERS AND CONTRIBUTORS IS INCLUDED IN THIS VOLUME:

Charles P. Alexander, Edward Barnes, Ginia Bellafante, Lisa Beyer, Massimo Calabresi, Margaret Carlson, George Church, James Collins, Richard Corliss, Howard Chua-Eoan, Sally B. Donnelly, Martha Duffy, Michael Duffy, Philip Elmer-DeWitt, Christopher John Farley, Kevin Fedarko, Nancy Gibbs, Elizabeth Gleick, Christine Gorman, Paul Gray, John Greenwald, Robert Hughes, Leon Jaroff, Daniel Kadlec, Michael Kramer, Michael Krantz, Richard Lacayo, Elaine Lafferty, Erik Larson, Michael Lemonick, Johanna McGeary, Lance Morrow, Bruce W. Nelan, Christopher Ogden, Karsten Prager, Andrew Purvis, Paul Quinn-Judge, Joshua Quittner, Joshua Cooper Ramo, Roger Rosenblatt, Richard Schickel, Michael S. Serrill, Walter Shapiro, John Skow, Jill Smolowe, Anthony Spaeth, Richard Stengel, Karen Tumulty, David Van Biema, James Walsh, Jack E. White, Steve Wulf, Richard Zoglin

SPECIAL THANKS TO:

Ames Adamson, Louella Armstrong, Ken Baierlein, Robin Bierstedt, Susan L. Blair, Andrew Blau, Wayne Chun, Jay Colton, Anne Considine, Richard Duncan, Osmar Escalona, Linda Freeman, Arthur Hochstein, Raphael Joa, Nancy Krauter, Morgan Krug, Charles Lampach, Joe Lertola, Robyn Mathews, Peter Meirs, John Meyer, Gail Music, Amy Musher, Rudi Papiri, Mary Pradt, Sue Raffety, Edel Rodriguez, Anthony Ross, Barrett Seaman, Michael Sheehan, Kenneth B. Smith, Robert Stephens, Michele Stephenson, Cornelus Verwaal, Carol A. Weil, Miriam Winocur, Carrie A. Zimmerman. Additional thanks to the TIME Imaging staff.

IN A YEAR OF RELATIVE PEACE AND PROSPERITY, THE REAL

surprises in the news came not from much anticipated

THE YEAR IN

REVIEW '96

events like the Olympics and the presidential campaign, but

from stories that carried the shock of the unexpected: the

nabbing of the Unabomber; the downing of TWA Flight 800;

sudden death on Mount Everest; indications of life on Mars.

THE POIGNANCY OF A CANDIDATE'S SMILE SET against the festive transience of confetti. A shard from a shattered jetliner transformed into a floating sculpture. As this gallery of pictures from 1996 shows, a photojournalist's work is both document and art.

IMAGES

ATLANTA

Michael Johnson after winning the 400 meters. He also took the 200—the first man in Olympic history to win both

SAN DIEGO

Former Senator Bob Dole accepts his party's nomination at the Republican National Convention

EAST MORICHES, NEW YORK

A wing section of TWA Flight 800 floats
in the Atlantic Ocean a day after the
Paris-bound plane exploded, killing 230

CALVERTON, NEW YORK

Wreckage from Flight 800 awaiting
reconstruction for investigators
in a hangar on Long Island

MOSCOW

Russian President Boris Yeltsin with his bypass-surgery team in November. Above, earlier campaign hijinks

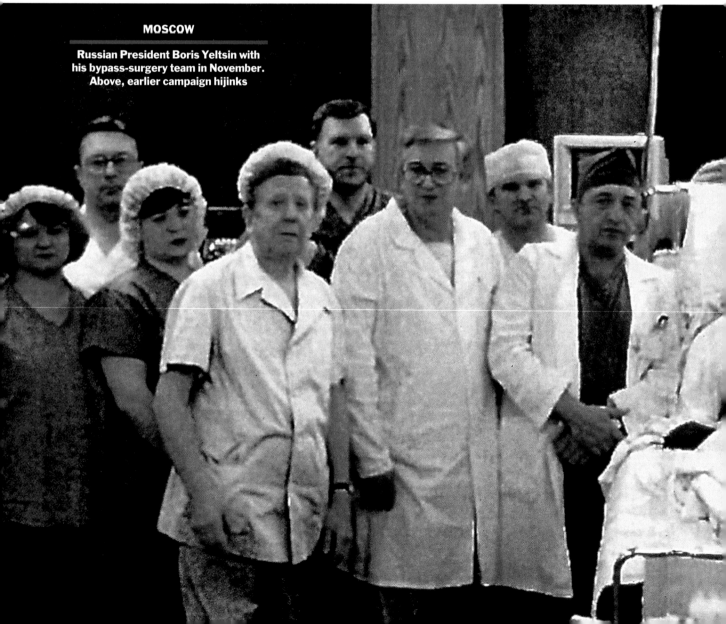

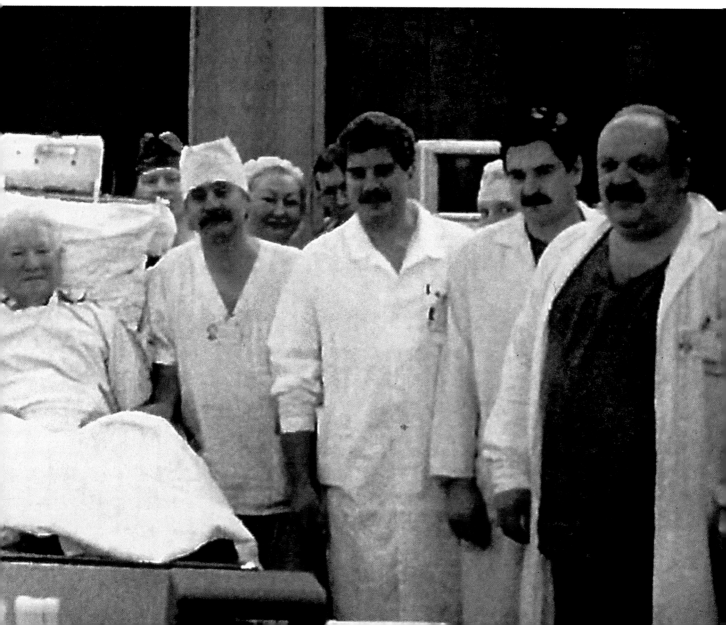

GROZNY, CHECHNYA

The body of a Russian soldier
smolders, as a Chechen freedom
fighter prepares to toss a grenade

GRBAVICA, BOSNIA

A resident of this Sarajevo suburb attempts—without success— to douse a fire lit by departing Serbs

CHICAGO

Workers apply finishing touches to a mural of Michael Jordan, shortly before his Chicago Bulls won the N.B.A. title

BROOKFIELD, ILLINOIS

Binti-Jua, clutching her own baby, rescues a human toddler who fell into the Brookfield Zoo's gorilla pit

KABUL, AFGHANISTAN

A woman mourns at the grave of her
brother, the victim of a rocket attack in
a nation still devastated by civil war

NETANYAHU & ARAFAT
As a fractious peace exploded into war,
the two leaders came under fire

GEOFFREY THE GIRAFFE
Say it ain't so, Geoff—Toys "R" Us
nabbed for restraint of trade!

JOHN & CAROLINE KENNEDY
"Don't let it be forgot, we really got
a lot … for selling Camelot"

MADONNA
She heard the ticking of the biological
clock, and unto her a child was born

MARTIAN LIFE-FORMS
The possibility of alien life stole the
spotlight from the G.O.P. convention

PRINCESS DIANA
Her Royal Di-ness gave up the initials
H.R.H. to go her separate way

FIDEL CASTRO
He gave up 1995's charm offensive
when he shot down American planes

HILLARY CLINTON & FRIEND
She 'fessed up to holding imaginary
conversations with role-model Eleanor

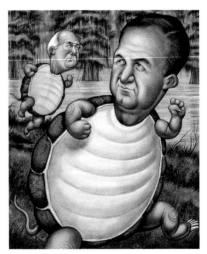

BUCHANAN & GRAMM
In the slo-mo G.O.P. primary field,
Pat's posturing beat Phil's funds

DWIGHT GOODEN
The onetime drug abuser changed his stripes—and pitched a no-hitter

TIGER WOODS
Forsaking amateurism, he won big Nike bucks—and big pro tournaments

JOHN MAJOR & MAD COW
Where's the beef? Not on European plates—and John Bull was bellowing

O.J. SIMPSON
Just when you thought it was safe to watch your TV again—he's back!

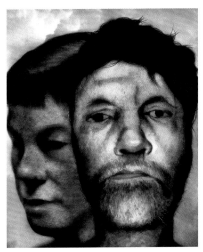

DAVID & TED KACZYNSKI
In a story as old as the Bible, David played his brother's keeper

SHANNON LUCID
After spending a U.S. record 188 days in space, she had gravitas aplenty

MARGE SCHOTT
The ornery Reds owner was in the doghouse again for praising Hitler

BOUTROS BOUTROS-GHALI
A U.S. veto walled off a second term for the U.N. sphinx-in-chief

MOBUTU SESE SEKO
Move over, Nero—he was convalescing on the Riviera while Zaïre burned

"God will destroy America at the hands of the Muslims."
-*The* REV. LOUIS FARRAKHAN, *during a visit to Iran*

"Everybody knows he was good at the beginning, but he just went too far."
-*Cincinnati Reds owner* MARGE SCHOTT, *on Adolf Hitler*

"I went home and bit her."
-*Democrat* JAMES CARVILLE, *on being called a "rabid dog" by his Republican wife Mary Matalin*

"They took all of my Tupperware."
-BARBARA JEWELL, *mother of the cleared Atlanta bombing suspect Richard Jewell, on the FBI search*

"Can you imagine me with a woman old enough to be my wife? ... My girlfriend is 25 years old—perfect."
-TONY CURTIS, 70, *in* GQ *magazine*

"Had Christ died in my van with people around him who loved him, it would be far more dignified."
-JACK KEVORKIAN

"Yes, I was married to a seducer. I had to make do."
-DANIELLE MITTERRAND, *widow of the French President, whose mistress prominently attended his funeral*

"You're toast"
-TED TURNER, *to his son when asked if the younger Turner's job would be safe after the Time Warner merger with Turner Broadcasting*

"I don't want to go around shaking hands and having babies pee on me."
-BARBRA STREISAND, *on why she has no plans to run for political office*

"All the dogs hated him."

-A RESIDENT *of Lincoln, Montana, on alleged Unabomber Ted Kaczynski*

"Obviously, we don't want it to smell like sweat."
-A SPOKESMAN *for Michael Jordan's new cologne*

"We can wear flat shoes now and be fat."
-*Flight attendant* ANN BARBOUR, *on improvements in United Airlines' working conditions*

"What's a disco?"

-THE DALAI LAMA, *on being told the Chinese were building a dance hall beneath the Potala Palace in Tibet*

"It's like trying to teach a dog to be a vegetarian."

-*Reform candidate* DICK LAMM, *on the ability of Republicans and Democrats to reform themselves*

"I need some security."
-*Former* PRESIDENT NAJIBULLAH *of Afghanistan, just before being captured and executed by Muslim rebels*

"But two Huangs don't make a right."

-*Clinton spokesman* MIKE McCURRY, *on two different John Huangs who often visited the White House*

"The Monster... The Twister... Stumpy."
-*Political adviser* DICK MORRIS's *terms for Bill Clinton, Hillary Clinton and George Stephanopoulos, according to call girl* SHERRY ROWLANDS

"I must say we're hoping that we have another child."
-HILLARY RODHAM CLINTON, *in an interview with* TIME

"You know, if I were a single man, I might ask that mummy out. That's a good-looking mummy!"

-PRESIDENT CLINTON, *on the frozen 500-year-old Inca "ice princess" on display at the National Geographic Society in Washington*

"All he has to do is not drool on himself, and he wins."
-KEVIN L. GEDDINGS, *media consultant to 93-year-old Strom Thurmond's opponent in the South Carolina senatorial election*

"In high school she dated Bob Dole."

-SENATOR JOSEPH LIEBERMAN, *in response*

SECOND WIND

Bill Clinton wins another term with a commanding victory over Bob Dole. But is the center he holds truly vital?

THE VOTE 96

IT WAS A STRANGELY SERENE AND businesslike display of exultation. Shortly after midnight in Little Rock, Arkansas, having achieved what had always seemed inevitable, William Jefferson Clinton stood in the glow of his happy hometown crowd as only the seventh Democratic President ever to be elected to a second term, and the first since FDR in 1936. "My fellow Americans," he began, "we have work to do, and that's what this election is all about." He must have used the word *work*

two dozen times in his short speech, which he concluded with, "Tomorrow we greet the dawn and begin our work anew"—as if six long months of a nation's listening to Bob Dole's gothic baritone and Clinton's pleading lilt had been a sideshow ending in one brief act of citizenship. Now the President and the people could return to the course they had agreed upon.

But what course had they agreed upon? By conventional standards, Clinton had won a sweeping victory over his Republican opponent and Reform Party candidate Ross Perot. The President just missed a cherished goal of topping 50% of the vote; he finished with 49% to Dole's 41% and Perot's 8%. And in the more telling electoral count, his victory loomed even larger: he accumulated 379 votes to Dole's 159. Perot took none.

On a map of America, Dole's states cut a north-south swatch through the thinly-populated Rocky Mountain West and then across Texas and into the South. But Clinton took everything else: the Northeast and the Midwest (except for Indiana), the far West, even the once-safe Republican bastion of Florida. His victory had been expected, but, even so, it did not feel as powerful as the statistics showed it to be.

WHY? FOR STARTERS, THE PUBLIC, playing it safe, returned the Republicans to power in both houses of Congress. The G.O.P. picked up two seats in the Senate, where such veteran Democrats as Bill Bradley, Sam Nunn and Howell Heflin retired. And though the Republicans' advantage in the House dropped from 38 seats to 20, Speaker Newt Gingrich would still be in command. With the conservative new Majority Leader Trent Lott of Mississippi running the Senate, Gingrich bossing the House and Clinton in the White House, the public had come solidly down in favor not of work, as Clinton had hoped, but of gridlock.

And that is why the election of 1996 had less whoop and holler than it might have had. The electorate had become a bit like Sherlock Holmes' dog in the nighttime: the dog did not stir because it knew its master. Not that people did not care about the election; they knew what was coming because they themselves had ordered it up. They felt that the country was doing well enough, and understood at the same time that the government they were about to put in place was unlikely to have much to do with their lives. Tellingly, the voter

GOOD SPORT
Bob Dole ran a clean race, but congressional Republicans had a nasty streak that hurt them

turnout was the lowest ever: a mere 49% of the electorate went to the polls.

Of course, the candidates had been railing against Big Government all along, so they ought not to have been crestfallen when the electorate believed them. Those who embodied Big Government had successfully argued themselves into a state of semi-irrelevance, with Clinton coming out on top because he was already on top, because his opponent's campaign had been a disaster—but mainly because the President had become that mold of moderation toward which the people had been edging for 25 years.

TAXING PATIENCE
Dole's proposed 15% tax cut failed to ignite the support he expected

Both parties had been railing against the perils of BIG GOVERNMENT all along, so they ought not to have been crestfallen when the electorate believed them

cans wanted no part of; Gingrich was no longer amusing as Newt the Menace, and was now seen as the Bad Seed; and the voters, who had not encountered a real vision since the days of Ronald Reagan, evidently did not think that one was needed now.

Clinton's campaign focus on such small-change matters as school uniforms, curfews and V chips was a tactic of genius. He could be appealing as the nation's ward healer, while decrying the presence of deep ills that no one felt a national leader could fix anyway. So an election that seemed spiritless in fact demonstrated positive satisfaction in the achievement of a clear, if unimaginative, centrism that most people had long desired: fewer guns, tougher laws, lower crime, higher culture, cleaner air, freer trade, better teaching, less deficit, less welfare and abortion rights unchanged. Naturally, one also wanted expressions of concern about affirmative action, entitlements and foreign policy, but if Clinton chose to express-and-dodge, that was all right. Most people did not know what they felt about such things either.

All that is what Clinton meant by the "vital American center." When it came down to it, people could settle specific issues or scores by addressing local propositions, as they did in California on affirmative action, deciding to curtail it severely. As for sending a message to Washington, Election Day was a bon voyage party without champagne: do everything you can about the poor, but don't give away the store. And have a nice day.

A new party system may be awaiting the Age of Somebody a few years from now, someone who may be so appealingly revolutionary as to make the election of 1996 in retrospect seem blindingly quiescent. But 1996 marked the Age of Popular Demand, because that—more than one man's malleability—is what has shaped national government. The country got the election it sought, befitting a people who are by conviction liberal, by impulse conservative. It got the President it sought as well—a reflection of the attitudes of the majority and yet as removed from the people as they are from him. It was a curious time: the people had created the government in their image, which is the way it is supposed to work, and then they waved goodbye.

On the morning of November 6, the newly elected President and Congress awoke and listened for the joyful noise of their country, which, resting its head on its paws, made not a sound. ∎

If the country did not get excited about the election, it was because it recognized the philosophy that stood before it. "Tonight," Clinton said in his victory speech, "we proclaim that the vital American center is alive and well."

Odd that the same voters who had scorned George Bush four years earlier for his lack of vision did not mind that the man they had chosen in Bush's place now seemed to have lowered his sights to the work of minding America's store. But a lot had happened since 1992: the Republicans in Congress had shown a nasty streak about Medicare and Medicaid that most Ameri-

HOW HE GOT THERE

Bill Clinton cleverly shed his skin—and got under Bob Dole's—to win a second term as President

THE VOTE '96

BILL CLINTON'S IMPRESSIVE ELECTION VICTORY OVER Republican Bob Dole made it difficult to recall just how far behind the Comeback Kid had started in his final campaign. Only 11 months before, in January of 1996 as G.O.P. candidates stumped Iowa and New Hampshire in the first presidential primaries, Clinton had seemed likely to join the ranks of one-term Presidents. He was an object of derision, a chubby, drawling, indecisive figure of fun. He was still the President of Lani Guinier and Whitewater and gays in the military.

In the *Doonesbury* comic strip, he was drawn as a free-floating waffle.

In fact, Clinton had already set in place the single policy that was ultimately to prove most responsible for his re-election— the 1993 deficit-reduction measures. These had gained his infant Administration credibility with the financial markets, which in turn helped keep America's economy purring throughout his first term. But the failure of his elaborate effort to reform the nation's health-care system had enabled the G.O.P. to portray him as a classic liberal in the 1994 mid-term elections and thus recapture Congress.

By April of 1995 the President seemed so marginalized that he was forced to defend his relevance. In the early days of 1996 House majority leader Newt Gingrich was the most powerful political force in the

THERE HE GOES AGAIN
Victorious veep Al Gore is ready to run in 2000

country; TIME had named him Man of the Year for 1995. Yet Clinton would rebound to trounce the Republicans, his success due in equal parts to his own nimble political adaptability and to the failings of Bob Dole.

The 73-year-old Dole, the Senate majority leader and a World War II veteran, had wanted to be President ever since he ran on the G.O.P. ticket with Gerald Ford in 1976. He tried hard in 1980 but lost to Ronald Reagan, tried harder in 1988 but lost to George Bush. Yet after the Republicans recaptured the House and Senate in the 1994 elections, and Dole became the Senate G.O.P. leader—back at the "center of the action," as he described it— he announced in April 1995 that he would seek the White House once again. His way became clearer when the popular former Chairman of the

KICKING DOLE'S BUTT
After Dole's tobacco gaffe, Democrats sent Mr. Butt Man to haunt him

Deadened to the siren call of quick fixes, voters became less enamored of Bob Dole's TAX CUT PLAN the more he publicized it

Joint Chiefs of Staff, retired General Colin Powell, announced late in 1995 that he would not seek the Republican nomination. After assiduously courting Gingrich, Dole secured the Speaker's promise that he too would not seek the presidency. "Two down and one to go," said Dole, thinking ahead to Clinton.

With Powell and Gingrich out of the race, no one emerged from the Republican field of challengers with the stature or momentum to stop Dole—even as the Kansan's flaws were highlighted in late January, when he offered a rambling, unconvincing G.O.P. response to Clinton's State of the Union address, in which Clinton tacked right by declaring that the "era of Big Government is over." Dole's uninspired turn alarmed Republican leaders. Yet it was already too late for a new candidate to emerge—the filing deadlines for the primaries had passed—so a roiled G.O.P. electorate turned to the existing, mediocre field for an alternative.

They did not find one. Steve Forbes with his flat-tax proposal and perennial firebrand Pat Buchanan threw a scare into Dole, especially when Buchanan won the New Hampshire primary *(see box)*. But Dole's team had astutely built a fire wall in the South. They had earlier recruited the players, like former Governor Carroll Campbell, who on March 2 delivered South Carolina, the state everyone deemed critical to capturing the entire region. After South Carolina, the rest of the primary march was anticlimactic. Dole was pronounced the candidate-apparent after winning primaries in California, Nevada and Washington on March 26.

But the primaries exposed Dole's fundamental weakness: he still could not say why he wanted the Presidency or what he

would do if he got it. "It's about us," he said. "It's about you. It's about America. It's about the future, which is where we are headed." Dole's aides hatched grand plans for the months before the August Republican Convention: national issues forums, a preview of likely Cabinet choices, the selection of a popular running mate. But Dole, broke (he had temporarily run out of campaign funds) and exhausted, was not interested: he watched from the sidelines with

GRAND OLD POPULISTS

A parade of populists faced Bob Dole in the Republican primaries, but they barely gave the front runner a scare.

GRAMM

Senator Phil Gramm bragged over the size of his Texas-scale war chest, but he never managed to con-

ALEXANDER

nect with voters, and he was the first to drop out. Plaid-shirted former Bush Education Secretary Lamar Alexander fared no better.

Steve Forbes, a millionaire magazine publisher, won wide early attention with his call for a "simple, flat tax." But finishing fourth in both Iowa and New Hampshire

FORBES

finished Forbes.

In New Hampshire fiery Pat Buchanan—peddling his patented antiestablishment elixir—upset the party favorite. But when Dole swept the South on March 12, the primary race was effectively over.

BUCHANAN

scarcely an answering volley as Clinton continued to co-opt Republican positions.

Clinton's transformation was guided by a mid-1995 survey conducted by political strategist Mark Penn. The "Neuropersonality Poll," as Penn called it, attempted to map the psyche of the American voter and became the campaign's blueprint. Every presidential remark, every action, every gesture was pretested and scripted using the poll's data. No detail was too small. Rather than amble off Air Force One, Clinton marched; the campaign's most famous line, about "building a bridge to the 21st century," was intoned because "building a bridge to the future" tested less well.

With the invaluable help of Dick Morris, the postideological strategist who had guided his 1982 comeback as Governor of Arkansas after a devastating defeat two years earlier, Clinton crafted a series of positions and actions that fixed him firmly in that holiest of political spaces, the center. In standing against Republican proposals to restrain the cost of Medicare, Clinton appeared both compassionate and firm. In embracing the G.O.P.'s call for a balanced budget, he laid claim to fiscal sanity.

THAT'S THE TICKET
Dole, Kemp and families
patched up old quarrels

In other small-bore but powerfully symbolic pronouncements, Clinton called for school uniforms, teen curfews and V chips to block violent television shows. A group of proposals aimed at women voters (including bills designed to increase child-support collections, extend the family leave act and mandate a longer hospital stay after giving birth) guaranteed that the gender gap, already in Clinton's favor, would grow to historic proportions.

In late June, the Clinton machine—flush with funds because no other Democrat had risen to challenge the President in the primaries—filled the airwaves with ads that defined the coming campaign: only Clinton could brake the Gingrich revolution's excesses. Clinton thus positioned himself not so much against Dole as against Gingrich, now viewed by the public as the blustering ideologue who had gleefully shut down the government twice in the budget battles of late 1995 and early 1996. It was a clever defining stroke from which Dole would never recover.

It was not all a straight line to oblivion. Dole got a lift by uncorking a dramatic surprise in May: he resigned from the Senate to concentrate on the election. Written by novelist Mark Helprin, Dole's tearful speech of farewell to the chamber where he had spent 27 years as a highly regarded Senator was heartfelt and moving. Dole's poll numbers lifted. But the euphoria was brief; Dole eventually came to seem adrift

ROSS, REFORM THYSELF

In 1992 billionaire maverick Ross Perot proved there was room for a third party in American politics. Yet four years later Perot and his new Reform Party earned only 9% of the vote, down from 19% in 1992.

Why? While Americans claimed to share many of his views, they still saw Perot as a loose cannon with an ego as big as his ears. Sure enough, after Colorado Governor Dick Lamm announced that he would seek the

PEROT

nomination of Perot's fledgling Reform Party, the feisty tycoon quickly entered the race and squashed Lamm's candidacy.

Whatever Perot's failings, his legacy will endure. Facing steep odds, he created a true third party whose candidate in the year 2000 will qualify for taxpayer funding. And he helped put two of his pet issues—campaign-finance reform and the need to overhaul Social Security—at the center of the nation's agenda.

without his attachment to the Senate, leading many political observers to believe that his resignation had been a major political blunder. He soon needlessly landed himself on the wrong side of a national debate with his claim, during a campaign speech in Kentucky, that tobacco was not addictive.

Dole tried yet again to create a new image for himself with a proposal to slash income taxes by 15%. But the plan bumped up against his own proud lifelong stance against just this sort of supply-side budget solution, and made him seem more wishy-washy than the President. In fact, the voters, deadened to sweet-sounding quick fixes, became less enamored of Dole's tax-cut the more he publicized it.

But at the least, the tax-cut plan allowed Dole to select longtime supply-sider Jack Kemp as his running mate. The energetically gifted former Cabinet member in the Bush Administration was not only a fervent believer in tax cuts but one Republican who could reach out to minority and poor Americans in the inner cities. Dole and Kemp had been bitter opponents for many years; in selecting him, Dole proved he could reach out to build a "big tent" for the Republicans to run under.

The Republican convention went off smoothly, presenting the illusion of a united party. But the platform battles between the party's moderates and its right wing revealed the G.O.P.'s fault lines. Facing the hostility of many women voters, Dole called

SKUNK AT THE PICNIC
Advisor Dick Morris ruined Clinton's big night

In bending himself out of shape, Dole negated his AUTHENTICITY, his single strongest card against Clinton

for a "declaration of tolerance" in the G.O.P. platform's pro-life plank. "That's non-negotiable," he said, but he quickly caved in to the party's hard-line antiabortion forces, then feebly tried to save face by claiming that he would not read the platform.

Once again, Dole could not convert the bounce he had gained from the convention into solid political capital. His verbal and tactical missteps took their toll, confirming the electorate's fast-hardening negative verdict: Clinton was far from ideal, but Dole simply wasn't up to the job. In becoming an overnight supply-sider, in pandering to the right to win over his party's conservative wing, in wavering between his own ironic take on politics and the smoother tactics designed by his handlers, Dole bent himself out of shape and negated his authenticity—which was the strongest card he held against Clinton.

By contrast, Bill Clinton kept getting stronger. By summer's end, nothing that hinted at liberalism was left of him. The President who had begun his term advocating the rights of gays in the military now signed the Defense of Marriage Act, which barred federal recognition of gay and lesbian unions. On July 31, in the action that most firmly anchored him in the political center, he agreed to support a Republican welfare reform bill; he had vetoed two earlier ones.

Even the revelation that his key political advisor, Dick Morris, had been involved in a long-term affair with a prostitute—which broke on the very day of Clinton's acceptance speech at the Democratic National Convention in Chicago—failed to slow the Clinton train. The lasting image of the convention was delirious Democrats dancing the Macarena in the aisles.

With his economic package actually losing him support, Dole cast about wildly for effective positions. He swung at Clinton for a rise in drug use among teenagers and derided the President as an old-fashioned liberal. Neither tack worked. Scandal was left, so Dole tried that, too: "Where's the outrage?" he demanded. The answer: there wasn't much.

Most voters, polls found, had long since concluded that, while inherently "untrust-

SCANDAL WATCH

Bill Clinton's second term comes with a price tag: more investigations into White House scandals. Among the Clintons' problems:
● **Whitewater** Independent counsel Kenneth Starr's investigation marches on, in two parts. An Arkansas team is probing the Clintons' dealings with former partners Jim and Susan McDougal. A Washington team is looking into the death of former legal aide Vincent Foster, Travelgate and Filegate.

KENNETH STARR

● **Paula Jones** The Supreme Court was expected to rule early in 1997 on the argument by the President's lawyers that Clinton should be immune from civil trial in the sexual harrassment case filed by Paula Jones over an alleged 1991 incident.
● **Campaign finance** Republicans called for an independent prosecutor to investigate Democratic fund raiser John Huang and other alleged violators of campaign-finance laws.

worthy," the President was nevertheless trustworthy enough for the White House, and in fact cared more about their own problems than did Dole. That mattered more to them than anything nefarious that the President, his wife or their minions might have done.

The television debates changed no one's mind. The first, held in Hartford, Connecticut, on October 6, was a genteel, unexciting affair. The second, in San Diego on Oct. 16, was held in a town-hall format, and though Dole had vowed he would zero in on the President's moral failings, he backed off after Clinton simply ignored a single early thrust.

In mid-October, the President was hit by yet another scandal, when news broke that a high-up Democratic fund-raiser, John Huang, had raised hundreds of thousands of dollars in campaign contributions, much of it from foreign sources. Republicans charged the donations were illegal. Huang, a Commerce Department employee, had been a frequent visitor to 1600 Pennsylvania Avenue, and had close ties to Indonesia's multibillion-dollar Lippo Group financial conglomerate. The news may have helped deny Clinton an even larger margin of victory, but it did not sway enough voters to put Dole back on track.

Near the end of the campaign, as desperation reigned, Dole's down-ticket Republican colleagues fled their leader, even running TV commercials suggesting that Clinton's second-term plans should be checked by a Republican legislature—just as the President had gained by avowing that he was needed to check them.

On election day, Bob Dole lost the battle, as Clinton swept to victory with 49% of the popular vote and 379 electoral votes. But the Republicans may have won the war, for Bill Clinton ran as a deficit-cutting, budget-balancing, welfare-reforming candidate. American voters had elected a moderate Democratic President to carry out a moderate Republican agenda. ■

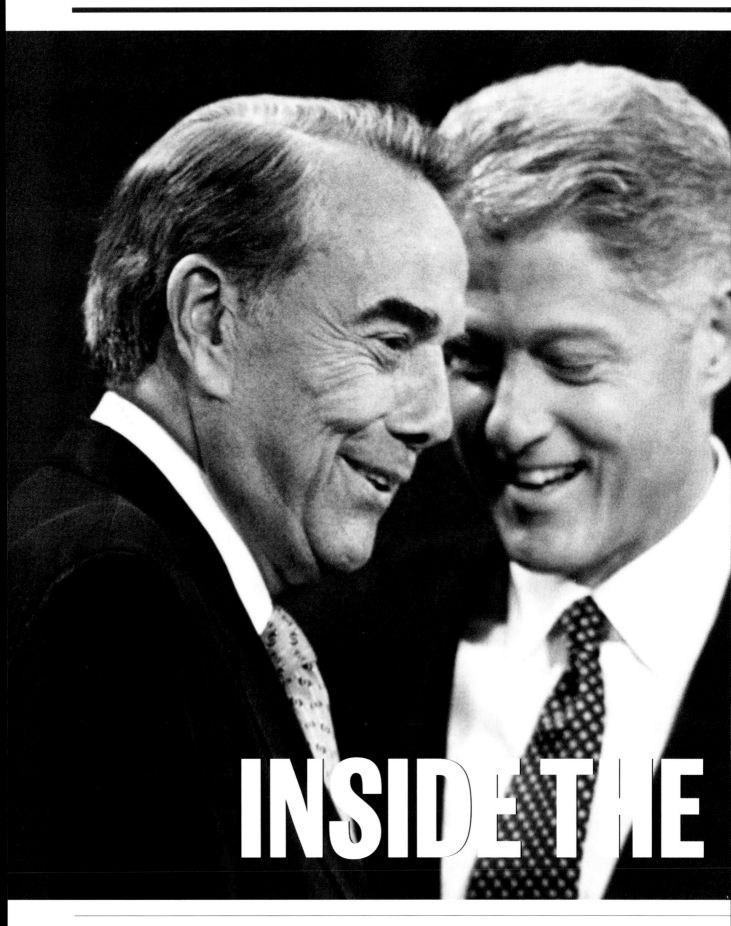

INSIDE THE

THE VOTE 96 In a campaign year, pictures of candidates are as common as postcards. The vast majority of these images are taken under the tight control of handlers who filter out all but the most flattering poses. But during the 1996 campaign, two TIME photographers— P. F. Bentley with the Dole campaign and Diana Walker with the Clinton campaign—were able to capture the two men, as Walker described it: "away from the theater of the photo op."

RACE

ALL ABOARD!
The President, who claims to have been an avid fan of railroads from his youth, exclaims with joy over the rolling Oval Office set up for him aboard his whistle-stop campaign train en route to the Democratic Convention in Chicago.

BROTHERS AT ARMS
Though different in many ways, Clinton and Dole respected each other. This picture was taken at the end of the first presidential debate, during which the President had noted: "I like Senator Dole. You can probably tell we like each other."

KING OF HEARTS
Bill Clinton plays hearts with aides Bruce Lindsey and Erskine Bowles aboard Air Force One as he flies to the first debate in Hartford, Connecticut. Guess who's winning.

HERE GOES!
The President gathers himself as he prepares to step onstage at the Democratic Convention in Chicago to deliver his acceptance speech. News of a scandal involving his political adviser Dick Morris had surfaced hours before.

ON THE BEACH
Senator Dole was known for his love of the sun; here he basks by the Pacific in La Jolla, California, during the Republican Convention. Three days after the election Dole went on the David Letterman TV show, where he joshed that he was amending his campaign slogan from "A better man for a better America" to "A better tan for a better America."

THE GAME PLAN
The President went to Chautauqua, New York, to rehearse for the first debate. Here he listens to longtime advisor George Stephanopoulos. Erskine Bowles, later named chief of staff for the second term, stands behind Clinton.

WHISTLE-STOP
The President eagerly donned the mantle of Democratic icon Harry Truman as his campaign train rolled across mid-America. He waves to voters in Michigan as his train passes between Battle Creek and Kalamazoo.

WAR STORIES
Flying to Louisville, Kentucky, in October, Dole shares a laugh with the enormously popular Colin Powell, who had turned down Dole's requests to join him on the G.O.P. ticket.

THE DECISIONS IN DETAIL

★ ★ ELECTION MONITOR ★ ★

In the year leading up to the election, a large proportion of voters switched from opposing Bill Clinton's re-election to favoring it. Here are the groups where Clinton made the biggest gains, according to the TIME/CNN Election Monitor, a survey that returned periodically to the same registered voters.

PARENTS AND PEROTISTAS

Percentage who switched to Clinton:

White, unmarried parents	26%
Fathers, age 18-29	24%
Perot voters, age 30-49	22%
White parents, age 18-29	22%
Suburban men, age 18-29	21%

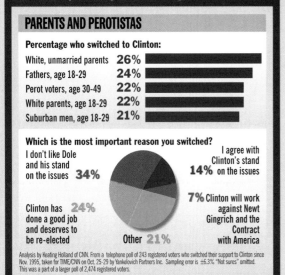

Which is the most important reason you switched?

I don't like Dole and his stand on the issues **34%**

I agree with Clinton's stand on the issues **14%**

Clinton has done a good job and deserves to be re-elected **24%**

7% Clinton will work against Newt Gingrich and the Contract with America

Other **21%**

Analysis by Keating Holland of CNN. From a telephone poll of 243 registered voters who switched their support to Clinton since Nov. 1995, taken for TIME/CNN on Oct. 25-29 by Yankelovich Partners Inc. Sampling error is ±6.3% "Not sures" omitted. This was a part of a larger poll of 2,474 registered voters.

PRESIDENT

How the states voted

Clinton

Dole

Electoral votes

WASH. 11
MONT. 3
N. DAK. 3
MINN. 10
W. VA. 5
ORE. 7
IDAHO 4
S. DAK. 3
WIS. 11
MICH. 18
NEV. 4
WYO. 3
IOWA 7
ILL. 22
IND. 12
OHIO 21
CALIF. 54
UTAH 5
COLO. 8
NEB. 5
MO. 11
KY. 8
ARIZ. 8
KANS. 6
N. MEX. 5
OKLA. 8
ARK. 6
TENN. 11
GA.
ALASKA 3
TEXAS 32
LA. 9
MISS. 7
ALA. 9
HAWAII 4

How the states voted, 1992

Clinton

Bush

THE HOUSE

	Republicans	Democrats	Independent
Old	236	198	1
New	227	207	1

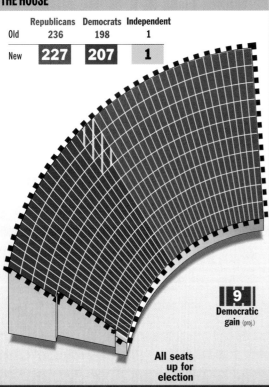

9 Democratic gain (proj.)

All seats up for election

THE SENATE

	Republicans	Democrats
Old	53	47
New	55	45

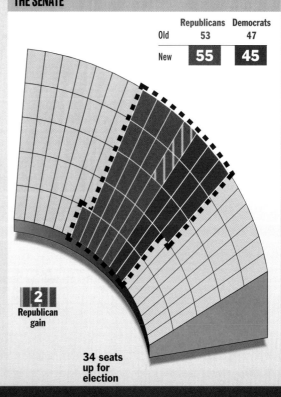

2 Republican gain

34 seats up for election

EXIT POLLS

How Americans voted

All

Males

Females

Whites

Blacks

Non–high school graduates

High school graduates

College graduates

Postgraduate study

Income $30,000-$50,000

$50,000-$75,000

$75,000-$100,000

Age 65+

Gun owners

Have children under 18

First-time voters

Smokers

Political talk-show listeners

Decided to vote in last three days

From the Voter News Service exit poll of 16,33... participants. Margin of error is ±1%.

The popular vote

49% Clinton
41% Dole
8% Perot

The electoral vote

Clinton 379

Dole 159

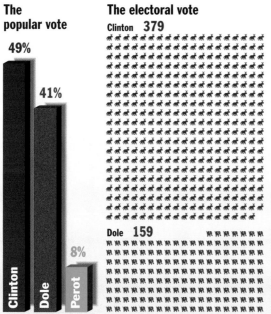

VT. 3
N.H. 4
ME. 4
N.Y. 33
MASS. 12
PA. 23
R.I. 4
CONN. 8
N.J. 15
DEL. 3
VA. 13
MD. 10
N.C. 14
D.C. 3
S.C. 8
FLA. 25

GOVERNORS

11 states held elections

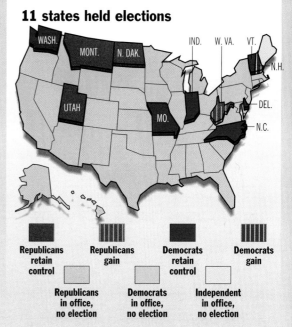

WASH. | MONT. | N. DAK. | IND. | W. VA. | VT. | N.H. | DEL. | N.C. | MO. | UTAH

Republicans retain control
Republicans gain
Democrats retain control
Democrats gain
Republicans in office, no election
Democrats in office, no election
Independent in office, no election

Clinton	Dole
49%	41%
44%	44%
54%	38%
43%	46%
83%	12%
59%	28%
52%	35%
43%	46%
52%	40%
48%	40%
47%	45%
44%	48%
50%	43%
38%	51%
48%	41%
54%	34%
53%	36%
45%	43%
34%	39%

INITIATIVES

AFFIRMATIVE ACTION — PASSED
Prop. 209, California—Prohibits preferential treatment based on race, sex, ethnicity or national origin in public employment, education and contracting.

TORT REFORM — NOT PASSED
Prop. 211, California—Makes it easier for an individual to sue for securities fraud and prohibits the legislature from making changes to attorney-client fee arrangements.

MARIJUANA — PASSED
Prop. 215, California—Allows use of marijuana for medical purposes.

PARENTAL RIGHTS — NOT PASSED
Amendment 17, Colorado—Gives parents an "inalienable right" to control the "upbringing, education, values and discipline of their children."

PARTY IN POWER

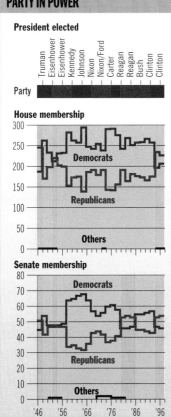

President elected

Truman | Eisenhower | Eisenhower | Kennedy | Johnson | Nixon | Nixon/Ford | Carter | Reagan | Reagan | Bush | Clinton | Clinton

Party

House membership
Democrats
Republicans
Others
(300, 250, 200, 150, 100, 50, 0)

Senate membership
Democrats
Republicans
Others
(80, 70, 60, 50, 40, 30, 20, 10, 0)

'46 '56 '66 '76 '86 '96
Election year

VOTER TURNOUT

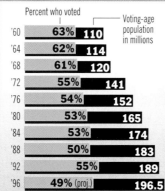

Percent who voted — Voting-age population in millions

Year	Percent	Millions
'60	63%	110
'64	62%	114
'68	61%	120
'72	55%	141
'76	54%	152
'80	53%	165
'84	53%	174
'88	50%	183
'92	55%	189
'96	49% (proj.)	196.5

STATE LEGISLATURES

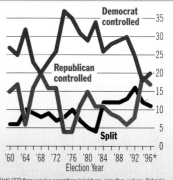

Democrat controlled
Republican controlled
Split

'60 '64 '68 '72 '76 '80 '84 '88 '92 '96*
Election Year
(35, 30, 25, 20, 15, 10, 5, 0)

Until 1972 there were two nonpartisan legislatures; since then, just one: Nebraska
Source: National Conference of State Legislatures *1 undecided

THE 10 BIGGEST CAMPAIGN BANKROLLS

Senate			Winner
John Kerry	Mass.	$8,333,197	✓
Robert Torricelli	N.J.	$8,269,457	✓
Mark Warner	Va.	$8,237,073	
Guy Millner	Ga.	$7,638,652	
Dick Zimmer	N.J.	$7,595,374	
Harvey Gantt	N.C.	$7,057,717	
Jesse Helms	N.C.	$6,725,515	✓
William Weld	Mass.	$6,639,759	
Carl Levin	Mich.	$5,730,793	✓
Paul Wellstone	Minn.	$5,161,767	✓

House			Winner
Newt Gingrich	Ga.	$5,625,093	✓
Richard Gephardt	Mo.	$3,249,849	✓
Charles Schumer	N.Y.	$2,859,681	✓
Michael Coles	Ga.	$2,344,912	
Ellen Tauscher	Calif.	$2,100,833	✓
Vic Fazio	Calif.	$2,054,088	✓
Greg Ganske	Iowa	$2,019,302	✓
Joseph Kennedy	Mass.	$1,885,342	✓
Martin Frost	Texas	$1,768,731	✓
John Ensign	Nev.	$1,748,956	✓

Financial activity Jan. 1, 1995, through Oct. 16, 1996

Source: Federal Election Commission

HOW THE UNABOMBER WAS
NABBED

After a 17-year manhunt, federal agents raid a remote Montana cabin—and seize the deadliest bomber in U.S. history

T HE QUARRY WAS found right where his hunters always suspected he would be, the place he had picked with the same care he brought to his other handiwork. Lincoln, Montana, sits as close as you can get to the spine of the western hemisphere and still have a post office and library within walking distance. Theodore John Kaczynski lived at heaven's back door, just below the largest stretch of unbroken wilderness in the continental U.S. No cars or roads mar the landscape, and on any given day there are more grizzly bears than people. This is America as the explorers found it, still sealed, unlit, unwired, resembling most perfectly the place the Unabomber wanted America to be.

Maybe it wasn't really so lonely at night in the woods at the edge of the Scapegoat Wilderness, where the trees sound like a crowd waiting for the curtain to rise. It is a place where a man who hates technology and progress and people would have plenty of time to

"Ted was a hard worker ... but he had a hard time with mechanical things."

FINALLY: Kaczynski is arraigned in Montana

practice what the Unabomber preached. He could listen to the forest sigh and hum, the tamaracks and the lodge-poles rustle in the wind. What he did not know was that, for the previous few weeks, the trees had been listening back.

The federal agents were everywhere, disguised as lumberjacks and postalworkers and mountain men. They had draped the forest with microphones, nestled snipers not far from the cabin. When they raided it on April 3, ending the longest, most expensive hunt for a serial killer in U.S. history, the lawmen finally got to look into the shaggy face of a man they had imagined and profiled and tracked like a grizzly for the previous 17 years.

Yet they restrained themselves from saying that they had finally caught the Unabomber. After 200 suspects, thousands of interviews, visits with clairvoyants, 20,000 calls to 800-701-BOMB, the agents were not about to rush to judgment. But when they finally, carefully entered the cabin, fearing booby traps, they found a whole bomb factory, including a partially built pipe bomb, chemicals, wire, books on bombmaking and hand-drawn diagrams. They even defused a live bomb found in the cabin.

Ted Kaczynski fit his hunters' expectations uncannily. He was, as they had surmised, a white male, middle-aged, who kept to himself—just as the entire town of Lincoln described "the hermit on the hill." He had built his home of plywood, with an outhouse out back and two walls filled floor to ceiling with Shakespeare and Thackeray and bomb manuals. Sometimes he would stay inside for weeks at a stretch. You could smell him coming, steeped in woodsmoke, wearing fatigues, riding a one-speed bike cooked up out of spare parts. He didn't make small talk.

"Ted was a hard worker," said his closest neighbor, Leland Mason, 57, "but…he had a hard time with every-day mechanical things." The bomb-squad cops had

THE LONG ROAD DOWN

Throughout his life—from high school to Harvard to the University of Michigan and then Berkeley—Ted Kaczynski cast no shadow, left no prints, made few friends. He finally vanished into the woods outside Lincoln, Montana, where the locals referred to him as the "hermit on the hill." These pictures trace his descent from honor student to his arrest as the suspected Unabomber.

**1958
HIGH SCHOOL**

always said they were looking for a "junkyard bomber," because his inventions were patched together from lamp cords, recycled screws and match heads. They imagined a smart, twisted man, carving and fiddling into the night. To kill three strangers with bombs sent through the U.S. mail, and injure 23 others, he had to be powerfully angry.

The first bomb went off at Northwestern University in 1978, bearing the name of a professor at the Technological Institute. A year later, a second bomb was left at the institute, injuring a graduate student. After that they came to an airline executive, the computer-science departments at Vanderbilt and Berkeley, a University of Michigan professor. The FBI shined up the bomber with an '80s nickname—Unabom, for his favorite targets, universities and airlines.

For 17 years he eluded the manhunt. And in the end it was not his bombs that gave him away. Perhaps it was the

HIS BROTHER'S KEEPER

David Kaczynski was seven years younger than Ted; the siblings (above, in 1954) shared a distaste for modern life. David bought land in Texas, where he lived in a hole sheltered only by a metal sheet (left). He also helped Ted buy the Montana land where he built his cabin (right).

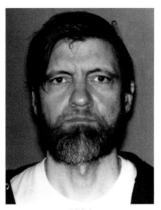
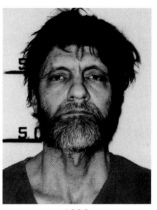

1962
HARVARD

LATE 1960s
AT BERKELEY

1994
DRIVER'S LICENSE

1996
MUG SHOT

Thackeray, the need for serial drama. In the wake of the Oklahoma City bombing in April 1995, the Unabomber seemed to need to bring himself back onstage, to get credit for his elusive prowess. Within five days another deadly package was in the mail, this time to the president of the California Forestry Association.

THE BOMBER THEN BEGAN THE EPISTOLARY striptease that would bring him down. Using, as was his custom, the madman's we, he wrote to the New York *Times* and the Washington *Post*, asking them to publish his magnum opus, a 35,000-word screed against industrial society and modern civilization. When Attorney General Janet Reno and FBI Director Louis Freeh consulted the publishers of the two papers, the *Times* and *Post* wrestled together over whether they should appear to give in to a terrorist. But the investigators wanted to take the gamble that someone who knew the killer would hear echoes of a friend or student or relative. They were hoping, in short, for David Kaczynski.

David was seven years younger than Ted; he shared his older brother's grudge against technology and revered his wilderness life-style. David had purchased the Montana land with Ted years before, and he occasionally retreated to his own isolated piece of land in West Texas, where he initially took shelter in nothing more than a hole in the ground covered with a metal sheet.

In the early 1990s David moved to Schenectady, New York to marry a high school sweetheart, Linda Patrik, an associate professor of philosophy at Union College. Late in 1995 he went home to Chicago to help his mother Wanda move out of the small gray house she had lived in for nearly 30 years. In sorting through their old boxes and trunks, David came upon some of Ted's journals and letters he had written to newspapers years earlier. Their tone—even specific turns of phrase—sounded darkly familiar to David, who had read the Unabomber's manifesto. Through Susan Swanson, an old friend of Linda's who now worked for a top private-investigating firm in Chicago, David contacted Clint Van Zandt, the retired former chief hostage negotiator of the FBI. After bringing in two experts who agreed that Ted's letters matched the tone of the manifesto, Van Zandt persuaded David to notify the FBI. David pointed the federal agents to Montana, and they began their stakeout of "the hermit on the hill."

Who was Ted Kaczynski? Born in Chicago in 1942, son of a Polish sausagemaker, Kaczynski was standout smart from childhood, but he sulked through grade school, perhaps because he was so much brighter than his peers. When he became a discipline problem in high school, he was put on an accelerated curriculum that shot him to Harvard at age 16. A loner in Cambridge, Kaczynski finished Harvard by the time he was 20 and headed off into the cauldron of '60s campus radicalism, first at the University of Michigan, where he got his master's and Ph.D. in mathematics, then to the University of California, Berkeley, to teach.

Kaczynski abruptly left his position at Berkeley in 1969, then wrote a long essay that opposed funding for scientific research, particularly in the field of genetics. In the hope of getting it published, he sent it to columnists around the country. In 1971 he set off for Montana, buying land and building his house and living on what he could grow or kill. He did odd jobs now and then but apparently got by on a few hundred dollars a year, with plenty of free time for his alleged growing vocation: the disruption of the industrial society he had left behind.

In June a federal grand jury in California charged Ted Kaczynski with 10 felony counts in four California bombings. Trials for bombings in other locations could follow. Meanwhile, further evidence emerged that seemed to identify Kaczynski as the Unabomber. One of three typewriters found in the shack appeared to match the one that produced the manifesto, and in September a federal prosecutor said that a diary found in the shack contained entries that amounted to a confession of the bombings.

But even if Kaczynski is ultimately convicted, one daunting task may never be completed: to determine how the Unabomber chose his victims—how, in his omnivorous reading of magazines, newspapers, journals and academic texts, particular names caught his eye, sparked his rage, and evoked his personal brand of justice. ∎

TERROR ON

230 die when a Boeing 747 plunges into the sea off the

THE SEA SPEAKS IN MANY VOICES. ON THAT FIRST MORNING after the explosion of TWA Flight 800, amid the stench of burning jet fuel and the plane's charred remains, hundreds of letters floated on the surface of the Atlantic: unanchored memories of diplomats, designers, doctors and teenagers. A postcard of the Statue of Liberty, a monument born in France, had become an interrupted souvenir, an image from the New World that never made its way across the Atlantic and home to Paris.

FLIGHT 800

coast of Long Island—and the cause is still a mystery

Out of a camera bag fished from the waters off Long Island came a list in pencil: Amy: light pink, size 8. Corry: dress. Steph: orange or hunter green. It was the plan for a shopping spree in Paris, transformed into a haiku of loss. And somewhere in the waters was an unuttered promise, a diamond ring to accompany a proposal to a lover who must now long for the rest of her life. The miasma off the beaches of New York was the cruelest of elements, mixing the memory and desires of the dead with the terror and fears of the living.

On that humid Wednesday evening in July, total strangers had gathered to share a common fate, waiting outside Gate 27 at New York's Kennedy Airport to board TWA's 7-hr. 15-min. flight to Paris. There was the contingent of high school kids from Pennsylvania off to France for a field trip; the mother who overcame her fear of flying so she could tour medieval castles in a "bonding"

A WING AND A PRAYER Rough seas hampered salvage operations as 100 divers searched for clues

THE FINAL DAY OF A BOEING 747-100

Wednesday, July 17

11:32 a.m. (Athens time): The 747-100, Flight 880 from J.F.K. in New York, arrives in Athens, Greece.

It spends two hours in Athens. The plane is guarded by police while on the ground, and all the luggage and carry-on baggage is passed through security checks.

1:25 p.m.: The plane, now Flight 881, takes off for its 10-hour flight to J.F.K. airport. It arrives in New York at **4:38 p.m.** (local time).

8:02 p.m.: After the engine-pressure radio gauge is replaced, the plane, now Flight 800, leaves the gate bound for Paris, with 230 people aboard.

8:48 p.m.: The plane disappears from radar, and witnesses see an explosion off the southern coast of Long Island.

trip with her daughter; the couple who fell in love as flight attendants 21 years ago and worked side by side on the New York-Paris route; the French "flat-picking" guitarist who was a protégé of Nashville's Chet Atkins. The other passengers ranged from TV producer to unemployed construction worker. All their lives, however, had come to a final intersection. At 8:02 p.m., the giant jetliner left the gate and taxied toward the runway. A few minutes later it would be in the air, flying eastward over the narrow, ragged strip of Long Island, on its way to Europe. There, at 8:48 p.m., startled residents reported looking up to see two fireballs burst in the sky.

In East Moriches, the town closest to the crash site in the Atlantic, residents and fishermen quickly headed out to find survivors. The crew of a National Guard C-130 practicing search-and-rescue procedures nearby had witnessed the crash, identified the wreckage and reported back to home base. Local law-enforcement and fire departments, large contingents from New York City and even rescue craft from Cape Cod, Massachusetts, responded to emergency calls. When Cecilia Penney first saw the explosion, she thought, "Is this a nuclear war? It was like I was watching it on TV." Her husband Randy then joined volunteers on a small rescue fleet of six boats. "The water was on fire from the fuel," he says. Soon he and his friends had "pulled three bodies out of the water. Two of them were still strapped to their seats. We had to get them out of there quick because we didn't want them to sink." Of the 18 people Randy saw pulled out of the

water, about half had had their clothes blown off. One was a pretty girl in her early 20s. "I tried not to get a good look at them, at their faces," he says hesitantly. "I didn't have time to think about what I was seeing—we were out there looking for survivors. And by about 3 a.m., it became apparent there were none."

In all, 230 passengers and crew—every person on board—died on that July night. What killed them? What could have caused such a swift and merciless catastrophe? Why did this plane, one of the oldest Boeing 747s in use, burst into flames 13,700 ft. in the air? Said a veteran pilot: "747s don't just fall out of the air." At first, it was widely assumed that such a swift and unexplained explosion could only be the result of a terrorist bomb—or perhaps even a hand-held missile. Or could it possibly have been a mechanical malfunction? The speculations proliferated. But they were cautious, with the ifs loudly iterated and "theory" worn like a reluctant fig leaf. For breathless days and weeks, then for restless months, the search for clues went on under the most challenging circumstances.

Two agencies were assigned to the case: the National Transportation Safety Board (NTSB), which is responsible for air safety in the U.S., and the FBI, in case the crash was a criminal act. Robert Francis, 58, of the NTSB was the chief federal official on the case; James Kallstrom, 53, the tough head of the FBI's New York office, was No. 2. Working under intense pressure, the two agencies and their leaders were later charged with acting more as rivals than partners as they struggled to solve the mystery.

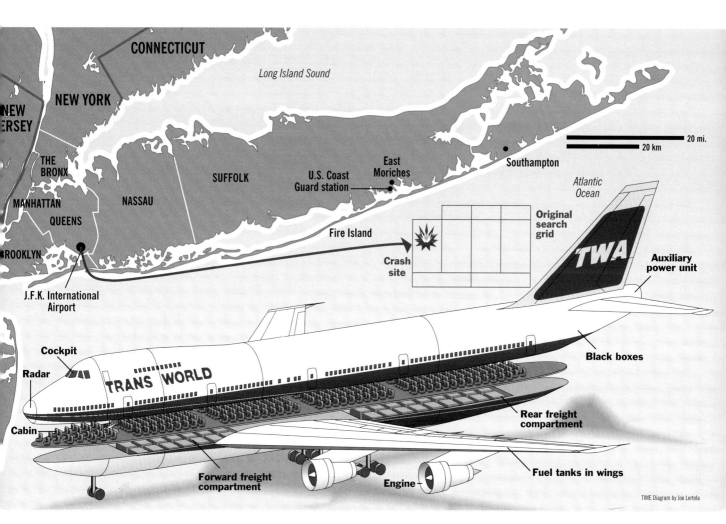

CONNECTICUT

Long Island Sound

NEW YORK

20 mi.
20 km

NEW JERSEY

THE BRONX

MANHATTAN

NASSAU

QUEENS

BROOKLYN

SUFFOLK

U.S. Coast
Guard station

East
Moriches

Southampton

Atlantic
Ocean

Fire Island

Crash
site

Original
search
grid

TWA

Auxiliary
power unit

J.F.K. International
Airport

Cockpit

Radar

TRANS WORLD

Black boxes

Cabin

Rear freight
compartment

Forward freight
compartment

Engine

Fuel tanks in wings

TIME Diagram by Joe Lertola

Again and again in the weeks after the crash, some 100 divers descended to an underwater hell: the silty tract roughly twice the size of Rhode Island containing the human remains and the wreckage of the plane, about 10 miles off the coast of Long Island, and 120 ft. below the surface of the Atlantic Ocean. At that depth, the water temperature dropped to 50 degrees, and pressure crunched face masks painfully against foreheads and chins. Visibility was limited to a few feet, but the visions were nightmarish. Scattered shards of the doomed airliner sprouted myriad electric wires and cords that waved medusa-like in the undersea currents. Some of the bodies were found swaying gently to the same tidal rhythms. Ultimately, divers brought back all but 15 of the bodies.

ALMOST EXACTLY A WEEK AFTER THE JETLINER took its fiery plunge into the sea came some promising news: the plane's two black boxes—the cockpit-voice and flight-data recorders—had been recovered. Both boxes were flown immediately to the NTSB lab in Washington, where experts deciphered them. But the cockpit-voice recorder quickly yielded only a tantalizing enigma: a fraction-of-a-second loud sound $11\frac{1}{2}$ minutes into the flight, followed by silence. This tiny glitch of noise reinforced the notion that Flight 800 was brought down by a bomb—or even a missile. One theory that arose the day after the crash —that a surface-to-air missile, perhaps of the shoulder-launched Stinger type, had brought down the 747—refused

to die. Gradually it mutated into a persistent rumor that the jet was downed by "friendly fire" from a U.S. Navy vessel. The government vehemently denied the story.

As the search for bodies and clues continued into the fall, theory after theory flickered across the news. One fact did emerge: the NTSB was able to determine that the explosion had begun in the plane's central fuel tank, though it still could not explain the reason for the blast. In late August came a welcome break: investigators found minute traces of bomb chemicals in several pieces of recovered wreckage from the plane. Now the bomb theory seemed most promising. But within weeks it was revealed that the chemicals had been deliberately sprinkled into the plane only five weeks before the crash, in an exercise to train an explosive-sniffing dog. The investigators were back at square one.

Slowly, very slowly, the bomb scenario and the missile scenario fell by the wayside. In November, Kallstrom, whose FBI team had been the strongest proponents of the theory that the crash was an act of sabotage, went on record as believing that it was "less likely" that evidence of a criminal act would be found. But he stressed that this conclusion was tentative—and that the NTSB still had no clues as to what might have caused an unprecedented mechanical failure. At the end of 1996, the story of Flight 800—as much an enigma as the disappearance of Amelia Earhart at sea 59 years before—was an unsolved mystery. And until that mystery was resolved, the wounds of the tragedy would not heal. ∎

A Farewell to Welfare?

Democrats and Republicans come together to reform a failing system

ISTORIC TURNING POINTS IN SOCIAL POLICY ARE NOT always obvious when they occur. Certainly President Franklin D. Roosevelt did not foresee that some provisions of the Social Security Act he signed in 1935 would burgeon over the next 61 years into a mammoth federally financed and regulated welfare program. But in late July 1996 the equally historic nature of the decision facing Bill Clinton was clear not just to the White House but the whole nation.

A Clinton veto of the Republican bill to overhaul welfare would have reversed the centrist stance—champion of family values, balanced budgets, more cops on the streets—that the President had been cultivating so assiduously since the rout of the Democrats in the 1994 elections. And, of course, there was that matter of his 1992 pledge to "end welfare as we know it."

SHAME! Bill Clinton's signing of the third version of the G.O.P. welfare bill was the most controversial—and defining—decision of his Presidency

Congress had stripped out of its new welfare bill many of the harsh provisions that had provoked the President to veto two earlier versions. But Clinton still branded as "just wrong" a provision excluding legal immigrants from getting most federal benefits. He also assailed a cut of $24 billion in federal outlays for food stamps over the next six years. These were the provisions that led most of Clinton's advisers to argue for a veto. The President, however, decided to support the bill, claiming that the two provisions could be changed by further legislation.

As for the core bill, though, Clinton said, "The current welfare system undermines the basic values of work, responsibility and family, trapping generation after generation in dependency. Welfare was meant to be … a second chance, not a way of life."

Democratic party liberals disagreed, and stridently: "shame" (protesters in the Senate gallery); "betrayal" (Ralph Nader); "moral blot on his presidency" (Marian Wright Edelman, head of the Children's Defense Fund and an old friend of Hillary Clinton's). Nonetheless, the final bill sailed through the House and Senate by lopsided majorities. Not only did Republicans vote for it almost unanimously, but large numbers of Democrats felt freed by the President's decision to take the popular side of the issue. House Democrats split down the middle, 98 for, 98 against. Democratic Senators voted for it, 25 to 21.

So the nation embarked on an immense experiment in social policy whose outcome will not be clear for years. The central themes of the law were straightforward enough. There would be no more guarantee of a federal check to poor people for as long as they might need it. Instead, Washington would make block, or lump-sum, grants for each state to distribute to the poor (along with some state funds) under guidelines intended to prod state and local authorities to goad the clients into finding jobs. There would generally be a two-year limit on payments for any one stretch of time, and five years lifetime for those who drift on and off welfare rolls.

Within those limits—and even they could be stretched—states could design pretty much any kind of program they wanted. They could decide just how hard someone applying for welfare must look for a job. They could vary the amounts paid for rent and food, even decide how much in day-care vouchers to give working mothers to pay for child care.

Now there would be 50 separate systems. In fact more, since many states may, and should, permit variations from locality to locality. No one can be sure how the whole process will turn out, but there is no uncertainty about the system's demise: it has contributed to, if not created, an underclass culture of idleness, dependency and self-perpetuating poverty. The new law had many flaws, and would lead to uncertainty and hardship for at least some of the poor. But Clinton was gambling that it is better to permit that to happen than continue a system that even the fiercest critics of the new law concede needs overhauling. ∎

Still Speaker, but Weaker

Battling ethics charges, Newt Gingrich keeps his job but loses clout

IT WAS A SQUEAKER FOR THE SPEAKER: NEWT GINGRICH, charged by a House ethics subcommittee with improper procedures, had to battle in 1996's final weeks to keep his job. As the new year began, his loyal House Republicans re-elected the man who first led them to a majority in 1994. Yet though Gingrich kept control of the Speaker's chair by a narrow margin, his prestige and influence emerged badly damaged.

Until just before Christmas, Gingrich thought he could tiptoe past the political graveyard. But on December 21 the House ethics committee released a report concluding that the nationally broadcast college course taught by Gingrich in Georgia, which was financed by tax-deductible contributions, had partisan intent. Most damning, the panel determined that Gingrich had misled committee investigators by signing false statements declaring that his political organization, GOPAC, had no involvement with the course.

On the same day that the committee offered its report, Gingrich issued a letter admitting that "inaccurate, incomplete and unreliable statements were given to the committee" over his signature. That gave him reasonable hope of getting away with just a reprimand, the lightest penalty, from the committee. While even that would be unprecedented for a House Speaker, it would fall short of censure, which would require Gingrich to step down. A few days later the ethics committee announced that it would not begin the final phase of its investigation of Gingrich until January 8—one day after the scheduled vote to re-elect the Speaker. Its schedule meant House members would have to decide Gingrich's fate without knowing what punishment the committee would recommend.

The Speaker's troubles deepened when Michael Forbes, a New York Republican and longtime Gingrich supporter, announced that he would not support the re-election of Gingrich as Speaker, thus becoming the first G.O.P. House member to call publicly for him to hand over his gavel. Hoping to prolong the agony, Democrats clamored for a postponement of the vote until after the committee's decision. Every one of them remembered how Gingrich had tormented Speaker Jim Wright until he resigned over ethics charges in 1989.

With early but clear signs of a meltdown flashing around him, Gingrich began dialing Republican representatives around the country to ask for their support. The effort reached a peak when the G.O.P. leadership pressured Representatives Porter Goss of Florida and Steve Schiff of New Mexico, the two Republicans on the four-member ethics subcommittee responsible for investigating Gingrich, into writing a letter announcing their intention of supporting the Speaker. Then, on the night before the election, Gingrich addressed a closed caucus of House Republicans, apologizing for his mistakes and asking for their votes, in a meeting that lasted three hours.

The full-court press worked: Gingrich took 216 votes, only three more than he needed to keep his seat; House Democrat leader Richard Gephardt received 205. Of the nine G.O.P. defectors, the most prominent was Iowa's Jim Leach, head of the House Banking Committee. Although Gingrich retained his chair, his reputation and position suffered. Restive committee chairmen were ready to reassert the independence Newt had once tried to curb, and new Senate majority leader Trent Lott was angling to spearhead the G.O.P. agenda in the next Congress. ∎

FIRES
In the Night

A wave of arson hits small
black churches in the South,
but federal agents find
no evidence of a conspiracy

**BRANDED: pages
of a burned hymnal**

IF ANY SOUTHERN TOWN could be said to have somehow avoided racial strife, Kossuth, Mississippi, might have made the claim. Situated far north of the old plantations in the Delta, the tiny, oak-dotted hamlet (pop. 248) has historically enjoyed a lack of tension between white and black communities. In the 1940s and into the 1950s, children of both races played and ate together, and Kossuth achieved legal integration without the horrible spasms that wrenched most of the South. It was always a point of pride to Linda Lambert, the wife of Kossuth's mayor, that 109 years ago her ancestors donated the land on which black ex-sharecroppers built the Mount Pleasant Missionary Baptist Church—a big, beautiful edifice that housed a $10,000 baby-grand piano, the congregation's pride.

On a Monday night in June, however, the Lamberts' phone rang: Mount Pleasant was ablaze. Worse, the town's fire engines were already fighting a fire a few miles away—at another black church, Central Grove Missionary Baptist. Finally, the county fire department arrived at Mt. Pleasant, but by then the church was lost. As the roof caved in and the steeple crashed to the ground, Linda Lambert glanced over at Sheriff's Deputy Billy Dilworth, a big, quiet man who serves as the church's deacon. Tears streamed down his cheeks. She thought to herself, "They had labored so for that church!"

Throughout the early spring and summer of 1996, Americans of all races labored to understand a nationwide epidemic of violence against black churches—and federal agents labored, without success, to discover if a conspiracy was to blame. Over the 18-month period from January 1995 to July 1996, more than 30 black churches were burned in an eight-state arc stretching from Louisiana to Virginia. The 50-some federal agents who swept down on Kossuth while the embers were still warm quickly determined that both fires were indeed the result of arson. (They also confirmed a failed arson attempt at an all-white church nearby.) They ruled out an insurance scam by church personnel. And, since no outsider would have known the tiny Central Grove church existed, they concluded that the culprit was probably a local.

For months, black leaders said the fires at small black churches represented a re-emergence of racial extremism. As National Urban League president Hugh Price put it, "The flames of bigotry and intolerance are soaring

NIGHTMARE: A church in North Carolina succumbs to arson

higher than they have in a generation." The charge reverberated. Bill Clinton made a pilgrimage to the site of a rebuilt church in Greeleyville, South Carolina. Shortly after, the Republican-controlled House unanimously passed a bill making it easier for the Federal Government to prosecute church-burning cases and allowing victims to be compensated by a federal fund. A Senate version added a $12 million appropriation for the Bureau of Alcohol, Tobacco and Firearms' arson investigations.

ACCUSED OF RESPONDING SLUGGISHLY TO THE EPIdemic early on, the FBI and ATF by June had a combined task force of 236 agents on the case. The ATF had success with both low-tech gambits (an accelerant-sniffing Labrador retriever established the Kossuth fires as arson) and cybersleuthing (a computer database helped pin arson charges on two Klansmen in two South Carolina cases). But investigators found that not all the fires were racially motivated.

Among those arrested: a white firebug, an emotionally unstable 13-year-old girl and two black contractors who had done restoration work on the church they allegedly burned. "If there was one group doing this, it would give law enforcement a single target," said Neil Gallagher of the FBI. "Much ... more unnerving is the fact that what we're facing isn't a national conspiracy but a mind-set of a large segment of our society."

Yet, in the end, the furor over the fires may bring some adjustment of that mind-set. Throughout the South, white citizens donated money, labor, prayer books and even choir robes to their burned-out black neighbors. Several groups volunteered for 24-hour vigils to guard churches. That thought was pleasing to the Rev. Joseph Darby of St. Phillip AME Church in Eastover, South Carolina. "We would love to have white volunteers serve on [our] watch squads," he says. "If you stand out in the countryside together in the middle of the night, you are going to have to talk." ∎

More Trials for O.J. Simpson

He is battered in a wrongful death suit, but wins custody of his kids

WHEN *THE PEOPLE V. ORENTHAL JAMES SIMPSON* concluded in October, 1995, it seemed that America's silly season had ended. Gone was O.J., nothing but O.J., from TV and the tabloids. What lingered, though, from the most avidly discussed criminal trial in the late 20th century was not fond memories of the Dancing Itos but bitter divisions and unanswered questions. Simpson was acquitted in a matter of hours by a mostly black jury after a yearlong proceeding tainted by race baiting and muddied by mountains of evidence and theories of police conspiracy. Nothing seemed the same: not juries, not police departments, not the reputations of anyone who came near the trial—and not civil discourse.

Yet as 1996 drew to a close, O.J. was once again prominent in headlines through two separate California trials. In the first, Simpson faced civil charges in a wrongful-death suit filed by the families of murder victims Nicole Brown Simpson (his ex-wife) and Ronald Goldman. In the second, the former football star battled to obtain custody of his two children by Nicole, Sydney, 11, and Justin, 8, who had been living in the care of Nicole's parents, Lou and Juditha Brown.

With the parties under a gag order and cameras banned from the courtroom, the civil trial, which started on October 23, turned out be very different from O.J.'s criminal trial, with key pieces of evidence—including the bloody prints left by a pair of expensive Bruno Magli shoes allegedly owned by O.J.—being cast in an entirely new light. Rulings by Superior Court Judge Hiroshi Fujisaki (nicknamed the anti-Ito for his decisive demeanor) led to significant shifts in strategy. For example, Fujisaki ruled that videotapes of former Los Angeles police detective Mark Fuhrman's testimony could not be shown to jurors; in earlier rulings he made it difficult

FAMILY FUN: Simpson with Sydney and Justin in 1994

for the defense to offer alternate scenarios of a police conspiracy or murderous drug lords without hard evidence.

The civil trial offered a spectacle long awaited by many: Simpson himself under oath, answering questions from a hostile lawyer. The plaintiffs gave it their best shot. For nine hours and two minutes, their lawyers tried to shake the defendant, to provoke an outburst, to spark a defining moment that would convince nine of the 12 jurors that Simpson was guilty. The defendant never lost his cool, but his testimony left his credibility in tatters. When plaintiff's attorney Daniel Petrocelli pointed to an enormous blow-up of Nicole's face, cut and purpled with bruises, looming on a huge screen, Simpson suggested they were caused by Nicole's habit of picking at her pimples. He denied ever having struck his wife, calling her accounts of battery "lies." The plaintiffs presented 31 witnesses who refuted almost everything O.J. said when he was on the stand. On December 9 the plaintiffs rested, and the trial adjourned for a holiday recess just as the Simpson defense team began introducing witnesses.

Yet for Simpson the holidays proved festive indeed. On December 20, in a 10-page decision, Orange County Superior Court Judge Nancy Wieben Stock ended Lou and Juditha Brown's guardianship of the Simpson children, declaring that they had failed to prove, as California law requires, that a return to Simpson's custody would be detrimental to the children.

The decision was not unexpected, given California law's bias in favor of biological parents, and given the judge's earlier decision to disallow evidence from O.J.'s criminal murder trial. The Browns were granted a hearing to ask the judge to stay her custody decision pending an appeal. But the year ended with California law maintaining a controversial maxim: Father Simpson knows best. ∎

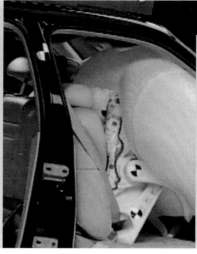

When Safety Devices Kill

Washington responds to fears about air bags by retooling the rules

AMID THE PUBLIC CONCERN OVER THE DANGER OF automobile air bags that surfaced in the autumn of 1996, it was rare to find anyone ready to declare that the bags were among the most effective safety devices ever developed for cars and trucks. Yet that is just what auto-safety experts like Ralph Hoar continued to believe. "The debate over air bags has always been distorted," argued Hoar, a consultant in Arlington, Virginia. "Air bags have been sold as the silver bullet that will save you or the lead one that will kill you. They have been oversold and demonized."

The demons were running rampant in the late fall. While air bags have saved more than 1,600 lives and averted thousands of crippling injuries since 1986, public attention fastened on the fact that the devices, which bang open at speeds up to 200 m.p.h., can be lethal as well. Since 1991, 51 victims—including 31 children—have been killed by air bags that slammed into them in low-speed crashes that might have been otherwise survivable. Many of the victims were not wearing seat belts. Among those particularly vulnerable: infants and small children placed in the front seat in rear-facing childrens' seats that put small heads within inches of the onrushing bags.

Faced with the rising anxiety over air bags, which were present in 50 million vehicles on U.S. roads, federal safety officials in November pulled in the rules that regulate the devices for a thorough overhaul. "Air bags are working well," said Dr. Ricardo Martinez, head of the National Highway Traffic Safety Administration, "but need to be improved to enhance the safety of children and small-stature adults." Martinez said his agency had been logging up to 500 phone calls a day from worried drivers and passengers who wanted to shut off or disable the safety devices. In response, the agency rolled out a five-part proposal for air bags that, if adopted after public hearings, would cover every passenger car and truck sold in the U.S. by the end of the decade.

The five points ranged from allowing consumers to disconnect air bags to requiring that a new generation of smart bags be phased in beginning with the 1999 model year. But the proposals raised hackles among safety advocates and their traditional foes, the Big Three automakers in Detroit. "It's bad public policy," said Joan Claybrook, who led the NHTSA in the Carter Administration and now runs the watchdog group Public Citizen. "For the government to tell people it is O.K. to disconnect their air bags is a terrible idea that sends the wrong signal." Claybrook blamed both Washington and the car manufacturers for failing to instruct the public in basic matters such as never allowing small children to ride in front seats and wearing seat belts to make the air bags most effective.

At the same time, carmakers enthusiastically endorsed the proposal to power down air bags, which reflected industry recommendations. Chrysler was already developing slower-speed air bags and expected to have them ready for the 1998 model year. The harmony ended there, however, because Detroit was likely to resist the proposal for smart air bags. Automakers insisted that elaborate systems tailored to the weight and position of each occupant would be difficult to engineer and test, and could add as much as $600 to the cost of each vehicle. But just as in its earlier opposition to air bags, Detroit may learn to live with all that extra trouble—and so too may the driving public. ∎

DEATHTRAP: Above, a test shows how a rapidly inflating air bag can be fatal to a child sitting in the automobile's front seat

G.I. JILL: The Army faces harassment woes

School for Scandal

In the most far-reaching scandal to hit the armed forces since the Navy's 1991 Tailhook incident, charges of sexual harassment were filed at two U.S. Army training centers: Maryland's Aberdeen Proving Ground and Missouri's Fort Leonard Wood. The Maryland troubles emerged first, when the Army announced in November that it was filing rape, assault and sexual harassment charges against three male officers responsible for training new recruits at Aberdeen, and investigating at least 17 others. A toll-free hotline set up at Aberdeen to receive calls concerning sexual harassment in the Army logged some 3,930 calls by the end of the week.

Terrorism in Saudi Arabia

On June 25, a truck bomb planted by Muslim extremists outside an apartment complex housing U.S. troops in Dhahran, Saudi Arabia, killed 19 U.S. airmen and wounded 50 more. The force of the bomb sheared off the outer wall of Building 131 and left a smoking crater 85 ft. across and 35 ft. deep where the truck was parked. The shock wave blew in windows and pulverized reinforced concrete, creating a blizzard of slashing, crushing

DEVASTATION: Crater from Saudia Arabia terrorist bombing

projectiles. The tragedy raised serious questions about how well the military had prepared for terrorist attacks—and highlighted the increasing power of Islamic extremists within the Saudi kingdom.

Of Death and Decorations

A stunned nation mourned when Admiral Mike Boorda, the Pentagon's Chief of Naval Operations, took his own life with a .38-cal. pistol in the yard of his Washington home. Boorda, 56, the first enlisted man to rise through the ranks to become boss of the Navy, was an affable man who was especially popular with rank-and-file sailors. He shot himself only hours before he was to meet with a pair of reporters he

VALOR? Boorda's pins

believed were going to question him about his wearing of two small bronze Vs—symbolizing valor in combat—on his military ribbons. Though he had never been awarded the medals, Boorda had worn the decorations for years.

Bad Lessons from Teacher

Just less than three years after the CIA accused its agent Aldrich Ames of spying, it arrested another of its own: Harold J. Nicholson. Since joining the spy agency in 1980, Nicholson had been quietly but smoothly rising through the agency ranks.

NICHOLSON: A new CIA traitor?

At the time of his arrest, he was working as an instructor at Camp Peary, the CIA training facility near Williamsburg, Virginia, teaching new spies. The agency accused Nicholson of spying for the Russians, claiming that he had turned over classified documents to their agents and may also have told them the names and assignments of Camp Peary's recent graduates, thus blowing their covers at the outset of their careers. Nicholson, who pleaded not guilty, allegedly received $180,000 for his services. After the election, President Clinton nominated his former National Security Adviser, Anthony Lake, to replace John Deutch as head of the espionage agency.

WHOOSH! Yet another snow job in the capital

In early January, Republicans shut down the government—and so did Mother Nature, as the most powerful **BLIZZARD** in years paralyzed Washington, D.C. and 20 states along the Northeastern seaboard, dumping 30 inches of snow in Philadelphia, 20 in New York City

New First Lady—at State

She is iron-willed, deeply political and media savvy. She is an immigrant to the U.S., the daughter of a Czech diplomat who fled with his family to London when the Nazis overran their country in 1938, and who sought asylum in the U.S. in 1948. She attended Wellesley and earned her Ph.D. at Columbia while mothering three young daughters. She is Madeleine Albright, and in December Bill Clinton named her the first woman ever to serve as U.S. Secretary of State. The outspoken Albright, U.S. Ambassador to the United Nations in Clinton's first term, is known for her tough, no-nonsense attitude as well as her considerable diplomatic skills. Under her soft-spoken predecessor, Warren Christopher, she became the most visible public promoter of U.S. foreign policy in the Administration. When Fidel Castro's pilots shot down two U.S. civilian planes in February 1996, the diplomat's brisk retort to the Cuban leader soon became famous. "This is not *cojones*, this is cowardice," said the outspoken Albright.

TOUGH: Albright takes no guff

"He Walked and Ran and Flew Through Life"

Commerce Secretary Ron Brown, 54, was an engaging study in contradictions: a fan of Hermès ties who liked to dine in deep-fry joints; a defender of the little people who enjoyed being chauffeured around in limousines; a dealmaker who could talk policy; a big-time Washington lawyer who never gave up public service; a man of conviction who often skirted the ethical edge; a keenly optimistic black man in the white establishment. His résumé contained a gold-plated series of civil rights achievements: first black chief counsel to the Senate Judiciary Committee; one of the first black partners in his Washington law firm; first black Democratic Party chairman. In early April, Brown was leading a group of 12 U.S. executives on a trade mission to the Balkans when their Air Force T-43 plane smashed into a rocky hilltop outside Dubrovnik in a heavy storm, killing all aboard. President Clinton eulogized Brown as a "magnificent life-force" who "walked and ran and flew through life."

RON BROWN: A magnetic and effective force at Commerce

No-Frills Tragedy

ValuJet Airlines was a no-frills airline that was growing fast. But a long series of non-fatal mishaps had placed it under safety surveillance by the Federal Aviation Administration. The scrutiny came too late: on May 11, a ValuJet DC-9 carrying 105 passengers and five crew plunged into the Everglades shortly after takeoff, killing everyone aboard. The cause of the crash: the ignition of volatile oxygen-generating canisters that had been incorrectly marked empty, packed in cardboard boxes that lacked required warning labels and stowed in the cargo hold without safety caps.

GOTCHA! Juveniles in custody in Denver

For once there was good news in the nation's **WAR ON CRIME:** In city after city across the country, crime rates dropped as much as 17%. Experts credited a proactive new approach, "community policing," that put more cops on the streets

MOSCOW CIRCUS

Heart surgery, a dirty war and re-election in a squeaker: How long can Boris Yeltsin survive?

THE RUSSIAN STATE "is not a country, it's a circus," tough-talking ex-general Alexander Lebed complained to journalists in October. Lebed's walk on the Kremlin tightrope had ended a few hours earlier, when he was ousted by President Boris Yeltsin after serving only four months as Yeltsin's national security adviser.

In 1996 Yeltsin, ringmaster of the Russian circus, put on a three-ring show as he struggled to control events in

Chechen fighters humiliated the Russian leader in the week of his inauguration

THIS JUST IN: Election results on Moscow TV

the republic he is trying to lead out of seven decades of stagnation under communist rule. In addition to the drain of war in the breakaway republic of Chechnya, Yeltsin had to come from behind to defeat a resurgent Communist Party in a presidential election in July. He prevailed by ruthlessly utilizing and then discarding Lebed. Yet through it all Yeltsin struggled against a more insidious nemesis: severe heart illness that led to bypass surgery in November.

In his first term, Yeltsin had succeeded in wrenching Russia from its statist past, but he had failed to shove it into a stable and prosperous economic future. Corruption, chaotic change and arbitrary rules were exploited by criminals and the well-connected nouveau riche, while ordinary Russians seethed over lost jobs, unpaid wages and a widening gap between rich and poor.

Yeltsin's popularity had slumped along with the country. With the presidential election looming, his approval ratings in February were not even reaching two digits, his policies were under siege, and his health was shaky. Those unsettled by economic reform were angry at Yeltsin, but reformers were too. He had dumped from his Cabinet most advocates of a market economy, and he had turned to a hardfisted style of leadership, surrounding himself with ever more authoritarian aides.

All this offered fertile ground for Yeltsin's most formidable opponents—the newly revitalized communists who in December 1995 won more seats than any other party in the Russian legislature. The party's standard-bearer was Gennadi Zyuganov, a smooth customer and an opponent of Yeltsin's in the last days of the U.S.S.R. The canny Zyuganov sounded like a social democrat when he met with Western businessmen and diplomats. To the party faithful, however, he put forth a harsher, anti-Western, sometimes anti-Semitic message.

The election was held in two rounds, a general election in June and a run-off between the two top candidates in July. As the first round of the election approached, Yeltsin pulled a typically shrewd political move. With polls showing he was running about even with Zyuganov, he struck an alliance with Lebed, who was running as an independent on an antiwar platform. Lebed commanded a wide following—wide enough to put a dent in Yeltsin's polls, but not enough to survive the first electoral round. Just weeks before the general election, Yeltsin and Lebed concluded a deal: Yeltsin would offer clandestine support for Lebed in the first election, thus draining votes from Zyuganov. Then Yeltsin would appoint the former general to a high position in his administration in return for Lebed's support in the run-off election.

The plan worked perfectly, fueled by Kremlin money. One major Moscow weekly received 2 billion rubles from the Yeltsin campaign to cover the cost of running Lebed's election propaganda. Yeltsin won 35% of the vote in the first election; Zyuganov got 32%, Lebed 15%. Two days later, Yeltsin tapped Lebed for two jobs: he became the President's national security adviser and secretary of the Kremlin's Security Council, which coordinates foreign

SURVIVOR: Yeltsin resting before surgery

"President Yeltsin will be able to return to his office and carry out his duties."

and domestic policy. Lebed's payoff: Yeltsin fired his loyal but hugely unpopular Defense Minister, Pavel Grachev. The President soon purged three more hard-liners, including the man closest to him personally, his drinking buddy and tennis partner Lieut. General Alexander Korzhakov, the President's chief of security. The firings amounted to an almost clean sweep of the so-called Kremlin war party, an inner circle of authoritarian, antireform power brokers.

Yeltsin went on to defeat Zyuganov by 13 percentage points in the July 3 run-off election. With his power base secure, he was free at last to confront the other problems he faced. First up was Chechnya, a thorn in Yeltsin's side since its leader, Jokhar Dudayev, had declared independence from Russia in 1991. Expecting a quick victory, Yeltsin in 1994 had sent the Russian army to put down the Chechens, but the situation became a quagmire. About 30% of Chechnya's 1 million people were killed or wounded in Yeltsin's vain attempt to impose his will on the tiny republic. After 20 months of war, the ill-trained Russian infantry was still no match for the tough, fast-moving Chechens.

Though the Russians struck a blow in May by killing Dudayev, that only redoubled the Chechens' defiance. In a ferocious surprise attack in early August—timed to embarrass Yeltsin at his inaugural—Chechen fighters reversed the course of the war, driving thousands of Russian troops out of the capital city, Grozny, inflicting hundreds of casualties and surrounding thousands of other Russians in their strongholds. It was a humiliating defeat.

Yeltsin now assigned Lebed to investigate the Chechen situation. Lebed immediately went to Chechnya and worked out an informal cease-fire with Chechen chief of staff Aslan Maskhadov. Lebed claimed he could end the war if he were given broad special powers to do so. After hesitating, Yeltsin decided to go along; he granted Lebed effective control-and-command authority over all army, Interior Ministry and security troops in Chechnya.

Lebed began shuttling between Moscow and Chechnya, holding a series of meetings with Chechen army boss Maskhadov and political leader Zelimkhan Yandarbiyev. On August 31, after eight hours of strenuous talks with the rebel leaders, Lebed announced a cease-fire that he claimed would "terminate this bloody bacchanalia." He promised he would soon produce a permanent political solution to Chechnya's bid for independence.

Lebed seemed triumphant—yet Yeltsin hinted at Lebed's suddenly shaky status by claiming that he was "not completely satisfied with Lebed's performance." Pointedly ignoring the cease-fire, Yeltsin claimed that during the recent election campaign, Lebed had "said if he had power, he could solve Chechnya. Well, now he has the power, and unfortunately, I still can't see any results."

By mid-October, Lebed no longer held the power. His brief ride atop the Kremlin tiger came to an end when Yeltsin fired him, claiming Lebed had been planning a coup. No one took the accusations seriously; they were clearly a pretext for Yeltsin's getting rid of Lebed, whose can-do approach to Chechnya had made him far and away the most popular political figure in the country—including the President. Lebed was also deeply feared by such Kremlin insiders as Anatoli Chubais, who was named presidential chief of staff after the elections, and Prime Minister Viktor Chernomyrdin.

LEBED'S DISMISSAL, WHICH SOLVED ONE OF YELtsin's problems, only underscored another: the President's continuing ill health. Making a rare live appearance on TV, the sadly feeble-looking Yeltsin at times stared blankly at the wrong camera and seemed to take forever to place his signature on the decree dismissing Lebed. Weeks before, the Kremlin had finally come clean about the President's health: he suffered from a serious heart condition that would require surgery before year's end.

The operation took place on November 5, with U.S. heart specialist Michael DeBakey in attendance. After seven hours in the operating room, during which Yeltsin's heart was stopped for more than 60 minutes, the clearly relieved surgeons announced that all had gone well. Their optimism was echoed by DeBakey, who said, "President Yeltsin will be able to return to his office and carry out his duties in normal fashion."

Spectators of the Russian circus were apprehensive about what those duties would involve. Rather than moving boldly forward to solve the country's problems, Yeltsin was likely to have his hands full running the greatest show in Moscow: the continuing struggles for power among the lions and tigers and bears—Lebed and Chubais and Korzhakov. ∎

POWER PLAYERS

It seems to come with the territory: whether Joseph Stalin, Leonid Brezhnev or Boris Yeltsin is boss, the Kremlin is a hotbed of intrigue and secretive power struggles.

With Boris Yeltsin recuperating from heart bypass surgery, three top aides will be the key players inside the Kremlin—and discarded aides like Alexander Lebed and Alexander Korzhakov, the former security chief, will be challenging from outside.

Viktor Chernomyrdin, the stolid Prime Minister, will present the administration's reassuring

Viktor Chernomyrdin

Anatoli Chubais

face—business as usual. Yeltsin's bright and ambitious chief of staff, Anatoli Chubais, formerly czar of privatization and sardonically nicknamed "the Regent" by his enemies, will be the strategic powerhouse of the regime.

A new face could be a strong force: Tatyana Dyachenko, Yeltsin's younger daughter, has become the most trusted channel of information to and from the President. A near contemporary of Chubais's and like him

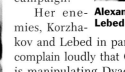

Tatyana Dyachenko

highly educated, Dyachenko is a discreet but crucial figure who first won her father's trust with her candor and analytical powers during the election campaign.

Her enemies, Korzhakov and Lebed in particular, complain loudly that Chubais is manipulating Dyachenko. Their outrage is understandable: she played a significant role in the downfall of both.

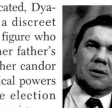

Alexander Lebed

HOW PLIANT IS

Clashing over Taiwan, trade and human rights, Washington and Beijing

CHINESE ARMED FORCES LAUNCHING missiles that splash down perilously close to Taiwan, putting its armed forces on high alert. A U.S. carrier task force cruising the area, another sailing toward it. Washington's policy of "comprehensive engagement" with Beijing under fire from Americans concerned about continuing Chinese violations of civil rights. The international financial community fretting over the 1997 transfer of Hong Kong to Chinese control. A severe trade imbalance, complicated by ongoing Chinese violations of U.S. copyrights. Even the Walt Disney Co. butting heads with Beijing over a motion picture dealing with the life of the Dalai Lama.

In 1996 one misstep and one misperception after another bumped America, the world's sole remaining superpower, and China, its sole up-and-coming superpower, closer to crisis. The year's most serious rupture was triggered by China's harsh warning to Taiwan in March, underlined by "test firings" of missiles off Taiwan's coast, that it must remain committed to eventual reunification and squelch whatever dreams of independence it might be harboring. President Clinton responded to the Chinese gambit by sending a "big stick," an aircraft-carrier task force, to cruise through the area.

True, the show of colors by both sides off Taiwan was pantomime rather than confrontation: eager to avoid a clash, both sides were merely using their military to lend muscle to political messages. But to date neither Washington nor Beijing has given much indication that it knows the other well enough to ensure that pantomime belligerence will not someday give way to the real thing.

Washington has a wide range of interests at stake where China is concerned. Foremost is trade. The U.S. and China, a huge and largely untapped market of 1.2 billion people, now do $50 billion worth of business with each other. The fate of Taiwan and the transfer of power in Hong Kong are highly complicating factors. Beyond that, the U.S. has both a moral and a financial interest in seeing China improve its human-rights record. A more humane China would benefit its people; a more stable China would benefit its trading partners.

A half-century after World War II, the U.S. remains the dominant power in the Pacific, and, to the degree it

CHINA?

work to keep alive an uneasy truce

tries to maintain influence there, will inevitably collide with China's rising importance. The peace and prosperity of the world in the next century depend in many ways on what Beijing does. How should the U.S. handle it? There are essentially two prescriptions: a policy called comprehensive engagement, and one that goes under its old cold-war name, containment.

Comprehensive engagement, the approach pursued by all U.S. Presidents since Richard Nixon, aims to bring China into the world community through broadly based dialogue and diplomacy, such as the Pentagon's contacts with the Chinese military through naval visits. The advocates of containment are led by an odd-bedfellow alliance of human-rights activists and old cold warriors. Angered by what they interpret as Beijing's uncooperative behavior, the containment forces are convinced that China is a bully that needs to be disciplined, not indulged.

Across the board, the critics contend that comprehensive engagement has amounted to giving in to China whenever the two countries have come into conflict. To some degree, the record over the past few years bears that out. In 1993 President Clinton "delinked" Beijing's human-rights record from the annual decision on whether to grant China most-favored-nation trading status, claiming the policy had made China more recalcitrant and threatened to hurt U.S. business there. By reinforcing trade ties, he said, the U.S. would be in a better position to influence China on human rights. But China's record has not improved. The State Department's annual report, made public in March, talked of "widespread and well-documented abuses," particularly in Tibet.

Nor has the trade front improved. Estimates of the U.S. trade deficit with China range from $22 billion to $34 billion, depending on how Hong Kong transshipments are counted. Moreover, Beijing has failed to vigorously enforce agreements with the U.S. that outlaw piracy of videos, CDs and software. The trade and human-rights issues came to an unusual flashpoint in the fall, when the Walt Disney Co., which had been assiduously wooing Beijing in order to open up the huge Chinese market for its entertainment products, ran afoul of Chinese sensitivities. China warned Disney not to produce and distribute a movie biography of the Dalai Lama, the exiled leader of Tibet. But Disney, putting principle ahead of profit, refused to submit.

A TALE OF TWO CITIES: At left, even as Shanghai sparkles with prosperity, U.S. financiers worry about the future of Hong Kong, whose new stamps no longer show the Queen

There are other sources of friction. Beijing has continued to test atomic weapons, transferred nuclear-arms technology to Pakistan and sold missiles to Iran. Washington has blocked China's membership in the World Trade Organization, which Beijing wants as a venue for reconciling trade disputes and obtaining more favorable tariff treatment. The U.S. has also explored a closer military relationship with India, against which China fought a war in 1962, and in 1995 established full diplomatic relations with Vietnam, a traditional enemy that repulsed a Chinese invasion in 1979.

ALL THIS MUST BE VIEWED IN THE CONTEXT OF Beijing's current state of fragility, with Deng Xiaoping on his deathbed and his designated successor, Jiang Zemin, not firmly in control. Despite the government's success in raising the standard of living, its problem list is long: money-losing state enterprises; more than 100 million basically unemployed migrant workers; rampant corruption; growing gaps between rich and poor as well as between the booming coastal provinces and the hinterland—all tinder for potential social unrest. Perhaps most important, an ideologically bankrupt Communist Party is relying on repression and nationalism to maintain power.

Taiwan remains a test case for America's China policy. On March 23, it held a presidential vote—the first time in the 4,000 years of Chinese history that a leader was chosen in a free election. President Lee Teng-hui, who had infuriated Beijing by seeking greater international recognition for Taiwan, was re-elected. Beijing insists that Taiwan is part of China and will eventually be reintegrated. Lee, at least officially, accepts the objective of reunification, although Beijing and his political opponents at home have been questioning his sincerity.

The U.S. is also officially pledged to a one-China policy, but Beijing has come to suspect that Washington is backing away from it. Yet even Beijing agrees that reunification will not take place until sometime in the future when the societies on the two shores of the strait are more closely synchronized.

Even so, the year ended on a positive note, as Presidents Clinton and Jiang had a cordial meeting at a pan-Asian economic conference in November. No breakthroughs were announced, but at least the two sides were talking. Comprehensive engagement may still be the right path, but it would yield better results if both sides also engaged in more mutual comprehension. ∎

CHAIN REACTION: When Iraqi troops marched into Kurdish territory, U.S. Tomahawk missiles hit back

Saddam Flexes His Muscles

A quarrel between Kurd clans draws in Iraq's Hussein and the U.S.

CRISES IN THE PERSIAN GULF ARE ALWAYS COMPLIcated, but the flare-up that seized Iraq in the late summer of 1996 proved byzantine beyond the norm. Iraqi leader Saddam Hussein's Republican Guard attacked Kurdish towns in northern Iraq, and high above the Persian Gulf aging U.S. B-52s responded by launching computer-guided cruise missiles at military installations far to the south. In the end, Saddam improved his political position while the U.S. says it circumscribed his military capability. American critics grumbled that President Clinton had not done enough; foreign friends complained that he had done too much.

In fact, the struggle involved two rather separate wars, connected by the thuggish intentions of Saddam Hussein. War A was a nasty struggle for autonomy, power, money and influence among the factious Kurds in northern Iraq and the sometime-friend, sometime-foe regional powers of Iraq, Iran and Turkey. War B, the long battle of attrition against Saddam, is the one that preoccupies Washington. It is a test of wills in which the Iraqi leader, driven by motives of survival and revenge, regularly seeks to frustrate or lash out at the U.S. while Washington strives to contain his disruptive ambitions.

The trouble started when Kurdistan Democratic Party leader Massoud Barzani—threatened by Iranian aid to an opposing Kurdish faction, the Patriotic Union of Kurdistan—made an unthinkable about-face. Barzani asked Saddam, the Kurds' common enemy, to fight the P.U.K. In effect, he invited Saddam to enter the autonomous Kurdish enclave in northern Iraq that was established after the Gulf War and remains under the protection of U.S., French and British air forces. On August 31, Saddam responded to Barzani's request by sending 40,000 troops to the town of Erbil, then controlled by the P.U.K.

Within hours, the P.U.K. was routed and the town handed over to Iraq's new Kurdish allies, the K.D.P. Saddam's forces reportedly rounded up and killed dozens of Iraqi defectors and blew up the broadcasting facilities of the main opposition party, the Iraqi National Congress. Saddam left behind a cadre of spies and goons to reassert his authority. In a fortuitous benefit, he had also chased away a handful of CIA operatives in the Kurdish zone running a covert campaign to overthrow him.

Clinton responded quickly, ordering U.S. forces to fire two volleys of high-tech, low-casualty cruise missiles against 15 air-defense sites south of Baghdad. Clinton also expanded the "no-fly zone" under which U.S. jet fighters force Saddam's airplanes to operate in only a limited airspace inside Iraq. The expansion was intended to humiliate Saddam before his military and to make it even harder for the Iraqi strongman to venture south against the crucial oil lands of Kuwait and Saudi Arabia.

But would the U.S. response—which was not supported by such key allies as France—frighten Saddam? While Washington has curbed his appetite for external adventures for now, it has failed to control the dictator's misbehavior at home. Saddam has buffed up his tough-guy image and maintains an unabated hunger for revenge. His hold on power seems as durable as ever. War B may end only with the demise of Baghdad's resilient bullyboy. ■

The Sword of the Prophet

Strict Muslim fundamentalists capture Kabul and much of Afghanistan

THE SOUND OF ARTILLERY AND MACHINE-GUN FIRE reverberated in the darkened sky over Kabul, capital of war-ravaged Afghanistan. When dawn arrived on September 27, residents cautiously crept from their homes in search of clues as to what had occurred during the long night and who had control of their city. Outside the presidential palace, they found the answer. Swinging from a concrete post were two bruised corpses—those of Najibullah, President of Afghanistan from 1987 to 1992, and his brother Shahpur Ahmedzi.

It was an appropriately medieval spectacle for a country that years ago degenerated into primitive warring bands, although equipped with frighteningly modern weaponry. When the Soviets withdrew after 10 years of occupation, the U.S.-backed *mujahedin* groups that had opposed the communists fought among themselves for control of the country. Moscow-backed Najibullah was ousted in 1992, but since then four years of warfare between Najibullah's successor, Burhanuddin Rabbani, and rival *mujahedin* leader Gulbuddin Hekmatyar had done more damage to the country than the Soviet occupation. Kabul was relatively intact when the Soviets departed in 1989; by 1996 it had been virtually destroyed in bombardments and street fighting that took 30,000 lives.

Najibullah's swinging body signified Kabul's fall to a new set of victors—the Taliban, a group of former Islamic seminarians who had enjoyed remarkable military success since their founding only two years earlier. Strict Islamic fundamentalists, the Taliban were led by a former *mujahedin*, or holy warrior, in his 30s named Maulana Mohammad Omar. Rabbani and his government fled before the Taliban arrived, and that spelled doom for Najibullah, 49. The new government was recognized almost immediately by Pakistan, which had been covertly lending fighting men and supplies to the Taliban in order to gain influence over neighboring Afghanistan.

The U.S. and many other nations also initially welcomed the Taliban victory, since it appeared it would put an end to the civil war. But as the depth of the Taliban's Islamic fundamentalism emerged, world opinion turned against them. In their first week the Taliban shut girls out of schools and ordered women workers from offices and hospitals. All women were forced to wear chadors, long robes and veils, when in public. At a press conference, two female foreign correspondents were forbidden to question a Taliban official, because, according to an aide, he "must not hear their voices." Strict Islamic law—like the amputation of hands for stealing—was imposed.

Meanwhile, men were given a month to grow beards, and the photographing of human figures—as well as "sensitive incidents"—was forbidden. Amnesty International claimed 1,000 people were jailed in a "reign of terror." The Taliban acknowledged only 70 arrests for looting.

The fall of Kabul did not end the fighting in the country, which was complicated by its tribal nature. President Rabanni's former army chief, Ahmad Shah Massoud, a Tajik, forged a tenuous alliance with onetime enemy Abdul Rashid Dostum, a powerful Uzbek warlord, to fight the Taliban; together, they controlled the northern sector of the country. Weeks after their victory, the Taliban, mostly ethnic Pashtuns, were going house to house in Kabul in search of Tajiks and Uzbeks. Afghanistan's woes—and the lines of refugees they produced—promised to stretch deep into the winter and spring of 1997. ∎

CLAMPDOWN At left, the first victims when the Taliban seized Kabul were former President Najibullah and his brother, routed out of a U.N. safe haven and hanged. Above, Afghan women were made to conceal their faces in public

RIGHT TURN?

When Israel elects a get-tough new Prime Minister, the peace process slows down—and a new *intifadeh* flares up

SOMETIMES STATESMEN STUMBLE BLINDLY OVER AN EPOCHAL CROSSROADS they do not know is there. Others are given the chance to see the fork in the road ahead and decide deliberately which way to go. Folly, wrote historian Barbara Tuchman, is when leaders knowingly choose the wrong path. The leaders of the state of Israel—its voters—faced a clear fork in the road on May 29, 1996. Struggling to find their bearings after the assassination of peace-making Prime Minister Yitzhak Rabin in November of 1995, voters that day would elect a

new Prime Minister. The stakes were manifest: the election was nothing less than a referendum on the future of the long-sought, yet still fledgling Arab-Israeli peace process.

At issue was not peace vs. security: all Israelis craved both. Each candidate—Rabin's heir, Prime Minister Shimon Peres, 72, of the Labor Party, and conservative Benjamin (Bibi) Netanyahu, 46, of the Likud Party—vowed he could deliver both, if by vastly different means.

The Israeli voters chose to turn right, electing Netanyahu by the narrowest of margins, just 29,507 votes out of 3.1 million cast, a decimal-point majority of 50.4%. By the fall, the consequences of the election were clear: Israel was refusing to honor the groundbreaking accords it had signed in Oslo in 1993, and Israelis and Palestinians had fought in the bloodiest clashes in the West Bank in thirty years.

VICTORY: Netanyahu won, but by the narrowest of margins

To win at all, Netanyahu claimed to embrace the peace process even as he promised actions that would thwart its success. He would negotiate with Syria but never give up the Golan Heights. He would abide by the Oslo agreements but build more Jewish settlements in the West Bank. He would undertake talks on the territory's final status but not discuss Jerusalem.

In Arab capitals, reactions to the election ranged from indifference to dismay, anxiety, bitterness and resignation. Even before the election, Arabs were angry when Peres bombarded targets in southern Lebanon—including a U.N. camp for refugees where more than 100 civilians died—in an offensive against Muslim terrorists. The reaction in Washington, where President Clinton had invested heavily in the peace process, was gloomy too, but officials decided to cast the outcome in the best light.

In his first three months in office Netanyahu assiduously shunned Palestinian leader Yasser Arafat and froze plans to expand self-rule in the territories, as promised in previously signed accords. Then Israeli intelligence agencies began warning that, as a result, Arafat was fast losing standing among his people and that instability, perhaps violence, might follow. Finally Netanyahu agreed to a summit, which was held on the Israeli-Gaza Strip border on September 4.

The meeting produced no breakthroughs on the next steps of interim Palestinian self-rule: an Israeli pullout from Hebron, the last big Palestinian city still under occupation, where 400 Israeli settlers vowed to remain, plus further withdrawals in the West Bank. To Palestinian dismay, Netanyahu insisted on reopening the Hebron agreement already completed by Rabin and Peres.

The diplomatic slump presaged more serious trouble. Only three weeks after the summit meeting, Palestinian and Israeli forces engaged in the most severe fighting in the territories since the 1967 Arab-Israeli war. Putatively, it was all about a hole in the ground, dug by the Israelis in Arab East Jerusalem to complete an ancient tunnel that led to the foundations of Judaism's sacred Western Wall. Because the passage runs alongside the Haram al-Sharif, the plateau on which Islam's holy Dome of the Rock and al-Aqsa mosque are built, Muslim authorities charged that the excavation might endanger those sites. More important, the tunnel opening became the inflammatory symbol of who was truly boss in East Jerusalem, the eventual sovereignty of which remained in bitter dispute.

The first Palestinian protests were spontaneous. On September 24, youths on the Haram al-Sharif threw rocks onto Jewish worshippers at the Western Wall below. Elsewhere in East Jerusalem protesters scuffled with Israeli police. The next day Arafat and the Palestinian Authority embraced the unrest. Soon there were all-out battles between Israeli troops and Palestinian civilians backed by Arafat's soldiers. The two sides clashed everywhere: on the roads, at military checkpoints, in Jewish settlements in the West Bank, at Jewish religious sites still under Israeli control within the Palestinian cities.

Moving to a war footing, Israeli commanders sent thousands of reinforcements into the territories. They also beefed up the available firepower. After three days of hostilities, 59 Palestinians and 14 Israelis had been killed and nearly a thousand others injured throughout the West Bank and Gaza Strip. For the first time in recent memory the Israelis flew Cobra helicopter gunships above Pales-

tinian towns, firing shells at Palestinian shooters. For the first time since the 1967 war, the Israelis also moved tanks into the territories. Eventually Arafat was convinced to reign in his police and armed forces.

With the entire peace process in danger, the U.S. convened a hastily-called summit in Washington, and pressured Netanyahu, Arafat and Jordan's King Hussein to attend. But the Israelis remained intransigent, shocking U.S. negotiators with demands to reopen agreements that had been agreed on in the Oslo accords. At best, the summit cooled off the two leaders and offered them a chance to talk face-to-face. But it gave little hope for forward progress. As Israel marked the first anniversary of the assassination of Yitzhak Rabin in November, it was still questioning the wisdom of its decision to turn hard right on the road to peace in the Mideast. ■

AGAIN, WAR: Fighting was heaviest in the West Bank, where a Palestinian policeman is carried toward shelter

Birth Pangs of a New Balkans?

With NATO's help, ballots and demonstrations replace bullets—for now

AN UNEASY TRUCE BROUGHT SOME SOLID PROGRESS in 1996 to the squabbling republics of the former Yugoslavia, bloodied in recent years by ethnic wars grounded in the region's three great social divisions: Catholic Croats, Orthodox Serbs and Muslims. A NATO force in multi-ethnic Bosnia supervised elections guaranteed by the Dayton agreements of December 1995. The brutal Radovan Karadzic was pushed from office as President of the Bosnian Serbs. And, at year's end, the long reign of Serbian strongman Slobodan Milosevic was threatened by protests against his iron rule.

Despite this tide of good news, the long-term prospects for the region seemed to promise at best a lasting partition along strict ethnic lines. With hard-core nationalists winning the September elections in Bosnia, it was clear that the tolerance once enforced by the firm hand of Marshal Tito would never return to those lands.

The year pivoted around two major elections. In Bosnia on September 14, voting places were protected by 52,000 heavily armed NATO troops and thousands of police, as an estimated 1.5 million Bosnians made their way to the polls. The high security made for a relatively peaceful vote marred only by minor technical problems and long queues. But the results gave little cause for rejoicing. Both the winners on the Muslim side, the Party for Democratic Action (S.D.A.), and on the Serb side, the Serb Democratic Party (S.D.S.) led by Karadzic henchman Momcilo Krajisnik, insisted they would work to oppose the unified Bosnia specified in the Dayton plans. Karadzic, twice indicted for genocide and crimes against humanity for his butchery of Bosnian Muslims, had been officially forced out of office in July by Milosevic, who was acting under strong pressure from the U.S. But with his right-hand man Krajisnik as his stand-in, the fanatical Karadzic remained the guiding light of Bosnia's Serbs.

Hope for change in neighboring Serbia blossomed in local elections on November 17, when an opposition coalition of three parties known as Zajedno, or Together, won a majority in 15 of the country's 18 major cities. Since city councils control chunks of the mass media and electoral organization, the outcome represented a significant threat to Serbian President Milosevic and his party's grip on the country. Milosevic moved quickly to reverse the victory, citing voting "irregularities" and staging a follow-up, rigged election in which his people emerged victorious. That was too much for Belgrade's long-suffering citizens, many of whom blame Milosevic's demagogic Serbian nationalism for plunging the former Yugoslavia into $5\frac{1}{2}$ years of bloodshed and punitive sanctions. As many as 100,000 marchers surged into the streets for daily denunciations of the President, defying riot-control units from part of Milosevic's 80,000-man Praetorian Guard. The protests continued right through the New Year, even taking on a festive air for the holidays.

The demonstrators remained generally peaceful, chanting demands for Milosevic's resignation and opting for eggs over paving stones as projectiles of protest. The Serb President nourished a diminishing hope that enthusiasm would wane as winter set in. He had worked hard to rehabilitate his image overseas, first by hectoring his Bosnian Serb brothers into signing the Dayton peace agreement, then by agreeing to jettison Karadzic. Those deeds won him a removal of crippling Western economic sanctions but not full diplomatic rehabilitation. The demonstrators faced stiff odds against success in either ousting their unpopular President or revalidating the election he stole from them. But they at least served notice that their fund of patience was running out. ∎

SLOBO MUST GO! Waving report cards, students take to the streets of Belgrade to denounce Milosevic as a tyrant

Rwanda: Ghosts of Genocide

Hundreds of thousands of refugees destabilize Central Africa

TWO YEARS AFTER A BRUTAL WAR between tribes rocked Rwanda, the effects of the bloodshed continued to disrupt Central Africa. In 1994 more than 1 million Rwandan Hutu, including the militiamen and former soldiers who had massacred more than half a million of their country's Tutsi citizens, fled in fear of reprisal and were succored in U.N.-sponsored refugee camps in Zaïre and Tanzania. Tens of thousands of armed Hutu militiamen took control of the camps and, through propaganda and intimidation, prevented the rest of the refugees from returning home. International relief agencies kept the refugees fed and housed; the militiamen exacted "taxes" from the agencies and sold food aid for weapons, holding the civilians as a shield against Tutsi reprisals.

Over time, the Hutu guerrillas turned the refugee camps into safe bases from which to maraud into Rwanda in hopes of overthrowing the Tutsi regime there. The destabilizing effects spilled over into Burundi and Zaïre, provoking their Tutsi populations to fight back. By November 1, 1996, at least four factions of rebel Tutsis and regular soldiers were at war. As the clashes intensified, aid workers were driven from the camps, leaving the refugees to fend for themselves.

At that point the U.S. found itself being drawn into action. The rising hullabaloo from aid workers, news reports and foreign governments warned of an imminent holocaust among the Hutu refugees caught in the midst of the warring factions. The advocates clamored for immediate military intervention to save them. The pictures out of Zaïre certainly looked sickening. Some 500,000 Hutu were said to be huddled in the Mugunga camp, held captive by Hutu militias, cut off from food deliveries. As they do so often, the images began to galvanize political leaders. Canadian Prime Minister Jean Chrétien decided that Canada should lead a humanitarian military mission—provided the U.S. took part. President Clinton quickly concluded he could not refuse to join in.

Even then, however, it was not clear what the interventionists were volunteering to do. Their aim was to "facilitate" both the delivery of food and the voluntary repatriation of the refugees. Yet their troops would not protect aid convoys, not conduct forced entry into camps, not police camps. It soon became evident that mission planners knew little about the reality on the ground.

On Friday, November 15, attacking Tutsis finally routed the Hutu militias, who fled west from the Mugunga camp. Freed of their coercive overseers, thousands upon thousands of Hutu then simply stood up and began pouring down the straight tarmac road toward Rwanda. By Saturday, 200,000 had crossed the border, and 350,000 more were on the way. The formerly intimidated masses for whom the rescue mission was planned had suddenly freed themselves and decided en masse to go home: they could now reach aid supplies on their own. Yet the mass exodus did not solve the refugee problem; it merely shift-

HOMEWARD BOUND: Freed from the refugee camps in Zaïre, Hutus head for Rwanda

ed it eastward. As 500,000 Rwandans returned "home," the government said there were no homes for them.

In mid-December another giant migration began. Some 500,000 Hutus encamped in Tanzania were given a U.N. deadline to return to Rwanda by year's end. Many refugees began trekking home. Others, fearing reprisals, headed east into the Tanzanian bush. Their destination—like that of the entire region—was unknown. ∎

BUM STEER: Europe avoided British beef

Mad Cows and Englishmen

Since it first appeared in England in 1985, mad cow disease—known to scientists as bovine spongiform encephalopathy (BSE)— has killed more than 150,000 head of cattle. The government claimed BSE was harmless to humans, but in 1996 scientists discovered that the malady was linked to cases of a new strain of Creutzfeldt-Jakob disease, a deadly affliction. As a result, British beef was banned across Europe, hundreds of thousands of cattle were slaughtered and the future of Britain's beef industry was placed in serious doubt.

New Leader for the U.N.

After an ugly struggle between the U.S. and France, the United Nations named Kofi Annan of Ghana as its new Secretary-General, succeeding the reluctantly retiring Egyptian Boutros Boutros-Ghali. The U.S. had vetoed a second five-year term for Boutros-Ghali, long a thorn in Washington's side, but he was the preferred choice of the French. The widely popular Annan is an expert on U.N. finances; since 1993 he has been Under Secretary-General for Peacekeeping, in charge of 17 military operations and as many as 80,000 multinational troops in places like Bosnia, Somalia and the Middle East.

NEW BOSS: The U.S. faced down the world to put Annan in his post

A trailer truck on a flatbed rail car burned up under the English Channel, and a nightmare came true: **FIRE IN THE CHUNNEL!**
No one died, but intense heat damaged 2,400 feet of track and the tunnel wall

TUBULAR INFERNO: The scorched locomotive

Massacre of the Innocents in Small-town Scotland

Mass murder: it seemed a phenomenon to be found only in America and other urbanized lands. But on March 13, the tiny town of Dunblane, Scotland, endured a massacre of its children when a failed youth leader, Thomas Hamilton, 43, killed 16 five-

TARGETS: The Dunblane first-grade class

and six-year-old first-graders and their teacher. Hamilton, described by townspeople as an oddball, began shooting in the school playground, then barged into the building and shot his way down a corridor before emptying four handguns into his victims as they screamed and cowered in the gymnasium. Two other teachers and 12 children were wounded, three critically, before Hamilton put one of the guns to his head and shot himself.

GLOATING: Joseph Goebbels with Nazi gold

A Nazi Hoard in Swiss Banks?

For 50 years the Swiss had kept the lid on their horrible secret. But in 1996 the truth began to emerge: Swiss banks had served as willing repositories for Jewish wealth stolen by the Nazis during the Holocaust. In May, Swiss banks and international Jewish groups organized a panel to search for accounts lost in the Holocaust and help return the assets to rightful owners. The accounting was designed to rectify a 1962 inquiry that had found only $4.5 million in Jewish accounts at Swiss banks. As newly invigorated probers dug into all aspects of Switzerland's unsavory history of wartime dealings with the Nazis, the Swiss parliament in December set up a panel to investigate all Swiss-Nazi financial dealings and the fate of all Jewish Holocaust-era deposits in Swiss institutions.

The I.R.A.: More War

They gave peace a try—at least for 18 months. Then, on February 9, the Irish Republican Army broke the truce it had established in August 1994, exploding a bomb in London's Canary Wharf district that killed two people. Would-be peacemaker Gerry Adams of the I.R.A.'s political wing, Sinn Fein, distanced his group from the attack, but refused to condemn the I.R.A. directly. The bomb left the future of the peace process in Northern Ireland—and Adams' ability to speak for the I.R.A.—in doubt.

Gala at Gunpoint

It was one of the most audacious acts in the history of terrorist hostage taking. On December 17, left-wing rebels of Peru's Túpac Amaru Revolutionary Movement stormed into the Japanese embassy in Lima while the ambassador was entertaining a glittering assemblage of diplomats and dignitaries. They took more than 600 hostages, including ambassadors from at least 12 nations, then demanded freedom for imprisoned comrades—or they would begin executing hostages. By year's end, quiet diplomacy had got most of the captives released—but the siege went on.

Haiti's Bittersweet Peace

The U.S. intervention in Haiti, begun in September 1994, quickly achieved its first goal: legitimate Haitian President Jean-Bertrand Aristide was restored to power and the flood of boat people was halted. In February 1996 the second goal was reached when René Préval took the presidential oath and Haiti experienced its first-ever peaceful transfer of power from one popularly elected leader to another. U.S. troops returned home after losing only one soldier. But critics charged that Haiti still has a dysfunctional government and an impoverished economy, while crime and mob rule fill the vacuum of authority.

HEADS UP: A U.S. soldier patrols a slum in Port-au-Prince

NEVER FORGET: A war memorial in Guatemala

And now for the good news: after a civil war that raged for 35 years, killing 100,000 and leaving 40,000 "disappeared," Guatemalans decided to **GIVE PEACE A CHANCE,** as rebels signed a Christmastime treaty that ended the war

THE INCREDIBLE SHRINKING COMPANY

A new surge in corporate downsizing leaves workers worried, Wall Street happy— and bosses with big bucks

Happy New Year! Two days after the tooting of New Year's Eve horns heralded 1996, telecommunications giant AT&T announced that it would be bidding *Auld Lang Syne* to 40,000 employees, or 13% of its entire staff, by the end of the year. It was hardly news, of course, that "at most major companies, downsizing is standard operating procedure, year in and year out," in the words of John Challenger, executive vice president of the Chicago outplacement firm Challenger, Gray & Christmas. Nor was it any longer startling to hear of new job eliminations, even at companies that had already gone through previous rounds of layoffs and were earning solid profits.

In his new book *Mean Business,* "Chainsaw Al" Dunlap gloried in his role as dean of the downsizers

But in 1996 the downsizing trend—and the controversy about its effectiveness—once again dominated American business. With a total of 410,208 workers downsized through the first 10 months of 1996, announced cuts were running 20% above the 1995 pace. Even so, AT&T's move was a shocker. For one thing, the layoffs were much more numerous than anyone had expected. Moreover, as a social phenomenon the cuts were the most decisive signal yet that the old bonds of mutual loyalty between worker and giant company that had long prevailed in American business were now being strained to the breaking point.

AT&T had been bouncing people at an average rate of around 900 a month since 1984, when an antitrust decree forced it to get rid of its seven "Baby Bell" regional phone companies. Not entirely by coincidence, it earned $4.7 billion in 1994 and $139 billion in 1995 (after a $4 billion write-off in the fourth quarter for severance pay and related costs). It had also been obvious that more firings were coming ever since AT&T announced in September 1995 that it would split itself into three unequal pieces: a telecommunications company, a communications-equipment company and a computer company.

Even though the AT&T layoffs dwarfed all others, the practice had become virtually endemic, justified far and wide as the way U.S. companies had to go if they were to become mean and lean enough to survive the great international business run-off that lay ahead. In September, for example, just one day after Campbell Soup reported record profits, the behemoth of broth announced its intention to lay off 650 U.S. workers, including 175 employees—or 11% of the work force—at its headquarters in Camden, New Jersey. As a result, Campbell stock rose 8% on Wall Street by week's end.

In early November, Albert J. Dunlap, who had held the position of chairman and chief executive of Sunbeam Corp. for only four months, announced that half the appliance maker's 12,000 employees would be let go through layoffs or sales of divisions. According to one expert, in percentage terms it was believed to be the largest work-force reduction of its kind in history. Dunlap, 59, was a talkative, roll-up-the-sleeves corporate turnaround specialist who avidly pursued the role of executive poster boy for the downsizing movement and gloried in his nickname, "Chainsaw Al." He burst onto the scene in 1994 with a remarkably short, lucrative and controversial tour as CEO of venerable Scott Paper, which asked him to shake things up. So Dunlap sold billions of dollars in assets, chopped 35% of the work force, paid down debt and refocused the firm. By the time Scott was sold to Kimberly-Clark late in 1995, its stock had tripled, and Dunlap, via generous stock options and grants, had tucked away $100 million for himself.

In his book *Mean Business*, published in September 1996, Dunlap called his pay a bargain for Scott, whose total market value rocketed from $2.9 billion to $9.4 billion on his watch. Others said he did little more than gut Scott and dress it up for sale. But for the most part his critics were not shareholders, the constituency he wanted to serve.

Labor Secretary Robert Reich spoke for many when he said, "There is no excuse for treating employees as if they are disposable pieces of equipment."

But it was the AT&T cuts that left the deepest scar on the psyche of American labor. Of all U.S. firms, AT&T in its "Ma Bell" heyday probably came closest to a Japanese-style identification of worker with corporation. It was once common for an AT&T employee, asked what he did, to reply simply, "I work for the phone company," rather than saying, "I'm an accountant" or "I'm an engineer," Such feelings had been weakened by the layoffs that began in 1984, of course, but they somehow stayed alive in some workers—particularly those for whom employment at AT&T had become a family tradition.

Now, in an interview with TIME just after the layoffs were announced, AT&T chairman Robert E. Allen said a job at AT&T "used to be a lifelong commitment on the employee's part and on our part. But our people now realize that the contract [the implied promise of lifetime job security in exchange for hard work and loyalty] does not exist anymore."

Of the 40,000 workers AT&T let go, 7,400 were managers who accepted a company offer of voluntary separation with generous benefits. An additional 4,000 were in operations that AT&T planned to sell, and could go with those companies. That, however, left about 30,000 people who could be fired outright. They were given generous severance. According to AT&T, a typical clerical employee in New Jersey—44 years old, 18 years of service, making $644 a week—would receive more than $64,000.

Critics of downsizing often charge that it is simply a short-term ploy to boost a company's stock price on Wall Street on the heads of laid-off workers. In AT&T's case, some analysts suspected that the corporation's equipment-manufacturing business took the heaviest hit—23,000 layoffs—because it was the only one of the three split-off companies that would sell new stock, in addition to distributing shares to present AT&T stockholders. But Allen insisted that the layoffs were being driven by unavoidable business changes.

In the wake of the AT&T news, downsizing once again became a charged political issue. Pat Buchanan tarred the big corporations as villains in his run for the G.O.P. nomination. And eventual candidate Bob Dole noted, "corporate profits are setting records, and so are corporate layoffs." Even the probusiness *Investor's Business Daily* said, "Stockholders put experienced leaders atop America's great corporations not to shrink them or their payrolls, but to expand them, to create wealth and, in the process, jobs and growth."

SOME CORPORATIONS TOOK MEASURES TO CUSHION the blows of downsizing. In April, as two Baby Bells—NYNEX and Bell Atlantic—prepared to announce a merger, NYNEX chairman Ivan Seidenberg called Labor Secretary Reich to assure him there would not be sweeping layoffs; instead, some 3,000 jobs "consolidated" under the merger would be more than offset by future growth as the merged company entered different businesses. Plus, he promised Reich, ex-workers would get first crack at the new jobs. In December, when chemical giant Du Pont tentatively agreed to outsource its computer and telecommunications operations, it promised to do so without cutting jobs. Rather, some 3,100 Du Pont staffers would be given the chance to switch employers, with 2,600 spots reserved for Computer Sciences Corp. and 500 for Andersen Consulting.

There was good news on the job front in 1996: the number of new jobs created in the year's strong economy far exceeded those wiped out by downsizing. But the quality of those jobs left much to be desired. One federal study found that only 31.4% of those laid off between 1991 and '93 found jobs equal in pay and benefits to those they lost. What's more, the psychological effect of downsizing in shattering the confidence of laid-off workers far exceeds its economic impact. What frightens many is that painfully acquired job skills and long years of seniority at a profitable company are no longer a guarantee against layoff.

David Noer, author of a book on the psychological effects of layoffs, traces stages of reaction in the newly downsized that are strikingly similar to those discovered by psychiatrist Elisabeth Kübler-Ross in people awaiting their death: denial; anger; bargaining ("Can I get a better package?"); depression; and finally acceptance. Better get used to those stages, he says. In today's business climate, "we are all temps." ∎

BUSY SIGNAL

Downsizing was just a warm-up: AT&T—the once-imperial "Ma Bell"—came under attack from all fronts in 1996:

For AT&T, 1996 was the year of the triple whammy. Ten months after it downsized 40,000 workers, America's 10th largest company was rocked by the hiring of a controversial new president and by a monster merger that promised to pump even more life into its chief rival, MCI.

In late October AT&T dialed long distance—to R.R. Donnelley & Sons, a Midwest commercial printer, of all places—to find John Walter, its new president and heir apparent to CEO Robert Allen, who will retire in 1998, two years early. Surprised that AT&T had looked outside its ranks—and to a non-telecommunications executive—for leadership, Wall Street sent AT&T stock, already in the dumper, down 9% in the two days after Walter was named,

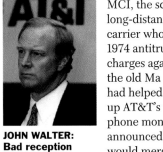

JOHN WALTER: Bad reception

clipping $5.7 billion off the embattled giant's market value. Ouch!

Walter, 50, found the ground shifting under his feet only two weeks after coming aboard. On Nov. 3, AT&T archrival MCI, the scrappy long-distance carrier whose 1974 antitrust charges against the old Ma Bell had helped break up AT&T's telephone monopoly, announced it would merge with massive British Telecommunications.

The merged company, to be called Concert, would have $42 billion in revenues and match AT&T in market value—if the merger is approved by U.S. regulators. Under the new 1996 telecommunications law, Concert's first gig could be the $100 billion local phone market in the U.S. Hello, Baby Bells: Competition calling.

BY THE NUMBERS

After tapering off in 1995, downsizing came on strong in 1996. Among the year's biggest layoffs:

AT&T	40,000
Wells Fargo/First Interstate Bancorp	7,500
Digital Equipment	7,000
ConAgra	6,500
Sunbeam	6,000
NYNEX/Bell Atlantic	3,000
Northrop Grumman	2,100
United Technologies	1,200

High Ride and HANDSOME

There's no dispute about "sputes": the popular sports utility vehicles are a shortcut to safari chic. But don't go off-road—you might scratch the paint

THE SIGNS WERE THERE TO BE READ, EVEN IF AT FIRST THEY didn't make a lot of what is usually thought of as sense. There was, yeah, that white Bronco in Brentwood. And the black Jeep that Tim Robbins, consummate Hollywood dealmaking lizard, drove in *The Player*. And Arnold's Hummer. Not a normal car among them. West Coast automotive analyst Christopher Cedergren read the signs in 1994 on Wilshire Boulevard, at the opening of a shrieks-with-chic Barneys boutique. His epiphany took place outside the store, not inside. Instead of Bentley Turbos, Mercedes sedans and the usual Porsches and Lamborghinis, so boring, there was a Lost Safari of Land Rovers, Ford Explorers and GMC Suburbans, all tricked out with steel brush guards, roof racks, off-roading spare-wheel mounts and black-leather car bras to ward off gravel and grasshoppers on the Paris-Dakar run. Cedergren flashed his perception to his clients, saying, "Cars are now history. The future belongs to trucks!"

Well, not trucks in the conventional sense as haulers of lumber or manure, but hybrid vehicles that combine the convenience of the four-wheel drive with the rough look inspired by a safari (the Land Rover) or even the battlefield (the Hummer). Whatever their pedigree, these new models are broadly known as sports utility vehicles, often called "SUVs" or "utes" or even, to those who sneer at them as wussmobiles, "sputes." Their popularity has given Detroit a jolt of renewed self-esteem and left foreign manufacturers struggling in the dust to imitate them.

When it comes to cars, something has happened to the American psyche, even in the highest tax brackets. Maybe the baby boomers, grown thick in the waist, were bored with being sensible. Without any question—the brief dawn a few years ago of the tiny, puppyish Miata sports convertible aside—cars had grown tedious and indistinguishable. A Lexus or a BMW or a Mercedes said, "I've got mine, and I'm rich." A Volkswagen Golf or Ford Escort said nothing whatsoever. Apparently a Jeep with a mountain bike or kayak rack bolted to the roof said, "I'm doing the Ironman next month." You have to drive something, and if your $299-a-month lease can get you a Ford Explorer and a largely painless reputation for living on the edge, why not?

Even conventional pickup trucks are hot. One truck model—Ford's F-Series pickup, the best-selling vehicle in the U.S. in 1995—sold more units than any of General Motor's seven divisions except Chevrolet. GM's truck-transmission plant in Toledo, Ohio, has operated almost every hour of every day for the past five years, and industry ex-

MERCEDES M-CLASS AAV The German entry, due in 1997, is to be built in the U.S. with a cost in the mid-$30,000 range

LX450 The luxurious new SUV from Toyota's upscale Lexus line will weigh in at a sticker-shock price of $50,000—and up

perts calculate that if GM could add two more truck plants, it could sell 450,000 more units a year, for an added profit of $3 billion. As things are, sales of trucks and SUVs, often also known as truckoids, rose to 41.5% of the U.S. automotive market in 1995, up from 30% a decade before. And while U.S. automakers hold barely 60% of a shrinking market for passenger cars, they build 90% of the trucks sold; without them, the Americans would still be losing money.

The foreign competition was caught off guard at first, but it is burning rubber to catch up, especially at the high end of the SUV market. Toyota has enlarged its rugged but cramped 4Runner, in 1996 Lexus came out with the pricey LX450 (in the $50,000-plus range), and Mercedes is putting the finishing touches on a $300 million factory in Alabama that will build a muscular growler it plans to call the M-class All Activity Vehicle, or AAV. This new-wave Mercedes will come equipped with a VIP price tag in the mid-$30,000 range.

MERCURY MOUNTAINEER Lincoln-Mercury's first stab at an SUV rolled out in 1996 with a price tag in the $30,000 range

But even the giddy sales figures don't exhaust the good news. Cars are now so complex and expensive to build, partly because of fuel-economy requirements, that there is not much profit left except in the luxury models. Trucks and truckoids, even with the power windows, CD players and pleated leather seats that suburban buyers are asking for, are still simple enough—many with rear-wheel drive and huge power plants outmoded 20 years ago—to return $4,000 to $6,000 in profit per vehicle. So far, buyers have absorbed sizable price rises—for pickups, from $18,000 to $24,000 in a few years—without much grumbling, except for wistful murmurs from carpenters and lawn-care guys who used to buy trucks to carry their tools around.

Television and magazine ads invariably show pickups and SUVs parked on a mountain spire or riverside gravel bar, with no pavement or traffic in sight. Whether the vehicles that leave the showroom ever go to such places isn't important. Even if they are filling-looseners that drive like trucks on washboard roads, which most of them do, these vehicles are unbeatable fantasy machines.

Sure, the the high center of gravity that feels good to the driver means the vehicle is easier to roll over, but the urge to live dangerously is probably why Donna or Dave bought the thing. Lincoln, in planning to bring out its Mountaineer model in 1996, found that only 15% to 18% of SUV owners ever used their machines to tow or haul anything. And as for off-road rowdiness, "They [the buyers] look at you as if you were crazy if you mention it," says GM designer Bill Wayland. "Why would I want to drive my $40,000 vehicle off-road and scratch the paint?" ∎

Chronicler of the Cubicles

Dilbert's Scott Adams manages to laugh at the traumas of corporate life

ELIZABETH HOAK, A NEW YORK city accountant, has been downsized twice in the past $3\frac{1}{2}$ years. In each case she was told that her fate did not reflect her performance: nothing personal. Right. "You never quite get over the feeling of unfairness," she says. "No matter what they call it, you always feel as if you've been fired, and fired for no good reason." Still, Hoak had no choice but to do as millions of Americans have done: she resumed the job hunt. The second time, she says, "it was tough. But it became a little ritual. Each morning I would sit at the table, drink my coffee, read Dilbert. And only then could I start typing my cover letters."

The Trojan war had its Homer. The Spanish-American war had its W.R. Hearst. Every calamity has its bard, and downsizing's is Scott Adams, the creator of Dilbert, a sack-shaped, ever threatened corporate loser. Dilbert, which already runs in more than 800 newspapers, is the fastest-growing comic strip in the country.

Dilbert is a phlegmatic, mouthless engineer at a nameless firm who, explains Adams, "is not fully drinking all of the passion and variety that other people might be." His sidekick, a dog named Dogbert, is far savvier—and merciless about his owner's many failings. From its debut in 1989, the cartoon featured some of what Adams calls "cubicle culture": a natural subject, since he himself occupied Cubicle 4S700R as an applications engineer at Pacific Bell. (He has also been a computer programmer, a commercial lender and a bank teller.) But in earlier strips the absurdities of Dilbert's workday shared space with his hopeless dating life and Dogbert's periodic attempts to conquer the world.

Then in 1993 Adams printed his E-mail address in the strip. The thousands of responses made it clear that his readers wanted more lampoons of corporate culture and had an endless supply of material to contribute. "There were about 35 million office workers in the United States all having this shared experience, but not knowing that it was shared," Adams found. "All going home and not being able to talk about it because they assumed that it could not be this bad anywhere else." Dilbert began to chronicle downsizing, hotelling (when a company has fewer cubicles than employees, and every morning is a game of musical chairs) and similar horrors. In one strip, Dilbert's boss uses humor as a management tool. "Knock, knock," he says. "Who's there?" asks a worker. The kicker: "Not you anymore."

Some might consider such humor crude; but some have not been downsized. Says Hoak, the New York accountant: "It was cathartic to watch the incompetent boss in the strip and know that the incompetent boss who let me go wasn't fooling everyone." Indeed Adams has now put forward the "Dilbert Principle" to supplant the outmoded Peter Principle. It is no longer true, he argues, that people are promoted until they reach the level of their incompetence. These days they ascend directly to management, bypassing the competent phase, promoted precisely because they fail everywhere else.

Adams says some 80% of his material comes from readers, which is a good thing, since he cleared out his own cubicle in 1995. He swears he was not downsized—"I had told my bosses that my energies were with the cartoon, and they just had to ask me and I would go peacefully." But the Internet, where his Web page, the Dilbert Zone, draws 55,000 visitors a day, was abuzz with concern. Truth to tell, his fans needn't worry—about him. Adams is earning more than ever, and the sad fact is that he will probably have ample grist for a long time to come. ∎

AAAHH! A young monk in Rangoon chills out

The New Cold (Cola) War

Only a couple of years ago, Pepsi rolled out an ambitious plan to close the global cola gap separating it from its great rival Coca-Cola—including investing $3 billion in international bottlers. In April Pepsi launched another salvo, a $500 million marketing campaign, called Pepsi Blue, to introduce a new, sky-hued can in 24 countries. But it was a tough year for Pepsi: Coke "owned" the Olympics in its hometown, Atlanta, and is now No. 1 in such longtime Pepsi strongholds as Russia and Venezuela. The final tally: Coke profits worldwide rose by 9%, while Pepsi's (gulp!) lagged behind with a 4% rise.

Pooch Hawks Hootch

When liquor distiller Seagram's ran a 30-second spot on a Texas TV station in June promoting Crown Royal whiskey as toted by an "obedient" dog, it broke the liquor industry's self-imposed ban on TV advertising, adopted in 1948. Reaction was swift: critics—including President Clinton—condemned the move and lawmakers threatened action. Why did Seagram's violate the old ban? Market share. With sales of hard liquor slipping and sales of beer and wine rising, TV is where tomorrow's customers—and all those beer and wine ads—are.

FETCHING CRITICS: If Bud had Spuds MacKenzie ...

Merger in the Sky

In what would be the 10th-largest merger in American history, Seattle's Boeing Company announced in mid-December that it had agreed to acquire the St. Louis–based McDonnell Douglas Corp. for $13 billion to form the world's largest aerospace company. The friendly merger would make Boeing America's only manufacturer of commercial jets. McDonnell Douglas, whose expertise is in military aircraft, was considered a good fit for Boeing, the world leader in commercial aircraft building.

Those Merry Media Moguls

After waiting 10 months for approval from the Federal Trade Commission, idiosyncratic media titan Ted Turner officially merged his company with Time Warner. The new corporation soon found itself at war with an old Turner foe: Rupert Murdoch, boss of another media giant, the News Corp. Murdoch was starting up a

HOWDY: Ted Turner joins Time Warner

new 24-hour news channel, Fox News, to compete with Turner's CNN. When Time Warner's New York City cable company chose not to carry Fox News, it sparked a brouhaha that involved New York mayor Rudy Giuliani. As the fur flew, Murdoch's New York *Post* tabloid ran a cartoon of Turner in a straitjacket, and Turner compared Murdoch to "the late Führer." Well—that's entertainment.

Freeing the Airwaves

After years of tinkering, Congress overwhelmingly passed a new telecommunications bill that opened local and long-distance phone service and cable TV to all competitors. The bill also required that new TV sets be equipped with V chips to allow parents to control kids' viewing.

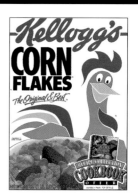

TOASTED: Kellogg's matched Post's move

The good news: A price war launched by Post sent cereal prices down about a buck a box. The bad news: Say goodbye to BOGOs— Buy One, Get One free

WAR FOR THE WEB

An epic battle for control of the Internet pits Bill Gates' Microsoft against James Barksdale's Netscape

O
N A CLOUDY MORNING in December 1995, as the white light of winter picked its way across the face of Mount Rainier, William H. Gates III, chairman and chief executive officer of Microsoft Corp., rolled out of bed after a brief night's sleep. There was no time for breakfast. He showered, pulled on his customary slacks, open-necked shirt and sweater, and climbed into his Lexus for the 20-minute drive from his suburban home to the Seattle convention

Gates chose Dec. 7—Pearl Harbor Day— to launch his full-scale surprise attack

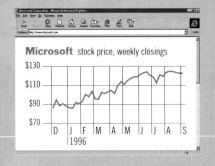

center. Gates had been at the center late into the previous evening preparing what he suspected would be the most significant Microsoft announcement in a decade.

For two years the rapidly expanding global computer matrix called the Internet had nagged at Gates like a low-level headache. Microsoft had long dominated the world of personal computing by providing PC operating systems, the software that controls the way users interact with their machines. With DOS in 1980, Windows 10 years later and the huge success of Windows 95 only months before, Microsoft had earned intimidating control over the computer industry—and lush profits that vaulted Gates to the top of the list of the richest Americans.

But the Internet could undo all that. Gates had been warning his top lieutenants that the Net could change everything about the way people used computers, perhaps even the fact that they needed an $89 copy of Windows to make their machines work. But he hadn't quite figured out Microsoft's proper place in the new terrain. This morning he planned to bring the uncertainty to an end. Microsoft would reorient every effort, every project and product to the new reality of the Internet. He was about to send a company with $6 billion in sales and 19,641 workers—all $70 billion worth—hurtling in that direction. In the future, as in the past, nothing was going to stand in Bill Gates' way.

Microsoft...

INTERFACE Explorer 3.0's user-friendly design reflects Microsoft's dozen years of selling software. It's the browser your mom will use.

COMPATIBILITY Explorer runs best on—no surprise—Windows-powered PCs. Mac versions are to come, but don't hold your breath.

PRICE Free! Microsoft hopes to build up its market share by giving Explorer away to any Web surfers who want to run it.

FEATURES ActiveX, a special Net language, makes it easy to embed sound, video and programs within Explorer Web pages.

NINE HUNDRED MILES DOWN THE PACIFIC coastline, in Mountain View, California, James Barksdale, president and CEO of Netscape, was bracing for another day of standing in Bill Gates' way. Barksdale slipped into a suit, grabbed a quick breakfast and pointed his Mercedes toward Netscape's Mountain View headquarters.

With $81 million in sales and 600 employees, Netscape had enjoyed its own dominance of the infant Internet world. Its killer application was a program that made navigating the Net as simple as pointing at what

you wanted to see and clicking on it. These so-called browsers brought order to the chaos of the World Wide Web, a corner of the Net stuffed with text, sounds and pictures. Netscape's Navigator browser was the best on the market, and it had propelled the company through a wildly successful initial public offering in August 1995. Some analysts said that Netscape had an invincible lead in the browser business, even against Microsoft.

Barksdale knew that Netscape's Navigator had the potential to be the next Windows: it could supplant the operating system and finally break Microsoft's hammerlock on the PC industry. Barksdale knew Microsoft wouldn't—couldn't—ignore the challenge.

It didn't. That morning in Seattle, addressing hundreds of analysts and media people, Gates hit a rare rhetorical high. To hammer the message home, he recalled the words of Admiral Yamamoto on the day the Japanese struck the U.S.: "I fear we have awakened a sleeping giant." The crowd chuckled its recognition: it was Dec. 7, 1995, and Bill Gates was taking Microsoft to war.

In 1996 Gates would spend the entire year backing up his martial rhetoric with action. In just six months, he refocused the work force onto Net-related projects, mercilessly eliminated a dozen others that had been Holy Grails a year before, even withdrew $1.5 billion in research-and-development money from a $6 billion cash stockpile Microsoft keeps tucked away against the sort of rainy business days seldom seen in Redmond. The result: Microsoft programmers released a stream of new products designed to seduce Net users away from Netscape.

Early in the spring Microsoft unveiled a new browser, Internet Explorer 2.0, but it proved to be a poor second cousin to Netscape's Navigator 2.0. Gates knew that Explorer 3.0 would have to be far better. So the company began throwing bodies at the problem. The results were phenomenal. On the release of Explorer 3.0 in August, critics of Explorer 2.0 were silenced by the new program's undeniable quality. The 8-megabyte behemoth

matched Netscape's franchise browser, Navigator, feature for feature, and at a much better price: it was free, while Navigator cost $79. Explorer's pricing was not an act of charity. Netscape later charged that a Microsoft executive told a gathering of software developers, "Our intent is to flood the market with free Internet software and squeeze Netscape until they run out of cash."

Available on the Web, Explorer 3.0 notched a million downloads in its first week. From around the Net, where Netscape had long trumpeted its 85% market share, word began to leak back that Microsoft browsers were accounting for 30%, then 40% and by September 60% of the hits on some servers. The result: Netscape's stock plunged sharply in value, while shares of Microsoft approached record highs.

Barksdale and Netscape wasted little time in counterattacking. Two weeks after the release of Microsoft's Explorer 3.0, Netscape unveiled blueprints for a new software firm called Navio that would try to outflank Microsoft by putting browser software on pretty much anything with a screen and a modem. The first stop was likely to be an Internet TV, followed by a $500 network computer, online video gaming machines and Net-surfing cell phones. Organized around a powerhouse electronics alliance that included just about everyone but Microsoft (Sony, NEC, Nintendo and IBM were supporting the venture), the new company had one aim: to use the Internet to make Gates' beachhead on most PCs— Microsoft Windows—irrelevant.

Gates' nemesis, Netscape CEO Barksdale, was less well known than the company's co-founders, entrepreneur Jim Clark and ace programmer Marc Andreessen, 25. But Barksdale had the toughest job of the three: getting Netscape to live up to its $3.1 billion market value. Barksdale, 53, had been wooed by Clark from his post as CEO of AT&T Wireless Services. A veteran of the Federal Express/UPS battles in the 1980s, Barksdale had also fought in the cellular-phone wars in the early 1990s.

... vs. Netscape

INTERFACE Navigator's stolid gray controls aren't sexy or fun to use, but they have captured the loyalty of millions of serious Netheads.

COMPATIBILITY Netscape browsers perform equally well on Mac, Windows and Unix machines. Microsoft can't match that.

PRICE Netscape built a customer base by passing out early versions of Navigaor for free. Now the company charges $79 a copy.

FEATURES Navigator 3.0 allows Web surfers to share documents, conduct online chats and even place phone calls on the Internet.

Andreessen, Barksdale and Clark (a triumvirate insiders refer to as "Marc, Bark and Clark") envision a future Netscape product that will assume many of the computer's operating-system functions, browsing local files as seamlessly as it browses today's Web. Of course, for a Web-based OS to have any real value to consumers, it has to have programs to run. To fill that hole, Netscape entered into a tight alliance with Sun Microsystems, a hardware and software company that had developed a Net-based programming language called Java, which is designed to run across the Internet on any computer, enabling it to act as a word processor, telephone, even a VCR. Though Microsoft has tried to embrace Java, analysts view Java more as a strategic weapon for Netscape, since Java software could one day compete with Microsoft software application products such as Word and Excel.

Opening a different front, Barksdale retained Gary Reback, a Silicon Valley lawyer noted for Microsoft bashing. In early August Reback mailed a legal letter bomb to the Justice Department's Antitrust Division on Netscape's behalf, accusing Microsoft of anticompetitive behavior. The charges infuriated Gates, who had already battled Justice on antitrust issues. Reback's tactics craftily played into the general perception of Netscape as a lonely underdog facing a domineering giant.

The war for the Web has only begun. Early in 1997, said Gates, Web surfers would be booting up Explorer 4.0, an even more advanced browser that would render obsolete Explorer 3.0, one of the hottest technologies of 1996. And that's where the real struggle in this battle lies. The victor may not be the company with the best browser but the team that can run the longest on an insanely fast product-development treadmill. Nathan Myhrvold, the physics Ph.D. who is a trusted Gates' deputy, told TIME in 1995 that "no matter how good your product, you are only 18 months away from failure." He was wrong. That span has been cut to six months. And it's shrinking. ∎

Net Worth Meets

JIM PELKEY USED TO CALL HIS BROker frantically the moment he heard breaking news about a company whose stock he wished to buy. A small investor by Wall Street's measure, Pelkey often had to try several times before getting through, hoping meanwhile that the stock wouldn't cool by the time his broker placed the order. For this the Cupertino, California, resident paid commission of around $70 a trade.

But that changed after Pelkey opened an account with an electronic brokerage service called E°TRADE Securities (www.etrade.com), which uses the Internet, rather than a traditional broker, to buy and sell stocks. Using E°TRADE and his personal computer, Pelkey now makes his own trades anytime, without a broker, at $19.95 a transaction. He also gets free stock quotes, free market reports and even free checking. "I used to feel like a lamb being led to slaughter. Now I'm the one who feels empowered," says Pelkey.

E°TRADE, as well as Lombard Institutional Brokerage (www.lombard.com) and discount pioneer Charles Schwab (www.schwab.com), is part of a new wave of brokerages that are shaking up the Wall Street establishment by trading stocks and bonds in cyberspace. Unlike traditional securities firms that operate out of storefronts and office buildings, this new breed connects to its customers mostly through PCs.

Elsewhere on the Net, online forums like the Motley Fool are breaking Wall Street's monopoly on information, and rumors, about companies and their business prospects. Drawing more than 200,000 visits a month, MF is the most prominent of a growing number of online sites, such as the Silicon Investor (www.techstocks.com) or the newsgroup misc.invest.stocks, where investors can ask questions and share knowledge.

Currently the upstart brokerages account for less than 1% of the 640 million shares traded daily, but they also account for nearly 100% of the anxiety that big Wall Street firms are feeling as technology reduces the complex world of securities to its barest minimum—carrying out a transaction. Wall Street's role then becomes something on the order of checkout clerk. This comes at a time when more and more investors are buying stocks. At one point, less than 5% of Americans owned stocks; now more than 20% do.

As increasing numbers of investors take financial matters into their own hands, trading companies like E°TRADE are expected to proliferate. The number of brokerage houses offering electronic trading nearly doubled from 1995 to 1996—to 22—including Jack White & Co. and National Discount Brokers. There are already 650,000 active online brokerage accounts, in contrast to 413,000 in 1995. By 2000, predicts Mary Doyle, senior analyst of mass-market interactive services at IDC/Link Resources, there will be 1.5 million online accounts. "The days are over," she says, "when brokers called all the shots and charged whatever commission they saw fit. Investors are plugging in and taking charge."

Trading stocks by computer isn't exactly new. The basic technology was first used in the mid-'80s by discount brokerages such as Trade°Plus, Charles Schwab and Quick & Reilly. On average, they reduced fees as much as 70%. To keep customers captive, the systems relied largely on special software and in-house investment services. Then brokerage firms like Donaldson, Lufkin & Jenrette began liberating customers by offering an electronic-trading service called PC Financial Network (AOL/Prodigy: PCFN) and making it available through the commercial online services.

But even these trailblazers are being upstaged by discount brokers, like E°TRADE and rival Lombard Institutional Brokerage, that use the wide-open information superhighway to offer lower commissions and inexpensive shortcuts to any investor with a computer and a modem. No money changes hands over the Net—only the trades are transacted over the open lines. A customer must first establish an account, often with cash or securities to cover trading costs.

The Internet brokers also allow investors to go online to monitor their portfolios, retrieve market data from brokerage databases and link them to other Websites oriented to business and finance. Says William Porter, the founder of E°TRADE: "The Internet lets us leverage our business in a way that old-fashioned brokerages never thought possible.

ROSENTHAL

the Net

Meet virtual Wall Street: consumers save money and gain autonomy by dropping traditional brokerage firms to buy and sell stocks via computer

Because cyberbrokers maintain little support staff, fewer offices and lower overhead, they can afford to low-ball traditional brick-and-mortar firms. WealthWEB (www.aufhauser.com), for instance, charges less than half as much in commissions as big brokers. If you were going to buy 100 shares of Wal-Mart at $25, Merrill Lynch, for example, would charge $78 for the trade. Some cyberbrokers would charge as little as $12.

One thing to consider when trading on the Net: you're on your own out there. Unlike full-service firms, which emphasize personal service and offer plenty of advice, electronic traders keep contact to a minimum. Many bare-bones Internet brokers do not even maintain a customer-support staff. Those that do have help lines often charge for the calls. And while the Internet is vast, it is not always fast. Moving from one Website to another takes time and a little luck.

With their core-investor market aging rapidly, old-line firms such as Merrill Lynch and Smith Barney know they have to expand into online trading to find new blood. And fast. The typical client at a full-service brokerage is 63 years old. Online investors are mostly affluent, computer-savvy males whose average age is 41. The big brokerages claim they aren't worried about the upstarts and point out that their traditional business is still growing. But the movement to trading stocks on the Internet is accelerating, rapidly, and Wall Street knows better than to swim against the tide. ∎

KORN: After being hyped over the Net, this little-known band sold 152,000 copies of its new CD in only two weeks

WIRED FOR SOUND

Rock 'n' roll is exploding over the Internet, changing how fans hear music and what music gets heard

WHEN EPIC/IMMORTAL RECORDS SIGNED UP AN AL-ternative band called Korn, the group was so alternative that it counted its blessings when 500 people showed up to hear it. Then Epic decided to promote the band over the Internet. The company opened a Korn page on the Sony Website (*www.sony.com*). It posted bios, concert-tour schedules and daily voice clips from Korn's lead singer, Jonathan Davis, and created a special electronic bulletin board for die-hard Korn fans. Not only has the Website been a big hit ("The Internet traffic is

melting us down," said Epic's West Coast general manager, Steve Rennie), but record sales took off. Korn's CD, *Life Is Peachy*, broke onto *Billboard's* album chart at No. 3.

After studiously avoiding the info highway for most of the 1990s, the music industry is getting wired with a vengeance, and that's changing everything: how bands get heard, how performers develop followings, even how music gets distributed. In the past two years thousands of Websites catering to millions of fans have sprung into existence, from tiny one-computer home pages for garage bands in Montana to world-class monster sites like New York City–based N2K (*www.n2k.com*), which offers thousands of titles and stages live Netcasts.

Why the music rush online? And why now? Part of the answer is technological. With stereo speakers and built-in CD players, today's multimedia computers have turned into surprisingly good sound systems. Throw in a telephone connection to the Internet, a fast modem and a software program like RealAudio 3.0 (which lets you hear "stereo-quality" sound in real time, as it downloads), and a world of online music opens up on your computer screen.

Another appeal of online music is economic. Electronic mail-order houses are one of the few businesses making money on the Web, and music CDs are among the biggest sellers (along with books, flowers and pornography). Buyers get to sample songs before they purchase, and they enjoy modest discounts (typical price: $9.95 a CD); sellers save a fortune on overhead and can carry a much wider selection of performers. Internet Underground Music Archive (*www.iuma.com*), one of the pioneers in the online-music business, got its start peddling the CDs of unsigned bands that nobody had ever heard of. Today the seven-person company carries 1,000 bands, draws more than a quarter-million hits a day and brings in nearly $1 million a year.

So will Sony and Warner see their record empires crumble? Not for a few more business cycles, at least. According to Jupiter Communications, online-music purchases probably won't exceed $25 million in 1996—about two-tenths of 1% of the U.S. industry's $12.3 billion total. Even if that number were to grow to 10% by 2000, as Jupiter predicts, most of the revenue is likely to end up in the pockets of the majors. Al Cafaro, president of A&M records, doesn't seem worried about losing Sting or Sheryl Crow anytime soon. "I don't want to say always," he says, "but generally artists want to reach as many people as they can."

If anyone is truly threatened by the rise of the Web, it is the record labels' longtime partners, the retail chains. Audio technology on the Internet is developing rapidly, and there is no technological barrier to downloading entire albums, in pristine digital quality, onto blank CDs—a prospect the Sam Goody stores of the world view with dread. But that's the way it has always been with rock. One person's dream is another's nightmare. ∎

A Machine Without Fear

Asked when he thought a computer would beat a human at chess, World Champion Garry Kasparov guessed the year 2010—or maybe never. Kasparov was off by a few years: in February, he sat down to a match against an IBM computer named Deep Blue—and lost the first game. Over the first four games, the machine played Kasparov dead even—one win, one loss, two draws—before the champ rallied and came away with the final two games and the match. Deep Blue is programmed to see about 200 million positions every second. But Grand master Yasser Seira-wan explained Deep Blue's real strength: unlike a human being, "the machine has no fear."

KASPAROV:Sunk in a Deep Blue funk

Merging TV and the Web

It is the industry's most coveted market: the 85% to 90% of American homes that are not yet connected to the Internet, but are heavy television viewers. To that end, some half a dozen companies launched new TV sets in the latter part of 1996 that were hybrids of TVs and PCs. The biggest push was behind the new set from electronics giants Sony and Philips, who licensed technology from WebTV Networks, a company partly financed by Microsoft co-founder Paul Allen. But critics charged that the Web's most exciting pages wouldn't work right on televisions, and pointed out the eye-straining challenge of reading screenfuls of text from eight to 12 feet away—the distance most people sit from their TV sets.

New Dimensions for Mario

Who was the virtual person of 1996? No doubt about it— the honor goes to Nintendo's veteran video-game warrior, Mario. The digital superstar was the standard bearer for Nintendo 64, the new 64-bit video game whose rich new 3-D graphics instantly rendered competitors Sony and Sega obsolete (at least for the short term).

HARD TO GET: Nintendo 64 systems were sold out by late fall

HOLY CYBERSPACE! Thanks to religious groups, the Web gets the Word

Naming the Nintendo 64 Machine of the Year, TIME's Technology editors heralded it as "a whole new standard in electronic entertainment, smashing barriers that the bug-filled Internet and clumsy personal computers have yet to approach."

The Internet Gets Religion

Like schools, like businesses, like government, religious groups rushed online in 1996, setting up church home pages, broadcasting dogma and establishing theological newsgroups, bulletin boards and chat rooms. Newsgroups like *alt.fan.jesus-christ* and *alt. religion.scientology* were among the busiest—and most contentious—of the nearly 20,000 discussion groups carried on Usenet, a major Internet area. A revamped Vatican site offered press releases, Pope John Paul II's schedule and most of the Pontiff's writings, translated into six languages. "The Internet is exploding, and the church has got to be there," said Sister Judith Zoebelein, the American-born nun who runs the site.

Couch Potato Heaven

Here it comes—the latest shortcut to couch-potato nirvana— the Digital Versatile Disc. Besides offering a picture that is purer than that of either VHS or even laser discs, DVD players can also play CDs and CD-ROMs. A 5-in. DVD disc can hold the equivalent of more than two hours of film. The players went on sale in 1996 at around $600; movies for them cost around $20.

The revolution in microelectronics began to work its magic in the medical world, as **TINY DIAGNOSTIC DEVICES** let doctors take their healing art on the road—in their pocket

MINI MARVEL: Reads blood oxygen level without breaking the skin

LIFE ON MARS?

NASA scientists claim a stone from Antarctica offers evidence that life forms may once have existed on Mars

Hurtling in from space some 16 million years ago, a giant asteroid slammed into the dusty surface of Mars and exploded with more power than a million hydrogen bombs, gouging a deep crater in the planet's crust and lofting huge quantities of rock and soil into the thin Martian atmosphere. While most of the debris fell back to the surface, some of the rocks, fired upward by the blast at high velocities, escaped the weak tug of Martian gravity and entered into orbits of their own around the sun. After drifting through interplanetary space for millions of years, one of these Martian rocks ventured close to Earth 13,000 years ago—when Stone Age humans were beginning to develop agriculture—and plunged into the atmosphere,

Tucked inside this small rock are immense issues of man's life and fate

ROCK ALH84001: only 4.2 lbs. in weight

blazing a meteoric path across the sky. It crashed into a sheet of blue ice in Antarctica and lay undisturbed until scientists discovered it in 1984 in a field of jagged ice called the Allan Hills.

In August that rock, dubbed ALH84001, seized the imagination of mankind—and set off a considerable scientific controversy. At a press conference in Washington, a team of NASA and university researchers revealed that this well-traveled, 4.2-lb. stone appeared to have brought with it the first tangible evidence that mankind is not alone in the universe. Tucked deep within the rock are what NASA scientists believe to be the chemical and fossil remains of microscopic organisms that lived on Mars 3.6 billion years ago.

That evidence was quickly subjected to intense scrutiny. While NASA researchers stuck by their guns, many other scientists maintained that they had not made an airtight case, and that the "organisms" in the rock may instead have been inanimate matter. What made the controversy so important was nothing less than the crucial question of whether life is unique to planet earth or a phenomenon that occurs on other planets. If such a possibility were to be confirmed, it would have staggering repercussions. It would undermine any remaining vestiges of geocentrism—the idea that man and his planet are the center of the universe—and support the growing conviction among scientists that life, possibly even intelligent life, is commonplace throughout the cosmos.

To A WORLD LONG FASCINATED BY LEGENDS AND fantasies about the Red Planet, however, a sense of awe and excitement overwhelmed any skepticism. Cornell University astronomer Carl Sagan, the most prominent champion of the search for extraterrestrial life, exulted: "If the results are verified, it is a turning point in human history, suggesting that life exists not just on two planets in one paltry solar system but throughout this magnificent universe." NASA Administrator Daniel Goldin echoed Sagan's excitement, but cautioned, "We must investigate, evaluate and validate this discovery." Members of the NASA-led team were thoroughly prepared for the fray. They bore copies of their peer-reviewed report, accepted for publication by the prestigious journal *Science*, and displayed some remarkable scanning electron microscope images of the tiny structures found inside the meteorite.

The most striking image clearly showed a segmented tubelike object, with a width about a hundredth that of a human hair, and to the untrained eye clearly resembling a life form. Another image revealed carbonate globules—circular features closely associated with fossils of ancient bacteria on Earth. Yet a third showed what seemed to be colonies of sluglike creatures. As startling as these images were, they constituted just one of several lines of evidence that team leader David McKay cites as "pointing toward biologic activity in early Mars." Besides the images, which McKay admits are the weakest link in the evidence, the scientists cited complex chemicals found close by or inside the carbonate globules. These included polycyclic aromatic hydrocarbons (PAHs)—organic molecules that on Earth are formed when microorganisms die and decompose (but also when certain fossil fuels are burned)—and iron sulfides and magnetite, which are often (but not necessarily) produced by living organisms.

Could these compounds have resulted from earthly contamination of the meteorite during its long Antarctic layover? Not likely, says Richard Zare, a Stanford University chemist who developed the analyzer that detected the PAHs. He noted that no PAHs were found on the rock's crust, but some were found inside it. Had any of Earth's abundant PAHs seeped in, more contamination would have been found on the surface than inside.

Moreover, the suspected fossils predated the meteorite's arrival on Earth: the NASA scientists pegged the age of the carbonate globules at 3.6 billion years, strongly suggesting that they formed in crevices of the rock while it was still part of the Martian crust. Observed

FROM MARS TO EARTH
What scientists think may have happened

1 Some 3.6 billion years ago, when Mars was about a billion years old, water covered at least part of the planet's surface. The new evidence suggests that microbes may have flourished in the Martian seas and fossilized in the cracks of rocks.

2 In time, the seas disappeared and the planet lost most of its atmosphere. Then, about 16 million years ago, a huge asteroid or comet slammed into the planet, gouging out a crater and spraying rock fragments into interplanetary space.

Mars

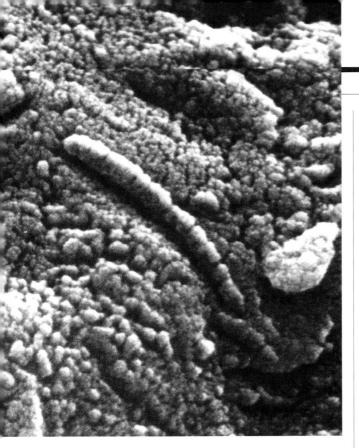

Sagan: "Mars was warmer and wetter [then] than it is today, with rivers, lakes and possibly even oceans. [This period is] just the epoch in Martian history when you expect that life may have arisen."

Whatever the nature of the material found on the meteorite, NASA researchers have little doubt that the rock is Martian in origin. They base their conclusion largely on the composition of gases trapped in tiny pockets within the meteorite. The NASA team found a strikingly close match between the constituents of the rock gases and those in the current Martian atmosphere, which the unmanned Viking landers sampled in 1976, transmitting the data back to

FOSSIL OR FOLLY? Far thinner than human hair

Inside the rock: Are the small tubes fossils of bacteria— or dried mud?

Earth. NASA's McKay conceded that "there are alternative explanations for each of the lines of evidence." But after 2½ years of study, the team became convinced that the evidence taken as a whole points to the existence of early life on Mars.

Still, paleobiologist William Schopf of UCLA, best known for discovering the world's oldest fossils, spoke for many who would urge caution. Invited by NASA to represent the skepticism of the scientific community, he repeated a familiar Sagan quotation: "Extraordinary claims require extraordinary evidence." It was clear that to Schopf such evidence was not yet forthcoming. He noted that PAHs are routinely found in outer-space debris as well as other meteorites, and not once "have they ever been interpreted as being biological."

Turning to the putative fossils in the electron-microscope images, Schopf pointed out that they are a hundred times smaller than any found on Earth, too tiny to be analyzed chemically or probed internally. Also, he noted, "there was no evidence of a cavity within them, a cell." Nor was there any evidence of life cycles or cell division. This led him to believe that NASA's proposed fossilized life forms were probably made of a "mineralic material" like dried mud. NASA researchers went back to gather ammunition for a long battle with their critics. But only months later, in October, British scientists reported finding similar signs of life on a different, younger Martian rock.

While scientists argued the microscopic evidence, most observers grappled with larger concerns. The discovery of evidence that life may exist elsewhere in the universe raised that most profound of all human questions: Why does life exist at all? Is it simply that if enough cosmic elements slop together for enough eons, eventually a molecule will form somewhere, or many somewheres, that can replicate itself over and over until it evolves into a creature that can scratch its head? Or did an all-powerful God set in motion an unfathomable process in order to give warmth and meaning to a universe that would otherwise be cold and meaningless? The rock from Mars did not answer such questions. It did, however, make them feel all the more compelling. ■

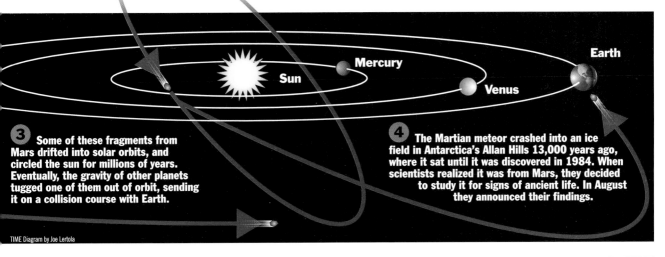

3 Some of these fragments from Mars drifted into solar orbits, and circled the sun for millions of years. Eventually, the gravity of other planets tugged one of them out of orbit, sending it on a collision course with Earth.

4 The Martian meteor crashed into an ice field in Antarctica's Allan Hills 13,000 years ago, where it sat until it was discovered in 1984. When scientists realized it was from Mars, they decided to study it for signs of ancient life. In August they announced their findings.

TIME Diagram by Joe Lertola

NORMAN SCHWARZKOPF

SIDNEY POITIER

MICHAEL MILKEN

BATTLING THE MAN'S CANCER

Prostate cancer is reaching epidemic levels in the U.S. The time for squeamishness is past

T HREE YEARS AFTER HIS TRIUMPH IN the Gulf War, General H. Norman Schwarzkopf was feeling invincible. But in March 1994, uncomfortable with nagging tendinitis in one knee, he stopped by a military hospital in Florida. While there, he decided to visit the base urologist for an exam. "I feel something not quite right," the doctor said, after making a routine rectal exam. "But if it's cancer, I can tell 90% of the time, and I don't think so."

Schwarzkopf, then 59, had reason to feel confident. He had recently undergone a PSA (prostate-specific antigen) test and had registered a count of only 1.8, well below the level considered indicative of cancer. But to play it safe, the urologist performed an ultrasound exam and took a biopsy of the prostate gland. A week later, the doctor called Schwarzkopf and said, "I don't know how to tell you this, but you have prostate cancer."

Shaken, and like most men woefully uninformed about prostate cancer, Schwarzkopf began devouring books and medical-journal articles. He overcame his squeamishness and started talking to friends and experts about this disease that seems to strike at the very core of masculinity. "For me, it was like war," he says. "First thing you do is learn about the enemy." Schwarzkopf had little idea how formidable that enemy is.

SURVIVORS New therapies help, but early warning of the illness is the key to beating it

FRANÇOIS MITTERRAND

AYATULLAH KHOMEINI

FRANK ZAPPA

The American Cancer Society estimated that in 1996, some 317,000 Americans would be told they had prostate cancer, well above the 184,000 new cases of breast cancer. That figure represents a staggering increase over 1995's 244,000 new prostate-cancer cases and the fewer than 85,000 recorded as recently as 1985. The ACS predicted that deaths from prostate cancer in the U.S. would reach a near-epidemic 41,400 cases in 1996; the annual breast-cancer toll is 44,300. The reason: demographics. The lifespan of Americans is increasing, and the disease most often strikes men in their 60s or 70s. As the baby-boom generation matures, the number of cases will balloon.

Although 1 in 5 American men will develop prostate cancer in his lifetime, most are only vaguely aware of the disease and its consequences. Unlike women, who usually talk freely among themselves about intimate health problems, most men shy away from discussing their physical disorders, let alone problems involving a gland that affects both urination and sexual potency.

Still, says Dr. William Fair, head of the urology division at Manhattan's Memorial Sloan-Kettering Cancer Center, "prostate cancer is beginning to come out of the closet. Fifteen or 20 years ago, you couldn't even mention the word prostate in polite mixed company." Indeed, popular awareness of prostate cancer may now be at a stage similar to that of breast cancer two decades ago, after Betty Ford and Happy Rockefeller revealed publicly that they were victims of a cancer that until then had been discussed only in private. Their role is now being played by Schwarzkopf, who, after learning that his cancer had not metastasized, quickly decided on major and somewhat risky surgery—a radical prostatectomy—to excise the prostate gland. Schwarzkopf made a speedy recovery from the surgery, is now cancer free and, as spokesman for Prostate Cancer Awareness Week, lectures regularly, warning men over 50 about their risks.

In his crusade, Schwarzkopf joined forces with an unlikely but powerful ally: Michael Milken, the famed junk-bond wizard of the 1980s. Milken, diagnosed with prostate cancer in 1993, was unable to fight his illness with a radical prostatectomy because it had already metastasized beyond the prostate. His doctors prescribed a hormone treatment that shut down his body's production of testosterone, which stimulates the growth of prostate-cancer cells. The hormone therapy worked: Milken's cancer went into remission. The billionaire went on to establish a public charity, called CaP CURE, dedicated to finding a cure for prostate cancer, and pledged $25 million to promote awareness of the disease and find a cure for it.

The biggest factor in the sharp rise of prostate-cancer diagnoses is the increasingly widespread use of the controversial PSA test, which in many cases can detect the disease early in its course, long before the tumor becomes palpable. By making early detection possible, the test could eventually reduce the number of prostate-cancer

VICTIMS Doctors say that one in five American men will develop prostate cancer in his lifetime

deaths. Paradoxically, it could also lead to a rise in premature, even unnecessary, treatments. The PSA test measures the blood level of a protein produced by all prostate cells. In general, readings under a PSA count of 4 indicate that cancer is highly unlikely. The probability of cancer increases with a rising count between 4 and 22 and becomes highly likely when the count is over 22.

Usually in a man at age 50, the prostate begins to enlarge, and the growing number of cells contributes to what is generally a steady but slight rise

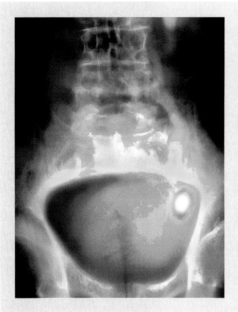

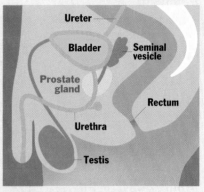

SPOTTED At left, a colorized frontal X ray of the lower urinary tract reveals a malignant prostatic tumor, colored light blue. The tumor can be seen shining through the bladder, here tinted orange. Above, the prostate gland is located near areas critical to both potency and urination

in the PSA count. But if prostate cells become cancerous and begin multiplying, the PSA level jumps dramatically. Often that is warning enough to prompt a doctor to view the prostate with a transrectal ultrasound probe, and frequently to take needle biopsies from the gland.

Men whose prostate cancer is detected early face a painful dilemma: virtually all the therapies available to them can drastically affect their quality of life, and the only one that can virtually guarantee a cure—if the cancer has not metastasized—is the most forbidding of them all.

That one is radical prostatectomy, surgical removal of the entire prostate gland. If the cancer has not spread beyond the prostate wall and the gland is removed, the cancer is gone. Period. Still, there are drawbacks. In performing a prostatectomy, the surgeon must reach the prostate by cutting through either the abdomen or the region behind the scrotum. Because the walnut-size prostate surrounds the urethra—the tube through which urine passes from the bladder—some of the sphincter muscle that controls the flow of urine may be cut away.

As a result, there is a substantial risk of incontinence. About 1% or 2% of prostatectomy patients will have complete lack of urinary control; from 20% to 50% will have partial control. A prostatectomy poses an even more intimate threat to a man's life-style. Because the two nerve bundles controlling penile erection run along the surface of the prostate, the operation until recently almost invariably rendered the patient impotent. Then, in the early 1980s, Dr. Patrick Walsh of Johns Hopkins Hospital in Baltimore, Maryland, pioneered a technique that in many cases enables the surgeon to move the nerve bundles out of the way before excising the prostate, allowing many patients eventually to have satisfactory erections.

For men who choose not to undergo a prostatectomy, external-beam radiation is often the therapy of choice. While it involves a series of exposures over several weeks to a finely focused X-ray beam, no hospital stay is required. But radiation often fails to kill all the cancer cells. While the tumor shrinks and PSA counts drop to low levels or even zero for several years, the cancer eventually returns. Also, in one study as many as 50% of such patients became impotent within five years of treatment.

A completely different radiation technique places dozens of tiny radioactive palladium or iodine seeds directly in the prostate, minimizing damage to nearby healthy tissue and maximizing the dose delivered directly to the tumor. Though seeds remain permanently in the prostate, their radioactivity sinks to negligible levels after several months. Yet even this relatively benign procedure is often followed by temporary incontinence—and impotence in about 15% of men under 70 and more often in older men. And while this method produces a lower rate of tumor recurrence than either prostatectomy or external-beam radiation, doctors cannot say with any certainty that the cancers have been cured.

Yet another form of treatment, cryotherapy, involves pushing metallic probes into the prostate and circulating liquid nitrogen at −195°F through them, forming an ice ball that freezes and kills the prostate cells. In the process, the overlying nerve bundles are usually frozen too, leaving more than 60% of patients impotent. Incontinence is seldom a problem, because a catheter is used to keep the urethra from freezing during the operation. One drawback: prostatic tissue immediately adjacent to the catheter does not freeze, leaving the possibility that some cancer cells will survive to resume their attack.

❝For me, it was like war,❞ says Norman Schwarzkopf.

EVERYTHING YOU WERE AFRAID TO ASK ABOUT ...

TREATMENT	PROS	CONS
RADICAL PROSTATECTOMY	Cures cancer that is completely confined to prostate	Long hospital stay and recovery, risk of impotence and incontinence
NERVE-SPARING PROSTATECTOMY	Same as above; 90% of men under the age of 50 retain potency	Same as radical prostatectomy except lower risk of impotence
EXTERNAL-BEAM RADIATION	No hospital stay, cure rate about 20%	Chance of recurrence, risk of impotence, some incontinence
"SEED" RADIATION	Outpatient procedure, less damage from radiation	Some risk of impotence and incontinence; no long-term studies
CRYOTHERAPY	Short hospital stay, less risk of incontinence	High risk of impotence, cancer cells may survive
HORMONE THERAPY	Outpatient procedure, temporary tumor shrinkage	Loss of libido; only a stopgap, cancer returns within a few years

EARLY WARNING

A man's PSA [prostate-specific antigen] count is measured in billionths of a gram per milliliter of blood. This antigen is produced only by the prostate and increases gradually with age. Its level jumps sharply when cancer is present. Until recently, a PSA level over 4.0 raised suspicions of malignancy. New studies have shown that somewhat higher levels in older men are not a cause for alarm.

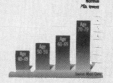

Faced with this bewildering array of draconian treatments—and their humiliating side effects—many older men and some younger ones opt for "watchful waiting." This controversial nontreatment calls for frequent blood tests, rectal exams and an occasional biopsy but no intervention unless the cancer becomes more aggressive.

Who should be treated, and who is a candidate for watchful waiting? Because the average prostate cancer takes a decade to develop symptoms that seriously affect quality of life, Dr. William Catalona of Washington University argues that any man whose life expectancy is 10 years or more should be treated. He supports widespread PSA screening to detect cancer early. Yet other experts point out that PSA readings sometimes raise misleading alarms, fail to differentiate between fast-growing and less threatening prostate cancer and can lead to debilitating treatment that may be unnecessary.

Much of the uncertainty could be eliminated, of course, if doctors could tell, while a prostate cancer is still small, if it is the lethally aggressive or relatively benign type. In other words, whether a man will die of it—or with it. Under the auspices of CaP CURE, University of Washington molecular biologist Leroy Hood is leading an effort to find biological markers that will characterize a tumor as either essentially harmless or dangerous while it is still small—which would eliminate much of the uncertainty about treating, or choosing not to treat—the cancer.

Hood's group is also trying to find its first prostate-cancer gene. All told, researchers believe, there could be as many as 10 of them. In November a team of 23 scientists from the U.S. and Sweden announced they had located the chromosome, though not the specific location within it, where one such gene resides. The finding was the first specific evidence that prostate cancer has a hereditary component. The incidence of the cancer in African-American men, for instance, is about 35 percent higher than that of white men.

In an effort to dispel some of the guesswork about prevention and the choice of treatment, the National Cancer Institute (NCI) in Maryland is conducting two large-scale prostate-cancer trials. One, called PIVOT (for Prostate Cancer Intervention Versus Observation Trial), is just getting under way, and will involve monitoring the progress over 15 years of 2,000 prostate-cancer patients in the Veterans Administration hospital system. The goal: to determine if radical prostatectomies save enough lives to justify choosing surgery over watchful waiting.

The other trial, organized in 1993, will eventually enroll 18,000 healthy men who are at least 55 years old and have a PSA level of 3 or less. Its aim is to determine if finasteride, a Merck drug, will help prevent prostate cancer. Medical researchers suspect that finasteride may be effective because it reduces the level of a testosterone by-product that promotes tumor growth.

As important as these long-range trials may be, however, they hardly address the urgency felt by men with advanced prostate cancer. Milken is convinced that a massive, well-financed effort, making full use of available high technology and advances in genetics, can find "a cure or a permanent delaying action" for the disease not in decades but in a few years. While most of the male prostate-cancer researchers are hardly that optimistic, they share the sense of urgency. "The odds that I'll get prostate cancer by the time I'm 70 are pretty good," said the NCI's Dr. Otis Brawley. For millions of other American men, that realization is beginning to hit home. ■

"First thing you do is learn about the enemy."

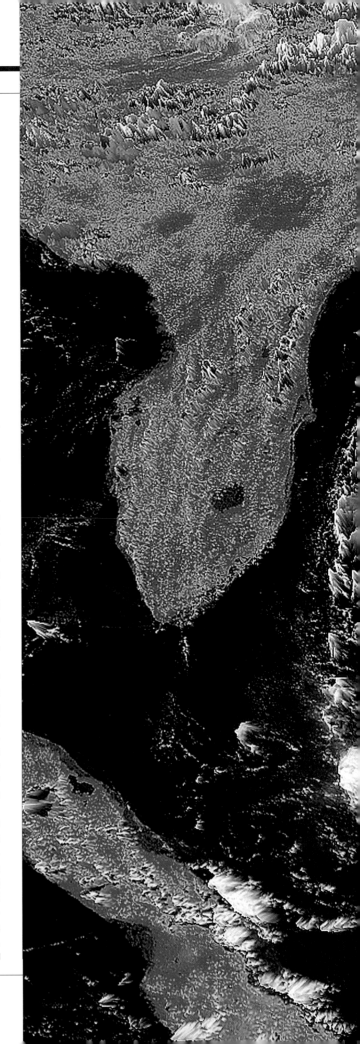

HIGH OVER THE EYE

Thanks to satellite photos, the world weathers hurricanes like Fran with earlier warning

O NE OF NATURE'S DARK IRONIES IS THAT THE MOST horrific expressions of its power are also the most beautiful. Think of Mount St. Helens or a Pacific tsunami. Add to these Hurricane Fran, pinwheeling toward the U.S. on September 4, prior to claiming more than 20 lives and damaging more than $1 billion in property. This picture of the mighty storm, dwarfing the Florida peninsula on its left and Cuba below it, was snapped by the GOES-8 weather satellite. The image includes several types of data. It captures the infrared spectrum that shows the temperature of objects—lighter for cold features like clouds and darker for warmer features like land. A software program was used to distort higher-altitude portions of the picture to create perspective, while another program gave the image its vertiginous tilt. Such photos are used to help give locals advance warning of a storm's path.

In 1996 the locals could have used some help, for America's weather pattern was marked by extremes. The year began with a monster blizzard—the biggest since 1947—that completely shut down New York City and much of the Northeastern seaboard for a long weekend. Later in January, a severe cold snap had residents of the upper Midwest enduring some of the coldest temperatures ever recorded. The chilly winds stretched as far south as Mexico, where a rare snowfall over New Year's weekend killed millions of wintering monarch butterflies.

America's West was also a land of extremes. In early February, states in the Pacific Northwest were hit by the worst flooding in 30 years, causing more than half a billion dollars in damage. Yet to the north, parts of Alaska experienced one of their driest winters ever. And to the south, the states of the Southwestern Plains suffered through a 10-month long drought, prompting recollections of the Dust Bowl of the 1930s. A final irony: in a summer when *Twister* was a smash at the box office, experts pronounced the year's tornado count "average." ∎

THE PROFITS OF PROPHECY

A generation after *Future Shock*, these are the good old days for professional prognosticators

PIONEERS: The Tofflers are still hocking the future

WHO WILL FIGHT THE next war in the Middle East? Where will the best new jobs be found in the coming years, and where will the most old ones be lost? How much will a gallon of gas cost in July 1998? What will be the hot consumer-electronics products of 2008? Where will the next environmental catastrophe occur—and what can be done to prevent it?

These are the kinds of questions that are asked—and, for a price, answered—by the forward-looking folks who call themselves futurists. Once the calling of wild-eyed Cassandras and 19th century writers and social scientists on the radical fringe, long-range forecasting has become a sophisticated and quite profitable industry. Its practitioners, who appear with increasing frequency in the press, on TV and on the best-seller lists, run the professional gamut from pop-culture chroniclers like Faith Popcorn ("cocooning") and Douglas Rushkoff (*Cyberia*) through digital-media stars like

M.I.T.'s Nicholas Negroponte and the Institute for the Future's Paul Saffo to management gurus like Peter Drucker and John Naisbitt (*Megatrends*).

But they all stand in the shadow of Alvin and Heidi Toffler, the husband-and-wife futurists whose 1970 blockbuster, *Future Shock*, blasted the infant profession into the mainstream and set the standard by which all subsequent imitators have been measured. A quarter-century later, having been catapulted back onto the front pages through their association with Newt Gingrich's "cyberbrain trust," the Tofflers are being repackaged for the digital era by Creative Artists Agency, the Hollywood agenting Goliath.

The vehicle for this effort: a multimedia clearinghouse called FutureNet, which is building everything from a site on the World Wide Web to a weekend televised magazine and an ambitious half-hour weeknight TV show called *Next News Now. NNN* will report not what happened

THE PAST, IMPERFECT

Accurately predicting the future is not an easy thing to do. History is filled with bold forecasts that didn't quite pan out. Here are a few examples:

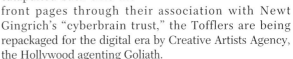

❝This "telephone" has too many shortcomings to be seriously considered as a means of communication. The device is inherently of no value to us.❞
—WESTERN UNION *internal memo, 1876*

❝"Heavier-than-air flying machines are impossible."❞
—LORD KELVIN, *Royal Society, 1895*

❝Everything that can be invented has been invented.❞
—CHARLES H. DUELL, *Commissioner, U.S. Patent Office, 1899*

❝Goddard does not know the relation between action and reaction and the need to have something better than a vacuum against which to react. He seems to lack the basic knowledge ladled out in high school.❞
—NEW YORK TIMES, *editorial about Robert Goddard's revolutionary rocket work, 1921*

today but what will happen tomorrow. "There's a History Channel but no Future Channel," says Alvin Toffler. "We plan to remedy that."

The Tofflers did not invent futurism, of course. H.G. Wells, Jules Verne and George Orwell were all practicing futurists working under a science-fiction guise. Modern futurism was born with the atom bomb—that fateful moment in history when it was suddenly possible to imagine a world without a future. It was Herman Kahn, a graduate of the Rand Institute, the Ur– think tank, who gave the nascent profession credibility with such pioneering works as *Thinking About the Unthinkable* (1962), which scientifically predicted the likely effects of a thermonuclear war.

But it was the Tofflers who brought futurism to the masses. *Future Shock* made the new profession cool. The book and its best-selling sequels, *The Third Wave* (1984) and *Powershift* (1990), examined not just tomorrow but today, not just one industry but all mankind, making the paradigm-shattering argument that what was really changing society was the radical acceleration of change itself. Future shock, the Tofflers said, is what happens when change occurs faster than people's ability to adapt to it. The book resonated for the 1960s counterculture, and in some ways it echoes

even louder in the digital era. "People today," says Alvin Toffler, "are scared silly."

That's the great thing about pondering the future these days: there seems to be so much more of it. Between the computer revolution and the end of the cold war, between the birth pangs of the international economy and the death throes of the traditional nuclear family, the demand for solid, scientifically based forecasting is greater than ever. Hard numbers are difficult to come by since so much "futurist" work goes on under the guise of economic forecasting or strategic analysis, but corporate America clearly has the religion.

The generation of strategic planners who came of age in the '60s and '70s has planted its forward-looking credo so firmly in U.S. boardrooms that it permeates the corporate hierarchy. "If you're in management at a modern company and you don't spend at least part of your day thinking like a futurist, you probably aren't doing your job," says Sharon Bennett, executive director of the Strategic Leadership Forum, an industry association.

But prognosticators who fatten at the corporate trough have their critics. "Futurism isn't prediction anymore," says futurist guru Douglas Rushkoff. "It's state-of-the-art propaganda. It's future creation." As he sees the process, two of the futurists' most potent tools are terror and exclusivity. "They put their clients in a state of fear and then explain that they hold the secret knowledge that can save them," says Rushkoff. He speaks with authority: his own shrewd brand of high-tech utopianism earns the 35-year-old New Yorker six-figure book advances and up to $7,500 an hour strategizing for the likes of the Sony Corp., Telecommunications Inc. and Interval Research.

The Tofflers, who made this market in the first place, hope to cash in as well. To that end, FutureNet is talking with cable and broadcast channels and several FORTUNE 500 companies about financial backing, and has recruited veteran Hollywood and network TV producers to add zip to its forecasts. The tone of FutureNet's offerings, Toffler says, will be "not just for the digerati and not heavy. After all," he laughs, "it's television."

Twenty-five years ago, the Tofflers wrote in *Future Shock* that "a well-oiled machinery for the creation and diffusion of fads is now an entrenched part of the modern economy." A generation after their first great sermon, the high priest and priestess of futurism may finally get to practice what they've been preaching. ∎

Now It's Rent-a-Shuttle

It's a bird … it's a plane … it's a flying piece of pie? No, it's America's next space shuttle, the VentureStar. Designed by Lockheed Martin and chosen by NASA after a heated competition among three entries, the fully reusable VentureStar is to be built using private funding, then rented out to NASA and others. It promises to be much cheaper to operate than current shuttles—and it won't even require astronauts aboard. A half-size prototype is scheduled to fly in 1999, the finished craft in 2006.

FOR HIRE: NASA will not own the new shuttle

Found: 11 Pyramids Lost: One Mummy

He designed and built the first true pyramids, but Snefru has long been overshadowed by his son Khufu (also known as Cheops). Because Khufu's Great Pyramid at Giza, on the outskirts of Cairo, is more accessible to tourists, it has become the landmark. Snefru's three pyramids, along with eight others, sat 13 miles away, concealed behind barbed wire on an army base. In 1996, Snefru's pyramids at last were opened to the public. Visitors marveled at the 4,600-year-old Red Pyramid,

TROJAN GOLD: A sauce-boat fit for a king

50 years after Soviet troops "liberated" them from Hitler's crumbling Berlin, the wondrous treasures of ANCIENT TROY unearthed by archaeologist Heinrich Schliemann were at last displayed in Moscow

the first to have the classic smooth-sided, rather than stepped, shape—as well as at the odd-shaped Bent Pyramid nearby. They marveled, too, at a mystery: Snefru's mummy, believed to have been found in 1948 in the Red Pyramid, disappeared shortly after and has not been seen since.

The Russians: Out of Money, Out of Space?

For the Russian space program, long beset by slashed budgets that led to fewer launches, the big comeback was to begin in November with the launch of its Mars '96 probe. The mission's importance was pumped up by NASA's reported discovery of life on the Red Planet. But the grand promenade to Mars turned into a fizzle when a booster malfunction sent the spacecraft plummeting back to Earth shortly after its launch. Five days later, Russian

HEALTH UPDATE

Redux: Dieters' Dream?

The first new diet drug in the U.S. in 23 years, Redux, was approved in April by the U.S. Food and Drug Administration (FDA). Within three months, doctors were writing 85,000

prescriptions a week for the drug, and one analyst predicted that sales would hit $1 billion within five years. Redux, a refined version of a compound popularly known as fen/phen, stimulates the production of the brain neurotransmitter serotonin, which is responsible for the

CRITICS: Exercise still beats diet pills physical and emotional sense of satiety and a general feeling of well-being. Yet critics charged that Redux was not a panacea for obesity. Besides such side effects as fatigue and diarrhea, the drug can trigger a rare but frequently fatal human disorder called primary pulmonary hypertension, which destroys blood vessels in the lungs and heart.

MYSTERY: The humped shape of Snefru's Bent Pyramid puzzles scholars

officials admitted that two of the country's spy satellites had recently fallen from orbit, leaving the military without any space-based reconnaissance capabilities. Nor were the Russians able to replace them. The future of Russia's once proud space program seemed very much in doubt.

Updating *Homo Erectus*

The prehuman species *Homo erectus* possessed little language and had limited skill in making tools. Anthropologists believe the species arose in Africa about 1.8 million years ago and later ranged from China to the Middle East. But *Homo erectus* was no match for our species, *Homo sapiens*, and not long after modern humans appeared, some 200,000 years ago, the more primitive hominid died out. Or so it seemed. According to a new analysis of fossil sites in Java, *Homo erectus* may have

lived there as recently as 27,000 years ago—long after he was believed to be extinct, and well into "our" time.

Shot Across the Bow

It was a heavenly near miss. In late May, a large asteroid whizzed by Earth, missing the planet by 280,000 miles—a hair-breadth in space terms. Perhaps a third of a mile across, the asteroid was the largest object ever observed to pass that close to earth—yet it was discovered only four days before it passed. The message: asteroids like this one present a clear and present danger. More than 100 NEOs (near-earth-objects) big enough to cause the kind of disaster that wiped out the dinosaurs have been identified; scientists believe some 2,000 more may lurk nearby.

WHEW! Earth got a scare from a passing asteroid

A fossil jaw found with stone tools in Ethiopia was dated at some **2.33 MILLION** years—arguably the oldest *Homo sapiens* bones ever found

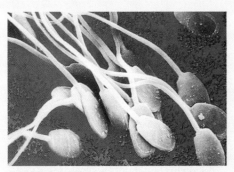
TOO FEW? Falling sperm counts, rising fears

Sputtering Sperm Counts

What's happening to men's sperm? Researchers in Edinburgh, Scotland, reported that men born after 1970 had a sperm count 25% lower than those born before 1959—an average decline of 2.1% a year. In an even more comprehensive analysis, Danish scientists discovered an alarming plunge of nearly 50% in average sperm counts over the past half-century. The quality of sperm—the percentage of healthy, vigorous cells versus malformed, sluggish ones—also appears to be in serious decline. Together, the factors add up to a significant drop in male fertility. The causes remain a mystery; stress, smoking and drug use are known to be factors, while an increasing number of doctors claim chemical pollutants in the environment are to blame. As more studies report a global problem, the pace of research is being stepped up.

Quick Fix for Strokes

Half a million Americans suffer strokes each year, in most cases as a wayward blood clot blocks the flow of oxygen-rich blood to the brain. Until recently, doctors could do little more than watch as stroke patients either recovered on their own or became permanently paralyzed. But in 1996 there was good news: the American Heart Association issued new guidelines for the use of a drug called tissue plasminogen activator, or TPA, that, if administered quickly, can dissolve the clot and prevent permanent brain damage.

The "Morning After" Pill

Many American women are not aware that the oral contraceptive "Pill" has another use: in a somewhat higher dose, it can serve as a "morning after" drug to avoid pregnancy after unprotected sex. After years of monitoring the situation, the FDA began encouraging such use of the Pill, noting that it can be used safely and effectively to avoid pregnancy as much as three days after intercourse. The push, which amounted to official government sanction of such use, was strongly criticized by pro-life adherents.

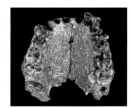
THE PILL: A controversial new use

HOW OLD? 400,000 years older than other *Homo sapiens* fossils

MAN OF THE YEAR

AIDS:

DR. DAVID HO

More than any other person, he
is responsible for the new
hope that AIDS can be overcome

S OME AGES ARE DEFINED BY THEIR EPIDEMICS. IN 1347 RATS AND fleas stirred up by Tatar traders cutting caravan routes through Central Asia brought bubonic plague to Sicily. In the space of four years, the Black Death killed up to 30 million people. In 1520, Cortés' army carried smallpox to Mexico, wiping out half the native inhabitants. In 1918 a particularly virulent strain of flu swept through troops in the trenches of France, then worked its way through the civilian population, killing 21 million men, women and children around the world.

Today we live in the shadow of AIDS—the terrifyingly modern epidemic that travels by jet and zeros in on the body's own disease-fighting immune system. More than 15 years after the first rumors of "gay plague" began, nearly 30 million people—gays and straights alike—have been infected by HIV, the virus that causes what has been, until now, an almost invariably fatal disease.

In 1996, for the first time, there is something that looks like hope. Early in the summer AIDS patients taking therapeutic "cocktails" that combine protease inhibitors with other antiviral drugs began experiencing remarkable recoveries. Their viral loads fell. Their T-cell counts climbed. Their health improved—perhaps temporarily, but often dramatically. Hospices and AIDS clinics across the U.S. began to empty.

Then in July, at an international AIDS conference in Vancouver, a virologist named David Ho reported on a most promising experiment. By administering the protease-inhibitor cocktails to patients in the earliest stages of infection, his team seems to have come tantalizingly close to eliminating the virus from the blood and other body tissues. Mathematical models suggest that patients caught early enough might be virus-free within two or three years.

This is, as an AIDS expert puts it, hope with an asterisk. Even if Ho's treatment works, there is still no magic bullet for patients in late stages of the disease and no vaccine that will inoculate against HIV infection. The cost of the cocktails (up to $20,000 a year) puts them beyond the reach of all but the best-insured patients—and out of the question for the 90% who live in the developing world.

Nevertheless, we have learned this year what may be the most important fact about AIDS: it is not invincible. This was not the work of one scientist: there is no Louis Pasteur of AIDS. Science today is too costly and too complex for that. Modern medical research is a richly collaborative effort. But in the shared achievement of the thousands of scientists and physicians who have helped bring AIDS to what seems to be a historic turning point in 1996, one name stands out.

Dr. David Ho was one of a small group of researchers who recognized from the start that AIDS was probably an infectious disease. He performed or collaborated on much of the basic virology work that showed HIV does not lie dormant, as most scientists had thought, but multiplies in vast numbers right from the start. His insights helped shift the focus of AIDS treatment from the late stages of illness to the first weeks of infection. And it was his team's pioneering work with combination therapy that first raised hope that the virus might someday be eliminated.

Ho is not, to be sure, a household name—like Bill Clinton, who dominated the front page this year, or Bill Gates, who deftly extended the scope of his software empire. But some people make headlines while others make history. And when the history of this era is written, it is likely that the men and women who turned the tide on AIDS will be seen as true heroes of the age. For helping lift a death sentence—for a few years at least, and perhaps longer—on tens of thousands of AIDS sufferers, and for pioneering the treatment that might, just might, lead to a cure, David Da-i Ho, M.D., is TIME's Man of the Year for 1996. ∎

HOPE *at* LAST

The DISEASE DETECTIVE

As the AIDS epidemic unfolded, Dr. David Ho had a knack for asking just the right questions

DR. DAVID HO DOESN'T LOOK LIKE A GAMBLER. WITH HIS BOYISH FACE and slender build, he could more easily pass for a teenager than for a 44-year-old father of three—or, for that matter, for a world-renowned scientist. In fact, when he was an undergraduate in the 1970s, Ho hung around the Las Vegas blackjack tables, memorizing each card as it was played. He got so good at counting cards that he was thrown out of several casinos.

Today Ho is still something of a gambler, though in a very different field and for much bigger stakes. The director of the Aaron Diamond AIDS Research Center in New York City, he has come up with a daring strategy for flushing out the virus that causes AIDS. As Ho explained at the 11th International Conference on AIDS in Vancouver, Canada, in July 1996, he (like more and more doctors) is using powerful new drugs called protease inhibitors in combination with standard antiviral medications. But unlike most doctors, he gives the so-called combination therapy to patients in the first few weeks of infection. Already the HIV in his patients' blood has dropped so low it can no longer be measured. Because he is attacking early, before full-fledged AIDS can develop, Ho told the conference, there is a good chance that within two or three years the virus could be completely eliminated from a patient.

Eliminated. Just a few months earlier, no reputable scientist would have presumed to imagine such a thing. Journalists, activists and researchers peppered Ho with questions. Had he found the cure? Could people stop worrying about AIDS? Could they throw away their condoms? The answers: No, no and no. What he had done, Ho explained, was begin an experiment that might, under the right circumstances, eliminate the virus from a small group of men caught within three months of infection. He couldn't offer the same hope to the estimated 100,000 patients in later stages of infection who in the past year have begun taking the same antiviral "cocktails"—often with encouraging results—but whose AIDS is probably too far advanced to permit a long-term recovery.

Like so many promising HIV treatments, Ho's strategy could fail. It could even backfire if it is mistakenly touted as a "morning after" treatment that allows people to engage in risky sexual behavior. By desensitizing the virus to medications, it could jeopardize a patient's response to future treatments. Worse yet, it could inadvertently create a mutant strain of virus resistant to all current drugs—a kind of super HIV—that could lead to a second, even more devastating AIDS epidemic.

Still, the tentative sense of hope that has sprouted in the AIDS community after the Vancouver conference is understandable. Ho's speech, for all its caveats, gave the first concrete evidence that HIV is not insurmountable. After 15 years of horror, denial and disappointment, the pendulum may at long last be swinging against AIDS.

A TEAM EFFORT

David Ho would be the first to say that he cannot take all the credit. It was an immunologist from Los Angeles named Michael Gottlieb who in 1981 reported the first cases of what was then called gay pneumonia. It was the U.S. Centers for Disease Control that alerted doctors to the gathering epidemic and found that the infection was transmitted through blood transfusions, tainted needles and unprotected sex. It was Dr. Luc Montagnier's lab at the Pasteur Institute in Paris that first isolated the killer virus in 1983. And it was Dr. Robert Gallo and his colleagues at the National Cancer Institute in

ON THE CASE

Ho in his headquarters
at the Aaron Diamond
AIDS Research Center
in New York City

show what the body does right in controlling HIV. His pioneering experiments with protease inhibitors helped clarify how the virus overwhelms the immune system. His work and his insights set the stage for an enormously productive shift in the treatment of AIDS.

Once, not so long ago, scientists believed that nothing much happened after HIV gained entry into the body. The virus simply hunkered down inside a few of the immune system's T cells—the linchpins of the body's defensive forces—for anywhere from three to 10 years. Then something, no one knew what, spurred the microbial invader to awaken. In this picture, the AIDS virus spent most of its life hibernating before starting its final, deadly assault.

In the past two years, Ho and his colleagues have demonstrated that this picture of the virus is wrong. There is no initial dormant phase of infection. Ho showed that the body and the virus are locked in a pitched battle from the very beginning. At first many AIDS researchers found this hard to accept, for it challenged some of their most cherished assumptions. If Ho was right, doctors would have to alter radically the way they treated AIDS.

It wasn't the first time that Ho had overturned conventional wisdom. During the past 15 years, he has displayed an uncanny ability to ask questions that seem obvious only in retrospect and to probe key issues others have overlooked. Ho also has an extraordinary knack for being in the right place at the right time. Two years after he received his M.D. from Harvard Medical School, Ho witnessed the birth of the AIDS epidemic.

The year was 1981, and Ho was chief medical resident at Cedars Sinai Hospital in Los Angeles. Across town at UCLA, Gottlieb had identified a new syndrome that seemed to target gay men. Each of the cases was different, but all had one thing in common: whatever was making the men sick had singled out the T cells for destruction. Eventually the body's battered defenses couldn't shake off even the most innocuous microbial intruder. The men were dying from what doctors termed opportunistic infections, such as *Pneumocystis* pneumonia,

Bethesda, Maryland, who made it grow in the laboratory, which led to the development of an antibody test.

But Ho, working alone or with others, fundamentally changed the way scientists looked at the AIDS virus. His breakthrough work in virology, beginning in the mid-1980s, revealed how HIV mounts its attack. His tenacious pursuit of the virus in the first weeks of infection helped

which attacks the lungs, and toxoplasmosis, which often ravages the brain.

Ho began seeing more and more of these patients in the intensive-care units at Cedars Sinai. Some doctors thought that amyl nitrate and other recreational drugs triggered the immune collapse, others that it was a bizarre allergic reaction from having too many sex partners. But Ho fell into the camp that suspected a virus. He quickly decided to specialize in AIDS research. In 1982 Ho landed in Dr. Martin Hirsch's virology laboratory at Massachusetts General Hospital in Boston. A prominent scientist in his own right, Hirsch is known for cultivating talented young researchers. Like many other ambitious young scientists, Ho wanted to be the first to isolate the virus that causes AIDS. Luc Montagnier and Robert Gallo beat him to it. Still, while working in Hirsch's lab, Ho became expert at detecting HIV in places where few were able to find it. He was the first to show that it grows in long-lived immune cells called macrophages and among the first to isolate it in the nervous system and semen. As important, he showed that there isn't enough active virus in saliva for kissing to transmit the infection.

To support his family, Ho started moonlighting in Mass General's walk-in clinics. It turned out to be the right time to be in that place too. "The clinics are where you see the flus, the colds, the common illnesses," Ho says. In the mid-1980s, however, he started seeing gay men with what appeared to be an unusually severe flu. They always got over their illness without any of the hallmarks of AIDS. Still, he wondered, could these flu-like ailments be the signs of the men's very first exposure to HIV?

Sure enough, blood tests showed that the "flu" corresponded with the sudden onset of HIV—and the total absence of influenza viruses. Then, after a few weeks, the antibodies in the immune system would jump sharply, while HIV disappeared from the circulation. It was the first evidence that HIV triggered an active infection.

LEARNING FROM FAILURE

Despite rising casualties, Washington kept tight purse strings on funding for AIDS research for much of the 1980s. By 1987, though, even Ronald Reagan knew that AIDS was a serious threat. The plague had encircled the globe, stretching from Africa to Asia. The antibody test revealed the presence of HIV in the blood supplies of the U.S., France and Japan. The FDA approved use of the antiviral drug AZT in a record 14 weeks. At that time, scientists across the U.S. were also excited about a possible breakthrough treatment: soluble CD4. They knew that HIV does not infect T cells at random. It must first attach itself to a particular protein,

called CD4, on the T cells' surface. Perhaps, researchers reasoned, if they flooded the bloodstream with free-floating CD4 molecules, the molecules would act as decoys and prevent HIV from infecting the T cells. Preliminary tests on viral samples grown under laboratory conditions showed that soluble CD4 worked beautifully.

Ho had taken a junior faculty position at UCLA and moved his family back to California. He contacted Dr. Robert Schooley of the University of Colorado Medical Center in Denver, and together they embarked on a clinical trial of soluble CD4 in two dozen patients, many of them in the later stages of AIDS. Unfortunately, Ho and Schooley wound up proving that soluble CD4 doesn't work. In the process, however, they discovered that there were tens of thousands of infectious viral particles in their patients' bodies, a lot more than anyone had expected.

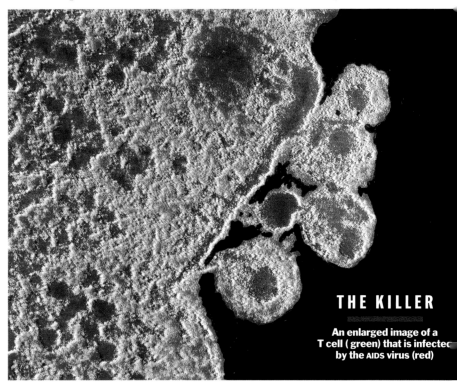

THE KILLER

An enlarged image of a T cell (green) that is infected by the AIDS virus (red)

It took Ho only a few weeks to figure out why soluble CD4 didn't work. The early tests on the treatment were done on much weaker viruses that had adapted to living under laboratory conditions. Somehow wild viruses could tell which CD4 molecules were decoys. Ho and the rest of the AIDS scientists had just learned a valuable lesson. They would have to test all their potential treatments on viruses that infected real patients.

BACK TO BASICS

The experience with soluble CD4 showed Ho that there were significant gaps in science's understanding of the life cycle of HIV. He decided to revisit his earlier Boston work on the first stages of infection. By hanging out in hospital emergency rooms and talking to colleagues, he and his team at UCLA identified four young homosexual men suffering from the flu-like symptoms of a primary HIV infection. Ho used a newly available tool of genetic engineering—the PCR test later used in O.J. Simpson's trial—to measure the amount of virus in the blood. Again, he was astonished.

By this time, most researchers agreed that people in the later stages of AIDS had large quantities of HIV in their blood. But the PCR test showed that millions of viral particles were coursing through Ho's patients' blood in the earliest weeks of infection as well—as many as could be found in someone with a full-fledged case of AIDS. Yet within a few weeks, the viral load plunged to low and in some cases undetectable levels. The patients recovered and seemed healthy.

Ho wasn't the only scientist who had observed this. Another team, headed by Dr. George Shaw, who runs the AIDS research lab at the University of Alabama in Birmingham, had seen the same spike in HIV particles followed

end stages of AIDS than anyone had thought possible. The next question was obvious: What is going on during those middle years, when patients are still in relatively good health? Ho suspected that the answer could dramatically change the treatment of HIV-positive patients.

All the blood tests indicated that the viral load was close to zero throughout the middle years, though it would gradually increase as time went by. Both Ho and Shaw realized, however, that zero doesn't always equal zero in the world of HIV. For one thing, the virus might be hiding out in the lymph nodes, where it could be producing thousands or even millions of copies of itself every day. As long as the immune system cleared those infectious particles as quickly as they formed, blood tests would show no change in viral load.

If the virus reproduced very quickly, it would eventually exhaust the body's defenses. At least that's what Ho and Shaw thought. The trick to proving their idea was to find some way to stop HIV's cycle of reproduction in the blood and to enable the immune system to rebound. By measuring that rebound, the scientists hoped to figure out just how rapidly the virus had been reproducing.

There was just one problem: no one knew how to stop HIV that quickly. AZT wasn't powerful enough to do it. The pharmaceutical companies, however, had just started looking at a new class of substances, called protease inhibitors, that might fit the bill. As it turned out, it took several years of testing to come up with a formula for a protease inhibitor that was effective against HIV.

LIFE CYCLE OF THE AIDS VIRUS AND HOW IT MIGHT BE STOPPED

1 The AIDS virus consists of two strands of RNA and some enzymes encased in a coating

1 VIRUS
CD4 RECEPTOR
CO-RECEPTOR
RNA

2 When the virus encounters a T cell (part of the immune system), proteins on the virus coating bind to both CD4 and co-receptors on the cell

3 The virus then enters the cell. Its RNA is converted into double-stranded DNA by an enzyme called reverse transcriptase (RT)

A RT inhibitor drugs, such as AZT and 3TC, can disrupt the early stage of viral reproduction

4 Next, an enzyme called integrase incorporates the virus' genetic material into the T cell's DNA

B Drugs called integrase inhibitors, which are designed to halt this process, are in development

5 The viral DNA uses the cell's manufacturing processes, directing it to churn out viral RNA and proteins

6 Protease enzymes cut the viral proteins into shorter pieces so that they can be incorporated into new viruses

C Protease inhibitors block this stage of reproduction

DNA
NUCLEUS
T CELL
PROTEIN
PROTEASE
VIRAL DNA
BUDDING

7 The viruses bud off and attack other T cells

TIME Diagram By Joe Lertola

REINFORCEMENTS

The year was 1994, and the new drugs were finally producing good results in the test tube. They worked against lab strains of the virus; they worked against viral samples taken from patients. Where AZT merely slowed viral reproduction, the protease inhibitors shut it down almost completely. But almost wasn't good enough. It often took less than a month for a few viral particles to mutate into a strain that was resistant to protease inhibitors. The new drugs were starting to look like another failure.

But a few weeks was all that Ho and Shaw needed to conduct their rebound experiments. The two laboratories raced to find the answer. Ho chose 20 volunteers whose T cells had dropped from a normal level of about 1,000 cells per ml of blood to fewer than 500. The newest PCR tests showed that the viral load of these patients was holding steady at about 100,000 copies per ml of blood. Ho started treating his subjects with one of the new protease inhibitors being developed by Abbott Laboratories. As expected, the amount of virus that could be measured in the patients' blood practically disappeared. But no one was ready for what happened next.

by a sharp drop. The two researchers learned of each other's work and decided to co-publish their findings in a 1991 issue of the *New England Journal of Medicine*. It was the beginning of a friendly but no less keen competition between the two.

This was also the beginning of a new phase in Ho's career. Philanthropist Irene Diamond had decided to found an AIDS research center in New York City and had chosen Ho, then 37, as its director. "Everybody said, 'He's so young, he's unknown.'" she recalls. "I said, 'I don't want a star, I want a wonderful scientist.'" For his part, Ho decided that the chance to gain more lab space, secure financial backing and attract top-level scientists to join him was too good to pass up.

Ho and Shaw had proved that there are high levels of virus in the first few weeks of infection. Ho and Schooley had already shown that there is a lot more virus in the

Preliminary calculations indicated that the immune system was rebounding faster than anyone had thought possible. The results showed that in every day of every year, in every infected person, HIV produced not thousands, not millions, but *billions* of copies of itself. And every day the body launched billions of immune cells in response. The wonder was not that the immune system finally crashed but that it lasted so long. Ho and Shaw found the answer at the same time and published their results in back-to-back articles in a 1995 issue of *Nature.*

Suddenly the entire picture of AIDS had changed. As long as doctors thought that the virus was not very active through the early and middle years of infection, it made sense to conserve forces and delay treatment so they would be ready for the virus when it emerged from hibernation. Now it was becoming clear that the immune system needed all the help it could get right from the start.

But where would that help come from? Cancer researchers knew that it is often better to combine the firepower of several different chemotherapeutic drugs than to rely on any single medication to destroy cancer cells. Too often, the one-drug approach allows a few malignant cells to survive and blossom into an even more lethal tumor. The AIDS researchers faced a similar problem with HIV. Whenever they prescribed a single drug, such as AZT, for their patients, a few viral particles would survive and give rise to drug-resistant HIV.

Now that the protease inhibitors had become available, doctors were eager to combine them with the old standby AZT and a third drug called 3TC. Mathematical models—created by one of Ho's collaborators, Alan Perelson of the Los Alamos National Laboratory—suggested that HIV would have a hard time simultaneously undergoing the minimum three mutations necessary to resist combination therapy. He placed the odds at 10 million to 1.

HOPE AT LAST

For once in the history of HIV, a strategy that ought to work seemed in fact to succeed. Within weeks of starting combination therapy, 7 out of 10 men and women with AIDS begin to get better. In many of them, the viral load has dropped below detectable levels. Relieved of the burden of fighting HIV, their long-suffering immune systems can finally tackle the deadly fungal and bacterial infections that have taken hold in their lungs, intestines and brains. Fevers break; lesions disappear; energy returns.

With the virus under control in at least some AIDS patients, doctors are considering how to rebuild their battered immune systems. After a decade of fighting HIV, many of the body's defensive reserves have been thoroughly depleted and cannot be regenerated from within. Researchers plan to grow replacement cells in the laboratory for transplant into recovering patients.

It all sounds so hopeful. But researchers know that any "cure" would have to do much more than clear HIV from the bloodstream. It must remove the virus from the lymph nodes, the brain, the spinal fluid, the testes—wherever it may be hiding. Today's combination therapies work in the blood, but not very well in the brain or the testes. Chances are that people in the later stages of the disease will have to stay on combination therapy the rest of their lives—assuming they can tolerate the often excruciating side effects. They also have to bear in mind that they are probably still infectious and that eventually—perhaps in a few years, perhaps longer—their immune systems will probably once again collapse.

But what if you could avoid all those problems, Ho wondered. What if you didn't wait until the end stages of the disease but started combination therapy during the first few weeks of the infection, before too many billion viral particles had formed? Would you have tilted the odds in the immune system enough so that it could wipe out whatever stragglers might be left, no matter where they were? To find out, Ho and one of his team, Dr. Martin Markowitz, recruited two dozen men in the earliest stages of HIV infection and placed them on combination therapy. All the men appeared healthy before treatment.

Some of them have been treated for more than a year now, and none of them show any trace of HIV in their blood. Ho has not forgotten, however, that zero does not always equal zero. He and Markowitz are looking for pockets of virus in the lymph tissue, the semen and the spinal fluid. Ho believes that prospects for success are good. Assuming that nothing has been overlooked, combination therapy should burn the virus out of the body in two to three years. Because treatment began so early, the men's immune systems should be able to replace any lost defensive cells. There is still a chance, of course, that bits of the virus, called proviral DNA, are lodged in the chromosomes, beyond the reach of even the most powerful drugs.

But even if the virus were to stage a comeback, that would not necessarily mean that combination therapy has failed. It may be that additional ingredients could eliminate the virus completely. Ho has already started using a combination of four drugs in another early-intervention trial. And he has access to new, experimental medications that can better penetrate the brain and perhaps the testes.

Much work remains, both in the quest for an effective treatment and in the search for a way to prevent infection in the first place. Some scientists are more hopeful about the prospects for gene therapy, which could possibly render the immune system impervious to HIV attack. Another promising line of research centers on a group of molecules called chemokines, which may one day be used to shield cells from HIV. Other scientists, including Ho, are intensifying their search for a vaccine.

It has taken the collaborative work of thousands of scientists and physicians to get this far. It will take even greater cooperation and well-funded coordination to overcome the remaining hurdles. But the worst fear—the one that seeded a decade with despair, the foreboding sense that the AIDS virus might be invincible—has finally been subdued. ∎

The TAO *of* HO

His tenacity and legendary tranquillity both spring from the immigrant experience

IF YOU LEAN IN CLOSE, CONSPIRATORIALLY, SONIA Ho may just let slip a secret she keeps about her son David. She will speak in a hush, as if to elude some spy's eavesdropping from behind the potted palm. Thus, slightly abashed but nonetheless proud, she will confide, "He's kind of a genius, you know. I'm not supposed to say that, but it's true."

Mothers are allowed to say these things. But one doesn't have to be David Da-i Ho's mother to be aware of his brilliance. He lays forth clearly and succinctly some of the boldest yet most cogent hypotheses in the epic campaign against HIV; at the same time, he operates nimbly through the budgetary and political pitfalls of the enterprise. And though he has been known to fling the occasional hot one-liner against naysayers, he is monumentally tranquil in demeanor.

Ho cuts too slight a figure to qualify as a force of nature, but his spirit is startling: a fierce competitiveness manifested as a subtle calm, a passionate transcendence. His fine-fingered hands do not punch out arguments; rather they escort logic through tangles of confusion, gently prodding reason his way. His genius emanates from the depths of his family's experiences, and it is not quite Asian to make a display of one's legacies. But this is America, and Ho's journey is also an extraordinary American success story.

FAMILY TIES

Sidney, David, Paul and Sonia Ho during their recent visit to Taichung

TIME's 1996 Man of the Year was born in Taichung, Taiwan, on November 3, 1952, and was given the name Da-i, two Chinese ideograms that literally mean "Great One," a Taoist term of vast cosmological consequence. Taichung was a quiet town in the Taiwan boondocks, and the Ho family lived in a modest four-room house. To forge a better life for his family, Ho's father took ship in 1956, traveling 18 days on a freighter to America. For nine years, Da-i would know his father only through letters and parcel post.

When his father sent for the family, a seriousness came over Da-i. The 12-year-old packed his own bags and stayed awake throughout the flight to watch over his mother and his younger brother. They were traveling to a land they did not know and whose language they did not speak. Their father, a devout Christian who now called himself Paul, had picked the boys' American names from the Bible. Thus it came to pass that Ho Da-i became David Ho and his younger brother became Phillip.

The family initially settled in a black neighborhood of central Los Angeles, not far from the University of Southern California, where Paul Ho pursued a master's degree in engineering. A diffident David did two things: he became an introvert and stuck close to the family, and he focused on school and achievement. It was A's in everything, math, science—and English. Six months after starting school, David settled into the language, thanks to an English-as-a-second-language program and the miracle of TV, particularly old *Three Stooges* movies.

Attending M.I.T. and Caltech as a physics major, Ho soon realized that the most glittering prizes in science weren't in physics; molecular biology was the cutting edge. So he made his way to Harvard Medical School, embarking on a path that led to the turning point of Ho's career, his decision to go into HIV research.

As he pursued the virus, Ho's introversion faded. At the same time he grew less temperamental and developed his legendary tranquillity. The equanimity deepened as Ho carved out time for his family. Even at school, he acted as a second father to his second brother Sidney, writing constantly with advice and encouragement. Ho became a father himself; he and his wife Susan Kuo, an artist, have two girls and a boy. Now and then, Ho sneaks away from his busy schedule to surprise his kids at school.

As a child, Ho had his math tables drilled into him in Mandarin, and to this day he does his calculations in Chinese. He plays down the importance of being Chinese to his success—but that is a very Chinese thing to do. Instead, he cites immigrant drive: "People get to this new world, and they want to carve out their place in it. The result is dedication and a higher level of work ethic." He adds, "You always retain a bit of an underdog mentality." Ho knows that if they work assiduously and lie low long enough, even underdogs will have their day. ∎

The Growing Epidemic:

AIDS is tightening its grip on the developing world, where new treatments are too costly to help

THE GOOD NEWS ABOUT AIDS THAT LED TO TIME's selection of Dr. David Ho as Man of the Year 1996 underscores a bitter truth: the new combination therapies are of little use to 90% of the people suffering from the disease. In Africa, India and Thailand, and to a growing extent in Central and Eastern Europe, the treatment's price tag—up to $20,000 a year—puts it beyond the grasp of all but the superrich. "With this discovery, the AIDS gap only becomes wider," laments Dr. Peter Piot, executive director of the U.N.'s AIDS program.

Meanwhile, AIDS is tightening its grip outside the U.S. and Western Europe. In India, researchers estimate, by the year 2000 anywhere from 15 million to 50 million people could be HIV positive. Central and Eastern European countries are seeing an explosion in the number of cases. And then there is Africa, across much of which the disease continues to rage unchecked. Already the sub-Saharan region accounts for more than 60% of all the people living with HIV worldwide.

For the majority of those with HIV outside the U.S. and Europe, the cost of the new "cocktail" treatments seems a cruel joke. A more effective alternative is prevention, through public education and safe-sex programs. Such efforts have made some progress in recent years in countries like Uganda, which launched a genuine anti-AIDS campaign in the mid-1980s that has helped HIV infections among young women drop by more than 30%. Elsewhere in Africa and in some parts of Asia, similar programs have stalled. Most of those dying from the disease in rural parts of Africa have no clear idea of what is killing them, let alone how to prevent it.

Virtually every AIDS expert agrees that only an effective vaccine can halt the epidemic. Yet vaccine research remains the poor stepsister of the anti-AIDS effort, because those pushing the hardest for AIDS research are Westerners who already have HIV, and thus are more interested in a cure than prevention. Private drug companies are disinclined to spend heavily on vaccine development because vaccines are generally less profitable than therapeutics. According to U.S. market researchers Frost and Sullivan, sales of antiviral drugs for AIDS and its accompanying infections reached $1.3 billion in 1995 alone. ∎

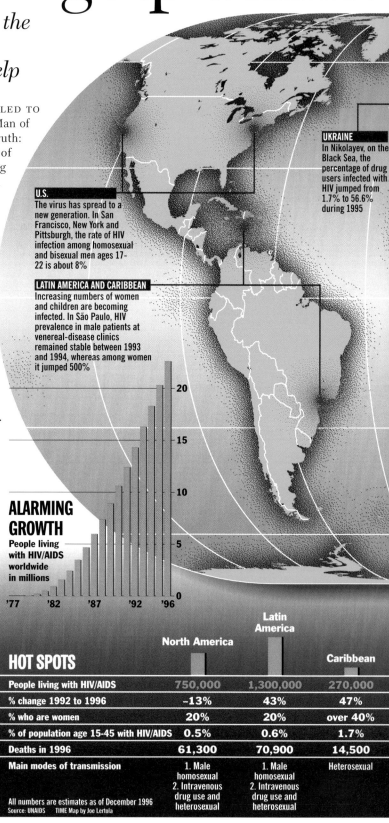

UKRAINE
In Nikolayev, on the Black Sea, the percentage of drug users infected with HIV jumped from 1.7% to 56.6% during 1995

U.S.
The virus has spread to a new generation. In San Francisco, New York and Pittsburgh, the rate of HIV infection among homosexual and bisexual men ages 17–22 is about 8%

LATIN AMERICA AND CARIBBEAN
Increasing numbers of women and children are becoming infected. In São Paulo, HIV prevalence in male patients at venereal-disease clinics remained stable between 1993 and 1994, whereas among women it jumped 500%

ALARMING GROWTH
People living with HIV/AIDS worldwide in millions

'77   '82   '87   '92   '96

HOT SPOTS

	North America	Latin America	Caribbean
People living with HIV/AIDS	750,000	1,300,000	270,000
% change 1992 to 1996	–13%	43%	47%
% who are women	20%	20%	over 40%
% of population age 15-45 with HIV/AIDS	0.5%	0.6%	1.7%
Deaths in 1996	61,300	70,900	14,500
Main modes of transmission	1. Male homosexual 2. Intravenous drug use and heterosexual	1. Male homosexual 2. Intravenous drug use and heterosexual	Heterosexual

All numbers are estimates as of December 1996
Source: UNAIDS   TIME Map by Joe Lertola

AIDS Around the World

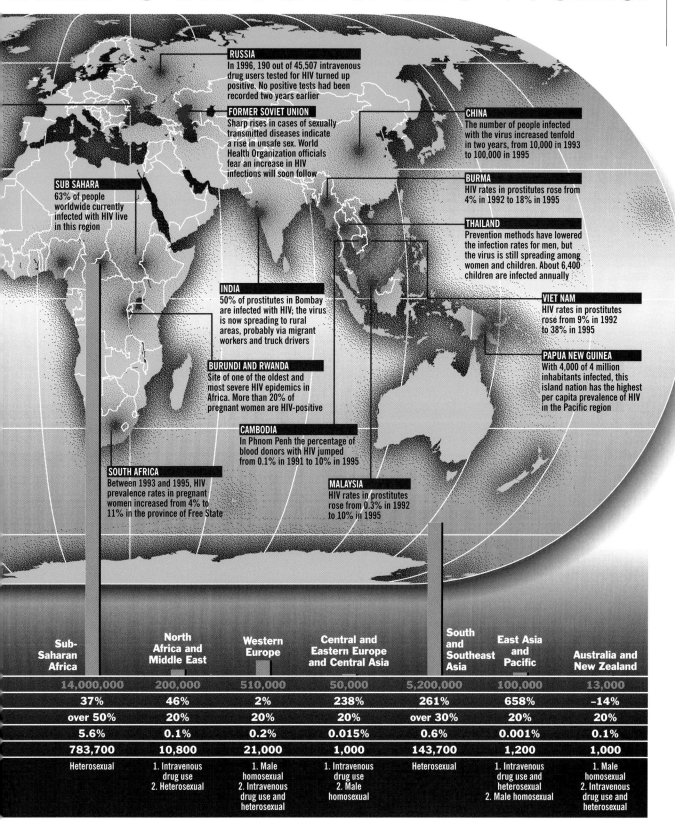

RUSSIA
In 1996, 190 out of 45,507 intravenous drug users tested for HIV turned up positive. No positive tests had been recorded two years earlier

FORMER SOVIET UNION
Sharp rises in cases of sexually transmitted diseases indicate a rise in unsafe sex. World Health Organization officials fear an increase in HIV infections will soon follow

CHINA
The number of people infected with the virus increased tenfold in two years, from 10,000 in 1993 to 100,000 in 1995

BURMA
HIV rates in prostitutes rose from 4% in 1992 to 18% in 1995

THAILAND
Prevention methods have lowered the infection rates for men, but the virus is still spreading among women and children. About 6,400 children are infected annually

SUB SAHARA
63% of people worldwide currently infected with HIV live in this region

INDIA
50% of prostitutes in Bombay are infected with HIV; the virus is now spreading to rural areas, probably via migrant workers and truck drivers

VIET NAM
HIV rates in prostitutes rose from 9% in 1992 to 38% in 1995

PAPUA NEW GUINEA
With 4,000 of 4 million inhabitants infected, this island nation has the highest per capita prevalence of HIV in the Pacific region

BURUNDI AND RWANDA
Site of one of the oldest and most severe HIV epidemics in Africa. More than 20% of pregnant women are HIV-positive

CAMBODIA
In Phnom Penh the percentage of blood donors with HIV jumped from 0.1% in 1991 to 10% in 1995

SOUTH AFRICA
Between 1993 and 1995, HIV prevalence rates in pregnant women increased from 4% to 11% in the province of Free State

MALAYSIA
HIV rates in prostitutes rose from 0.3% in 1992 to 10% in 1995

Sub-Saharan Africa	North Africa and Middle East	Western Europe	Central and Eastern Europe and Central Asia	South and Southeast Asia	East Asia and Pacific	Australia and New Zealand
14,000,000	200,000	510,000	50,000	5,200,000	100,000	13,000
37%	46%	2%	238%	261%	658%	–14%
over 50%	20%	20%	20%	over 30%	20%	20%
5.6%	0.1%	0.2%	0.015%	0.6%	0.001%	0.1%
783,700	10,800	21,000	1,000	143,700	1,200	1,000
Heterosexual	1. Intravenous drug use 2. Heterosexual	1. Male homosexual 2. Intravenous drug use and heterosexual	1. Intravenous drug use 2. Male homosexual	Heterosexual	1. Intravenous drug use and heterosexual 2. Male homosexual	1. Male homosexual 2. Intravenous drug use and heterosexual

Learning To Live Again

Fifteen years into the AIDS epidemic, optimism is a foreign state.
Should we let the new drugs take us there?

PEOPLE WHO HAVE LIVED FOR A WHILE WITH AIDS, or with any other life-threatening illness, will tell you what it does to their hearing. They put it in different ways, but what it comes down to is that the most ordinary conversation can cut like a knife. To begin with, the present tense has a whole new pitch. When you don't know how long you have, the simple words "I am" are enough to remind you of the unbearable lightness of being. With the past tense the problem is that you catch yourself saying, "I was ... " and feel the tip of the wing of the angel of death. But the trickiest form of speech by far is the future. One of the first things lost to real illness isn't alertness or vigor. It's the simple pleasure of saying, in full confidence, "I will be."

When he tested positive for the AIDS virus, in 1984, Caleb Schwartz was 28. What that means is that for most of his adult life he has expected to die prematurely. A while ago, when he was looking for a new apartment in Manhattan, he would only consider elevator buildings. He was in good health at the time, but he had to keep in mind the day—in two years? in five?—when he would be too weak to climb stairs.

Year after year, Schwartz looked handsome and sturdy. All the while, his T cells ticked downward. In 1992, when they dipped below 500—the normal level is around 1,000—Schwartz's doctor put him on AZT, one of the few drugs then available that attack the virus directly. Both understood that it would fail after a while. Later Schwartz added 3TC, another antiviral. AIDS took a first cuff at him anyway. He began experiencing memory loss and having difficulty concentrating. Every few weeks, something that felt like the flu would send him to bed for days. In the summer of 1995 he took a disability leave from his New York law firm. A few months later he had his first AIDS-related hospitalization, for meningitis.

By that time his T cells had dropped to 201. This is the stage at which AIDS starts to behave like an abusive mate. It simmers alongside you in bed. It sits quietly at your table. And from time to time it goes berserk, pushes you into a corner and makes a fist. "I was starting," says Schwartz, "to accept the possibility of something catastrophic."

What he got was something else. In March, his doctor put him on a third drug, Crixivan, one of the new protease inhibitors. Up to this point, Schwartz's story had been like most in the epidemic, none of them very encouraging. But 1996 reinvented the genre and put at its center the AIDS

patient who bounces back on the three-drug cocktail. Over the past year—like a character plucked from a drama and dropped into what, exactly?—Schwartz moved from one story to the other. His T cells are back above 500. His viral load, meaning the presence of the HIV virus in his blood, has dropped to—the magic words—undetectable levels.

After years of coming to terms with the prospect of death, Schwartz is mulling over the prospect of life. For his own peace of mind, he's being very, very careful. The drugs may not work forever. Or the side effects may worsen. Sometimes HIV-positive people refer to themselves as carriers. But the virus is only one of the things they carry. Along with it comes a weight of isolation, fears for the future and deep rage, humiliation and grief. After all of that, naive hope is one indignity they are in no hurry to accept.

In the history of the epidemic, there has never been a moment as intricate as this one. AIDS once again, as in the first years after it appeared, presents a predicament so new that no one is sure how to talk about it. When we say protease inhibitors work, what do we mean? Whom do they work for, how well and for how long? The only thing we know with certainty is that the conventions of language and sentiment that fit an earlier moment of AIDS, meaning all the years when death was at the end of every struggle, are unsuited to this one. Something powerful is happening. The new prospects for effective treatment insist that despair is an outmoded psychological reflex. Yet among people who live with AIDS, optimism is a suspicious character. Too many bright hopes of the past didn't pan out.

To begin with, buying time isn't cheap. For his three-drug combination therapy, Schwartz pays $11,280 annually, plus about $4,000 in test fees and doctor's office visits. Schwartz has insurance to cover most of the expense. But only 20% of the 1 million Americans who carry the virus are so lucky. Taking the new drugs properly—three times a day, with no food for one hour before or two hours afterward—also requires discipline. Patients who neglect the regimen risk developing drug-resistant strains of the virus. The side effects can be murderous.

Above all, for many people the wonder drugs don't work any wonders. Estimates of how many patients don't improve or can't tolerate the side effects vary from 15% to about 33%. For them, the promising developments only threaten to deepen their isolation. They worry about being left behind, artifacts of an earlier stage of the epidemic. "I've taken them all, and failed them all," says Ron Wilmot, 46, a Vietnam vet whose weakened condition led him to sell his half of a San Francisco real estate firm.

"These new treatments are like hope with an asterisk," says R. Scott Hitt, chairman of the White House Council on AIDS. Yet the signs of something changing are everywhere. In California, Sherman Oaks Hospital has shut down its AIDS unit, which used to hold 40 or more patients. In Los Angeles the AIDS Healthcare Foundation closed one of its three hospices. "This is the most important year in the history of the AIDS epidemic," says the foundation's president, Michael Weinstein. "For the first time, we made more progress than the virus did."

There are worse problems than hope. For years, in any of the gay neighborhoods around the U.S., it was common to meet old friends turned stick figures, men carved to the bone by illness. Thirty-year-olds studied the writings of Elizabeth Kübler-Ross, the psychologist who identified the stages in which the dying accept their fate, and dryly marked their own progress, good schoolboys acing their last assignment.

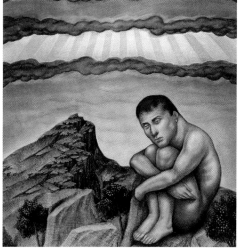

Now, however provisionally, the gloom is lifting. People are trying out the words "I will be," again. In the U.S., insurance companies and Social Security pay more than $1.5 billion in disability benefits each year to about 100,000 AIDS patients. But newly revived patients are now thinking about giving up disability and returning to work. First, there are major questions. Federal law bars discrimination against people with AIDS, but how many employers will hire someone with an expensive health problem? And if the benefits of protease inhibitors prove to be short-lived, how easy will it be for people with AIDS to resume disability?

People who work with the epidemic fear that upbeat news coverage is playing havoc with a decade of AIDS education. Doctors complain about patients who think that because their viral load is undetectable, the virus must be gone from their bodies. AIDS counselors talk about teens who think that science has discovered a morning-after pill to undo last night's unsafe doings. And everybody is concerned that a false message will go out that AIDS has been defeated. With that, they figure, will come a return to the '70s, the whole goatish and unbuckled funfest. The cycle of infection will go wild again.

Even before the appearance of protease inhibitors, there were signs that younger people were shrugging off the danger of AIDS. On average, half of new HIV infections in the U.S. occur in people under the age of 25. Doctors talk about a rising incidence of HIV-positive teenage girls, who get the virus from infected men. They worry about a "second wave" among younger gay men.

And for many of the poor—about half of AIDS patients qualify for Medicaid—protease inhibitors are somebody else's miracle. All 50 states have ADAPS, AIDS drug-assistance programs, which are partly funded by Washington. But in 28 states they won't cover protease inhibitors. The rest face a funding crisis as requests for the drugs flood in.

Even as some people struggle to get the drugs, others refuse them. With further breakthroughs reportedly coming, there are AIDS patients concerned that today's medications will make their bodies less responsive to better ones tomorrow. "There are 18 new treatments in the pipeline," says Teresa Nieves, 30, an AIDS patient in Brooklyn, who wouldn't take the three-drug cocktail her doctor prescribed. "What I fear is that using this concoction will disqualify me for more promising ones."

That's a risky decision, since researchers want patients to start protease inhibitors as soon as possible after being infected, before the immune system is too weakened to rebound. But they also acknowledge that the people who appear to be responding best to the new drugs are those who never used earlier ones.

Over the past few years, AIDS encouraged a lot of clean living. People started to take their health seriously. There were vows of chastity, some of them kept. The epidemic also helped forge a new sense of solidarity among gays. But many people found a way to go through life with one foot in the grave, one flooring the accelerator. They let their drinking get out of hand. They indulged big-ticket impulses.

Now, a return to life means a return to life's responsibilities. "A lot of people I know are facing troubles because they spent their credit-card money to the hilt, mortgaged their homes," says Dr. Jerome Goldstein, a San Francisco physician. "They have all these bills, and are wondering how they're going to pay them." Besides causing a small social revolution, protease inhibitors may also produce an upheaval in purely personal relations. AIDS opened a quiet split between positive and negative men, for instance, and the new drugs may add yet another fine fracture.

B
UT ALL THESE ARE THE PROBLEMS OF PEOPLE who have begun to imagine that they may have the time to work them out. For healthy people, the future is elastic; it stretches before them to whatever length their peace of mind requires. In 1996 a lot of people with AIDS began to find some flexibility in their own dealings with time. "I don't think about the future past a manageable point," insists Caleb Schwartz. "I stopped doing that the day I got the news I was positive." But ask him bluntly whether he expects to be alive a few years from now. The answer he gives may be the same one he would have offered before the new drugs came into the picture. But now you hear it differently. So does he. What he says is, "I will be." ∎

JOHN-JOHN, 1962
*Several sets of Jackie's simulated
pearls were auctioned off*

WHAT PRICE

An auction of Jackie Kennedy's possessions draws

CAMELOT?

throngs eager to pay any amount to touch celebrity

$211,500

*Sotheby's estimated value of the
simulated pearls: $500-$700*

WE DENIZENS OF THE LATE 20TH
century like to think we are the beneficiaries of humankind's
slow, lurching ascent from the fens of superstition toward the cool
empyrean of reason. After all, we can map the human genome
system and fling spacecraft past Jupiter. We are much too progres-
sive, thank you, for the magic charms and amulets
that so bedazzled our dim ancestors. We clasp at
this faith and hold on in spite of the myriad irra-
tionalities of daily life. But every so often some
public event gives our congratulatory self-image
a sharp blow to the chops.

> **When I
bought the tape
measure, the
first thing
I measured was
my sanity.**

The year's reminder of man-
kind's boundless capacity for irrational behavior
came in late April during a four-day mania on the
Upper East Side of Manhattan. The setting was
the U.S. showroom of the auctioneer Sotheby's,
the occasion the public sale of 5,914 personal
items belonging to the estate of Jacqueline Bouvier
Kennedy Onassis. And the outcome was not only

CAROLINE, 1961
In the White House nursery

a bewildering blend of conspicuous consumption but also a perverse tribute, crass in some eyes and innocently romantic in others, to the allure of nostalgia and of the woman who single-handedly, and in many ways involuntarily, redefined the culture of celebrity.

Everyone knew that Jackie's belongings would draw crowds. Sotheby's auctions of the effects of the Duchess of Windsor in 1987 and of Andy Warhol in 1988 had done so, and those people were not as famous and charismatic as Jackie. Her personal possessions figured to be irresistible to plenty of people, and Sotheby's was not disappointed. Its fat, glossy catalog of the lots up for auction sold more than 100,000 copies (at $90 hardback, $45 paper).

BUT THE HYPE FELL STUNNINGly short of what happened when the bidding finally began. Experienced auctiongoers understood that the estimated sales prices in Sotheby's catalog reflected an assessor's evaluation of fair market value, i.e., what an object would bring if it did not possess the added cachet of having belonged to someone famous. For things owned by Jackie, fair market value was just the starting point. The tension and electricity at the auction hummed around the question: How high would the markup go?

Once the bidding and the gavel pounding began, an answer quickly emerged: Very high, unbelievably high. On opening night, the best indication of the stratospheres that lay ahead came with the offering of a small stool with a torn, faded and stained satin cover. Sotheby's had previously estimated its market value at $100 to $150. After a furious competition between three bidders, two in the room and one on the phone, the homely little piece was sold for $33,350.

And so it went for the next three days of cascading inflation. Many of those who showed up to bid on the desiderata of celebrity were themselves celebrities. Film star Arnold Schwarzenegger, spouse of J.F.K.'s niece Maria Shriver, muscled up $772,500 for J.F.K.'s MacGregor Woods golf clubs, $134,500 for a Norman Rockwell painting of the President and $189,500 for a leather desk set. From a different latitude, singer Jimmy Buffett telephoned in a winning bid of $43,700 for a Jamie Wyeth

lithograph of the President on a sailboat. Manhattan interior designer Juan Molyneux bought Jackie's engraved sterling-silver Tiffany tape measure for $48,875. Sotheby's had ruled it would be worth $500 to $700. "When I bought the tape measure," says Molyneux, "the first thing I measured was my sanity."

And then there was the suddenly famous cigar humidor given to J.F.K. in 1961 by comedian Milton Berle. Marvin Shanken, publisher of the magazine *Cigar Aficionado*, set his sights on it because he had worked as a

$48,875
Sotheby's estimated value: $500-$700

$25,300
Sotheby's estimated value: $50-$100

$85,000
Sotheby's estimated value: $2,000-$3,000

THE BEGINNING, 1953
*John F. Kennedy and his bride at
their picture-book wedding in Newport, R.I.*

$63,000 to buy J.F.K.'s putter, a Robot K-44, and gave it to his business partner, Christopher Heymeyer, who instantly became a minor celebrity at the Board of Trade, where the two work. By late Friday afternoon, with the final session winding down and the supply of Jackie and Camelot memorabilia drying up, the feeding frenzy at Sotheby's reached a climax. Three modest cushions, assessed at $50 to $100, were snapped up for $25,300. When it was all over, the total proceeds from the auction, which the upper ranges of Sotheby's estimates had placed at about $4 million, came to $34.5 million.

Even before the auction's astronomical proceeds had materialized, there were some nasty returns for the principal beneficiaries, Jackie's children Caroline Kennedy Schlossberg and John Jr. As the buying orgy intensified, a Kennedy-family intimate who would comment only off the record called the auction "the pits."

But other insiders assert that the auction, while its public garishness might have mortified Jackie, was her idea. Pierre Salinger, J.F.K.'s press secretary, confirms that Jackie discussed the idea of an auction with her children.

He adds that the children rigorously culled their mother's mountains of things to select important items for the John F. Kennedy Library in Boston (the library will also receive most of the $2.5 million from the catalog sales). In April 1995, Caroline and John donated a huge trove of items to the library, including Jackie's wedding dress, 38,000 pages of documents, 4,500 photographs and 200 works of art.

But what can explain the behavior of those who spent such outlandish sums to relieve Jackie's children of parcels of their property? Class and taste are not, by definition, available for purchase. The Jackie auction represents an apotheosis of a new sort of cultural aspiration—a personal connection to celebrity at, quite literally, any cost. A common refrain expressed among those at the auction was the desire "to buy a piece of history." This impulse was vain in two meanings of the word, even if, also understandably, foolishly human. Ennobling myths and fairy tales are not passed on through the knickknacks of heroes and heroines. ∎

$547,500
*Sotheby's estimated value:
$2,000-$2,500*

$772,500
*Sotheby's estimated value:
$700-$900*

$85,000
*Sotheby's estimated value:
$300-$400*

$415,000
*Sotheby's estimated value:
$6,000-8,000*

high school volunteer during Kennedy's 1960 campaign for the presidency and, well, because he's the publisher of *Cigar Aficionado*. He expected to "pay a lot," he says, "but to me a lot was under $100,000." He wound up shelling out $574,500. Berle himself joined in the bidding for the humidor, which cost him $800 in 1961, but dropped out at $180,000.

Auction fever crossed time zones faster than Air Force One. In Chicago, Ralph Goldenberg, whose wife Helyn is a senior vice president of Sotheby's, spent

WHERE DEATH

TOO MANY ON THE MOUNTAIN?
Scott Fischer's group heads up
Everest. An excess of climbers
created delays that proved fatal.

WEARS WHITE

A routine ascent turns into a desperate ordeal as an icy blizzard rakes Mount Everest and claims eight lives in the ultracold "Death Zone"

T O MOST OF THE WORLD, THE great mountain is known as Mount Everest, named for a 19th century official in British India. But the Tibetans who live beneath its mighty shadow call it Chomolungma, or Mother Goddess of the World. They worship it as a giver of life through the rivers that flow from its glaciated flanks. And they fear it as a taker of life, the killer of scores of mountaineers, both native Sherpas and foreigners, who have presumed to ascend the Mother Goddess and stand at the top of the world.

Seaborn Beck Weathers was one foreigner who believed that his chances of success were good. He knew Mount Everest would be a tough climb, but he never doubted his success. Weathers, 50, a wealthy pathologist from Dallas, is not a professional mountaineer, but he was in the best shape of his life. He had clothing designed to protect him to 80°F below zero. Moreover, he had paid $60,000 for the services of Rob Hall, a renowned New Zealand climber and guide who in the previous four years had helped 39 people like Weathers to the top of the world. "Rob felt we all had a very good chance of reaching the summit," Weathers would say later. "We had prepared correctly and were climbing at the right time. We knew what we were doing."

Three days after Hall's optimistic assessment, Weathers, his face burned black and his arms nearly useless, would be a survivor of one of the worst mountain-climbing disasters of the century. On the night of May 10, while the party struggled through the summit's fearsome "Death Zone"—the area above 25,000 ft. where the air

Everest

CHINA
Tibet

NEPAL

Camp 4
26,200 ft.

Lhotse
27,887 ft.

Nuptse

Camp 3
23,622 ft.

Camp 2
20,977 ft.

Camp 1
20,013 ft.

On Friday, May 10, a dozen separate groups set out from Camp 4 to reach the crown.

Everest's higher reaches are the bodies of dead climbers. Says Jeff Blumenfeld, editor and publisher of *Expedition News:* "You can be hooked up to a Website, you can call anyone on a sat phone—and the mountain can still win."

Most Everest expeditions take place in early May, when the weather is best. Friday the 10th was temperate and clear, a day to rival the one in 1993 on which 40 people reached the top. Now a dozen groups, swarming like ants on a piece of cake, set out from Camp 4, the launch pad at 26,200 ft. for the grueling 12-hour hike up the mountain's final 2,900 ft. Fischer's and Hall's parties set out around midnight and eventually merged, pushing through waist-high snow up Everest's last 250 ft. Despite delays because of the number of people crowding through narrow passes, the mood was good. The daughter of Washington State postalworker Douglas Hansen had earlier faxed in her support: "Come on, Dad, do it." By 2:30 p.m., Hansen and more than 20 others had reached the peak.

But the delays—and excessive lingering at the summit by some climbers—proved fatal. As Jonathan Krakauer, a journalist covering the climb for *Outside* magazine, stood at the top of the world, he noticed something ominous: clouds were approaching from the valley below. Within

lacks enough oxygen to support life for long periods, a fierce storm swept into the zone, bringing snow, bitter cold and hurricane-force winds. Within 24 hours, eight of the more than 30 climbers on the peak were dead, among them Hall and another highly respected mountaineer, Scott Fischer of Seattle, who was also conducting a commercial tour.

By May 1996, Everest had become the accessible behemoth—or so it seemed. Never as murderously tricky to climb as K2, the world's second highest peak, it nonetheless constituted a daunting challenge because of the brute facts of its extreme altitude, occasional storms and inaccessibility. As clothing and equipment manufacturers mitigated the first problem, and a sprawling base camp sprang up at 17,500 ft. to provide warmth and food for

of cake, set out from Camp 4, the launch pad at 26,200 ft. for the grueling 12-hour hike up the mountain's final 2,900 ft. Fischer's and Hall's parties set out around midnight and eventually merged, pushing through waist-high snow up Everest's last 250 ft. Despite delays because of the number of people crowding through narrow passes, the mood was good. The daughter of Washington State postalworker Douglas Hansen had earlier faxed in her support: "Come on, Dad, do it." By 2:30 p.m., Hansen and more than 20 others had reached the peak.

But the delays—and excessive lingering at the summit by some climbers—proved fatal. As Jonathan Krakauer, a journalist covering the climb for *Outside* magazine, stood at the top of the world, he noticed something ominous: clouds were approaching from the valley below. Within

❝The most enduring mementos on Everest are the

dozens of would-be peak beaters, the issue for élite climber-guides was no longer whether they could reach Everest's pinnacle but rather how many paying customers they could take with them. It was not exactly a risk-free ticket to Disneyland, but for less than $100,000 a wealthy and dedicated amateur could buy a decent chance at summiting. Money could buy altitude.

Communications breakthroughs increased the impression that Everest was accessible to nearly anyone. Climbers can call home from the summit using satellite phones. They can send E-mail. During the two months before the final assault on the peak, New York socialite-alpinist Sandy Hill Pittman had been describing her ascent with Fischer's group on the Internet and throwing in remarks about books and recipes. One of her cyber-correspondents inquired as to whether there were "any permanent markers at the summit. Flags or plaques or anything like that? A gift shop, perhaps?" Pittman did not tell her new friend that the most enduring mementos on

two hours they had arrived and metastasized into a monster: shrieking winds blew sheets of snow horizontally at 65 knots. A whiteout dropped visibility to zero, and the wind chill plunged to −140°F. "It was chaos," said Krakauer. "The storm was like a hurricane, only it had a triple-digit wind chill. You don't have your oxygen on, you're out of breath, you can't think." In one horrifying vignette after another, the mountain began picking off its conquerors.

The first to die may have been Yasuko Namba, 47, one of Hall's Japanese clients; her frozen body was discovered the next morning, 1,200 ft. above the South Col, the valley between Everest and its neighbor Lhotse that is the most popular route up to the summit. Another guide, Andrew Harris, came within yards of Camp 4 before apparently walking right off the mountain face. His body was not found. Scott Fischer, a vastly experienced climber known as "Mr. Rescue," lagged behind his clients, perhaps to help stragglers. Searchers found him two days later high above the South Col. In the same area they found Taiwanese

climber Makalu Gau, half buried in the snow and mumbling. Gau could be awakened, but Fischer was comatose; and so, by the stark rules of mountain triage, the overtaxed rescuers saved whom they could.

Leader Rob Hall, meanwhile, had stayed on the ridge to tend Hansen, who had expended all his energy on the summit. Exposed and out of oxygen, Hansen died during the night. Hall hung on: at 4:35 the next morning, his startled friends in camp heard his voice on the two-way radio. Rescuers tried twice but failed to reach him: his only hope was to make his own way to the South Col. "We tried to get him to move," mountaineer Ed Viesturs told *Outside* Online. "And we thought he was moving down the ridge. But after three hours, he mentioned, almost casually, 'You know, I haven't even packed up yet.'" Instead, Hall asked to be patched through to his wife, Dr. Jan Arnold, back in New Zealand and pregnant with their first child. Arnold had reached the summit with her husband in 1993. Now they talked for several hours. She later said that his final words were, "Hey, look, don't worry about me." Then he turned off his radio.

On the northern approach to the peak—a more difficult climb than the popular route up the South Col—three members of an Indian team became stranded on their way down from the top. Their frantic comrades thought they had persuaded a late departing Japanese group to forgo its summit attempt and stage a rescue for the trio. But when next heard from, the Japanese were announcing a successful climb to the top. The appalled Indians believe that the Japanese found all three men and left at least two to die in their haste to reach the top. The Japanese insisted they found the Indians, who were beyond help, on their way down from the summit. Responded an Indian: "They [the Japanese] will have to live with their consciences."

There were miracles amid the death and chaos. Scott

HIGHER CALLING
Sandy Hill Pittman, top left, survived, but legendary guide Scott Fischer, top right, died in a rescue attempt. Above, Beck Weathers' hand is treated for frostbite; it was later amputated. At right, Fischer crosses a crevasse.

bodies of dead climbers.❞

Fischer's climbers, now led by guide Neal Beidleman, survived because Beidleman glimpsed the Big Dipper during a storm lull and was able to navigate them back into camp. Makalu Gau's Sherpa managed to wake him and get him down to the high camp, where Gau could receive fluids intravenously.

But the most remarkable revival was that of Beck Weathers, the Dallas doctor. At 9 a.m. on Saturday, fellow climbers left behind his apparently lifeless body; that morning the news was relayed to his horrified wife in Texas. Later that day, she got another phone call. People in the high camp had been astonished to see a zombie-like figure staggering down the slope toward them, face blackened from the sun, arms held rigidly outward, eyes closed to slits. Weathers had refused to die.

Neither Gau nor Weathers, both in critical condition, would have survived were it not for Lieut. Colonel Madan Khatri Chhetri, a Nepalese helicopter pilot. Choppers seldom venture above 20,000 ft.: at a certain height, the thin air reduces their lift. Yet Madan flew up to a giant cross the climbers had painted on the Everest ice with red Kool-Aid. There he hovered, runners just touching the snow's treacherous surface, as Gau was loaded onboard. Madan flew Gau down to the base camp, the staging area for most expeditions, located at 17,500 ft., then repeated the process with Weathers. They were the second highest helicopter rescues in history.

Mount Everest—Chomolungma—no longer seems so accessible. Krakauer, one of the two survivors in Hall's summiting party, believes that commercial expeditions "need to be reconsidered" because the customers put the guides' lives in additional danger and also because when treacherous conditions arise, "there is nothing any guide can do for any client." To which Sir Edmund Hillary, now retired in New Zealand, added, "I have a feeling that people have been getting just a little bit too casual with Mount Everest. This incident will bring them to regard it rather more seriously." ■

Do Gay Rights Stop at the Altar?

A ruling in Hawaii turns same-sex marriage into a new battleground between gays and conservative critics

IT IS BETTER TO MARRY THAN TO BURN.
— *Paul, I Corinthians 7: 9*

THE FUNNY THING IS, ON THE ISSUE OF SAME-SEX marriage, both sides agree with Paul. In fact, advocates of same-sex marriage and their opponents concur that it is better to marry than almost anything else. They both embrace the idea that marriage is the bedrock of a stable society, and that it is the ideal method for civilizing wayward and wanton males, something every society must do. In short, hooray for 'til-death-us-do-part. The only problem is that both sides disagree vehemently on who should be allowed to take that vow.

Same-sex marriage became a hot social and political issue in 1996 because of a 1993 Hawaiian supreme court ruling that denying marriage licenses to gay couples may violate the equal-protection clause in the state constitution. Sending the case back to the trial court, the supreme court directed the government to show that it has a "compelling" state interest in maintaining the ban—a test it is unlikely to meet. Although the case remained on appeal in Honolulu, Hawaii was expected to rule that such marriages are permissible. Christian conservatives, in particular, worried that if gay marriages were allowed in Hawaii, the Full Faith and Credit clause in Article IV of the U.S. Constitution would require every other state to recognize the legitimacy of such unions.

In a campaign year, the Hawaiian case stirred fury in statehouses across the country. Thirty-eight states considered action against same-sex marriage, with 18 states enacting such bans and 20 refusing to do so. In Washington, Bob Dole co-sponsored the Defense of Marriage Act to deny federal recognition to same-sex marriages. When Congress passed it in September, President Clinton said "I do" and signed it, presumably showing that he was not beholden to the homosexual community. He chose to make the point just after the U.S. Supreme Court had struck down a Colorado law nullifying civil rights protection for homosexuals, a significant victory for gay rights.

Whatever electoral points were scored, same-sex marriage is less a political issue than a moral, philosophical and legal one. The debate on precisely those grounds has engaged prominent thinkers on both sides of the argument.

NEVER MARRY BUT
FOR LOVE.
— *William Penn*

One of the most persuasive advocates of same-sex marriage is Andrew Sullivan, the former editor of the *New Republic* who in 1996 announced his resignation. Sullivan's writings suggest two syllogisms: Marriage is for people who love; homosexuals love; ergo marriage is for them. He and others push the argument further by claiming that denying homosexuals access to this fundamental societal institution is a denial of their basic civil and human rights.

Advocates also argue that legalizing gay unions is a way of getting the spousal benefits—like health insurance and pension-plan inheritance rights—that long-term domestic partners receive. One of the fundamental contentions of Sullivan and other same-sex advocates is that marriage—for homosexuals as well as heterosexuals—"domesticates" young men. The eminent social scientist James Q. Wilson asserts that nothing is better than marriage for civilizing men, a necessary task in every society.

IF A MAN ALSO LIE WITH MANKIND, AS
HE LIETH WITH A WOMAN, BOTH OF THEM
HAVE COMMITTED AN ABOMINATION.
— *Leviticus 20: 13*

The primary argument against same-sex marriage is really a religious animus against homosexuality. In short, homosexuality is a grave sin in the eyes of God and should

FIRST COMES LOVE: Then comes marriage, say many gay couples. Should their partnerships be legally recognized?

teachings in all three of America's dominant religious traditions: Judaism, Christianity and Islam.

THE FIRST BOND OF SOCIETY IS MARRIAGE.
—Cicero, De Officiis

Cicero's statement reflects what is known as the natural-law argument against same-sex unions: marriage evolved in society over thousands of years as a childbearing union between a man and a woman, and there is a profound wisdom in the tradition that should not be lightly discarded. Bennett argues that stretching the definition of marriage would jeopardize an already shaky institution. The Christian right suggests that gay activists are attempting to poison the youth of America with same-sex propaganda. Christian conservatives fear that children are being exposed to gay alternatives too early in life, when they are not old enough to make a mature judgment about their own inclinations.

THE NATURAL AND INHERENT RIGHT OF MARRIAGE ... IS TO INCREASE AND MULTIPLY.
—Pope Leo XIII

Sullivan answers those who argue that marriage is for procreation by saying that same-sex marriage is no different from sterile or elderly heterosexuals' marrying. Why should they have the right to marry and not homosexuals? But social scientist Wilson believes the raising of children remains the central role of marriage because "we have found nothing else that works as well." Besides, both Bennett and Wilson say, Sullivan undermines his own argument that the absence of children should not be an impediment to gay marriages when he says that it will give gay couples "greater freedom" to enjoy "extramarital outlets." Marriage, Bennett says, is not an open construct; "its essential idea is fidelity."

THE WEDLOCK OF MINDS WILL BE GREATER THAN THAT OF BODIES.
—Erasmus

Despite the glaring differences between the two positions, there are signs of consensus and compromise. Both sides are united in the desire to strengthen the foundations of civil society. But is there a way to accomplish this in a manner that satisfies all concerned, an evolutionary middle ground? Some cities, including New York, offer bereavement leave and health insurance to the domestic same-sex partners of city employees.

Stuart Kelman, a California rabbi, has proposed an alternative to traditional marriage: a ceremonial "covenant of love" for gay couples wishing to sanctify lifelong monogamous relationships. Ancient Roman law recognized three categories of marriage—a legally sanctioned union, marriage by purchase and marriage by mutual consent. Perhaps states might recognize different types of unions for both same-sex and heterosexual partnerships. Such a compromise would meet the standards, if not of the Bible, at least of Shakespeare, who said: "Let me not to the marriage of true minds admit impediments." ∎

not be condoned or comforted by the mystical union of marriage, which is a covenant with God. Such opponents of same-sex marriage as virtuecrat William J. Bennett point to the fact that disapproval of homosexual behavior is one of the most deeply rooted and consistent moral

WIGAND: Tweet!

FOR THE TOBACCO INDUSTRY, THE WHITE HOUSE ROSE GARDEN WAS EXACTLY the wrong place for President Bill Clinton's September announcement of new federal restrictions on the sale and advertising of cigarettes. In 1996 absolutely nothing was coming up roses for Big Tobacco. All year it was battered by mounting lawsuits, unfavorable publicity, defectors among its former executives, incriminating scientific research and seesawing stock prices. And the new rules, part of a bid to stop smoking among teenagers, established a precedent the industry has feared for decades. Clinton signed an Executive Order that subjected tobacco to regulation by the Food and Drug Administration. As a twist of the knife, the FDA claimed its new authority over cigarettes by defining them as the delivery system for an addictive drug, nicotine. Alphabetically, that would put nicotine after morphine and just before opium. Not exactly wholesome company.

"Joe Camel and the Marlboro Man will be out of our children's reach forever," said the President—wistfully. The changes are likely to be tied up in the courts for years. If they ever do take effect, cigarette sales would require a photo ID offering proof of age. In magazines read by a significant number of teens, tobacco ads under the new rules would be limited to a black-and-white, all-text format—no photographs, no cartoon camels with phallic snouts. The same rules would also apply to billboards, which would be banned entirely within 1,000 ft. of schools or playgrounds. Sponsorship at sporting events would be forbidden, as would tobacco-brand-name logos on products such as hats, T shirts and gym bags.

Even before Clinton's Rose Garden initiative, tobacco was in a droop. Five grand juries were looking into possible perjury and malfeasance by industry executives. At the same time, a novel legal strategy, which would hold the tobacco industry responsible to taxpayers rather than individual smokers, was gaining momentum around the country. "The current round of attacks on the tobacco industry is better thought out, better funded and better organized than at any time in history,"

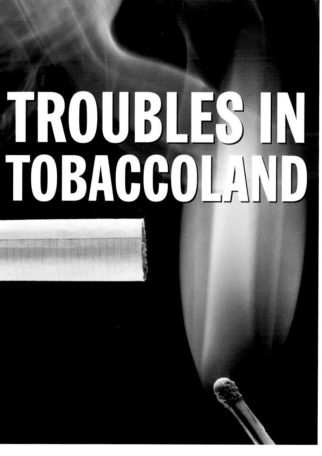

TROUBLES IN TOBACCOLAND

said Matthew Myers, a lawyer who litigates tobacco cases on behalf of the Coalition on Smoking OR Health. "And it comes at a time when the tobacco industry is more vulnerable than ever, given the disclosures from inside the industry."

Myers was referring to the testimony of former employees of tobacco companies who had come forward with highly damaging information about the inner workings of the firms. Jeffrey Wigand, formerly with Brown & Williamson, was the highest-ranking tobacco executive ever to testify against the industry. Among Wigand's allegations: that B&W manipulated nicotine levels in cigarettes, knowingly employed a carcinogenic additive to make pipe tobacco taste better, and covered up research into "safer" cigarettes that were not as addictive and thus would not create a customer forever.

A second group of whistleblowers was led by Ian Uydess, an associate senior scientist at Philip Morris for 11 years. In affidavits released by the Food and Drug Administration, Uydess and two other former Philip Morris employees directly contradicted the testimony of former Philip Morris CEO William Campbell before Representative Henry Waxman's 1994 congressional subcommittee investigating tobacco. At those hearings Campbell, along with six other tobacco CEOs, swore that he did not believe nicotine was addictive, and that Philip Morris did nothing to manipulate or increase nicotine levels in its products.

Campbell told the Waxman subcommittee that "nicotine levels in tobacco are measured at only two points in

our manufacturing process: prior to the tobaccos' being blended, and then 18 months later when those leaves have been manufactured into finished cigarettes." But, according to Uydess, "Nicotine levels were routinely targeted and adjusted by Philip Morris."

Jerome Rivers, who was a shift manager at the plant where the company made reconstituted tobacco, stated that the nicotine level in the product was measured "approximately once per hour." Why? Because, said Uydess, management was acutely aware of nicotine's addictive powers, euphemistically termed "impact." For instance, Uydess said, the company test-marketed a low-nicotine cigarette but gave it up when it did not sell and focus groups reported that it seemed to be "missing something." Philip Morris, explained Uydess, "clearly understood they would have trouble sustaining the sales of a good-tasting product that was too low in nicotine."

The whistleblowers' allegations exacerbated the industry's legal troubles. In March, Liggett, the smallest of the nation's major cigarette makers, broke ranks with other companies by agreeing to settle a class action suit filed in Louisiana on behalf of all smokers, as well as five state Medicaid suits against tobaccomakers. In real dollars, the terms of the agreement had little bite: Liggett could wind up paying less than $2 million a year over the next 25 years toward antismoking programs. But the capitulation was the first crack in the industry's once united wall of resistance.

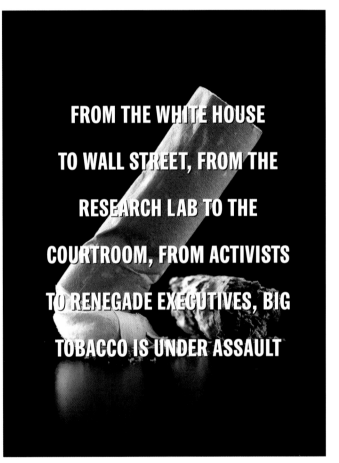

FROM THE WHITE HOUSE TO WALL STREET, FROM THE RESEARCH LAB TO THE COURTROOM, FROM ACTIVISTS TO RENEGADE EXECUTIVES, BIG TOBACCO IS UNDER ASSAULT

Liggett was prescient: after years in which the industry beat back lawsuits from health-impaired smokers, it lost a worrisome one in August. Following the disclosure of the whistleblowers' allegations, a Florida jury awarded $750,000 to a longtime smoker who had developed lung cancer. Though an Indianapolis, Indiana, jury later handed the tobacco industry a break by finding it not guilty in a similar case, there was much more litigation to come. More than 200 individual lawsuits nationwide await trial, plus 14 others by states that are suing tobacco companies to retrieve tens of billions of dollars in Medicaid costs for smoking-related illnesses.

Tobacco's legal troubles soon translated into setbacks on Wall Street: August was a meltdown for industry stocks. Philip Morris plunged from $104.66 a share to $88, and RJR Nabisco from $30.75 to $25.50. Loews Corp., parent of Lorillard Tobacco, slipped from $80.66 to $74.75. But by the end of the year overall profits and sales in the industry were up, international sales were strong, and Wall Street was having a change of heart. Tobacco stock prices rebounded—at least for the short term.

Channeling their profits into political influence, tobacco firms donated heavily to the Republican Party, an investment that paid dividends in the G.O.P.-controlled Congress, with its hostility toward government regulation in general and the FDA in particular. Thanks to a bill approved in March, Congress had 60 "legislative days" to overturn all new agency regulations. However, the industry's support for G.O.P. presidential candidate Bob Dole was a failure on two counts: Dole lost the election, and his June claim on the campaign trail that cigarettes are not addictive was greeted with derision by the public.

Short weeks after Dole's remarks, a team of Italian scientists released further proof that nicotine is addictive. In tests on laboratory rats, they found that a small dose of nicotine dramatically increased the amount of a powerful brain chemical called dopamine in an emotional center of the brain. A virtually identical pattern of biochemical activity , they found, accompanies injections of cocaine, amphetamines and morphine. The brain, in short, appears to make no distinction between addictive drugs and what smokers like to think of as just a bad habit.

As the year ended, the industry was planning to fight the new federal advertising rules in court as an unconstitutional restriction on free speech. "The evidence is clear," said Brennan Dawson, spokesman for the Tobacco Institute, "that the FDA's rules do not address the reasons youngsters smoke, will not work to reduce youth access to tobacco, and are an illegal expansion of this federal agency's authority." Or, as they used to say in the old cigarette commercials: We'd rather fight than switch. ∎

Mad About Martha

The Empress of Elegance is in the house—and she's on a mission!

MARTHA STEWART'S FACE IS EVERYWHERE BUT ON A WANTED POSTER: IN HER magazine; on four videos and a dozen books; on TV (twice a day); unofficially on the Internet; at K mart; and in her catalog (Martha by Mail). In an interview with TIME, conducted as she shuttled among her farm in Westport, Connecticut, her two Hamptons beach houses on New York's Long Island and her Manhattan office, she said her aim is nothing less than to take over Christmas. "It is our intention to own areas in communication. I don't mean to sound egomaniacal, but Perry Como used to own Christmas on TV. By own, I mean monopolize and influence."

Stewart had already claimed a chunk of Christmas in 1995 with her *Home for the Holidays* TV special featuring Hillary Clinton. Many people ceded Easter to her after 1994, when she counseled readers to celebrate by taking a fresh ham, roasting it for five hours and serving it garnished with organically grown grass that had been cut early that morning with the dew still on it. Never mind that most of her magazine's 5 million readers still buy the honey-baked version at Boston Market or, horrors!, take it right out of a can. Even the subscribers who don't work anyone without a staff, or who sleeps more than Martha's four hours a night, that there is no obligation to actually do it. Being in Martha's thrall is like buying a treadmill and instantly feeling fit even though it serves mainly as a coat rack. Acquiring the Martha oeuvre makes you think you will conduct a beautiful domestic symphony one of these days—when the kids grow up, when you lose your day job and perhaps the lunkhead you've married who likes meat loaf loaded with catsup. The magazine and television show bearing her name and developed with Time Inc. (she and the company are talking about restructuring the relationship to bring more of the control—and profits—Martha's way) have the rich glow of a Merchant-Ivory movie set. Actual people, as opposed to imported guests, would only muss the sheen of perfection.

MARTHA GUTS! An outmoded kitchen bites the dust

MARTHA GARDENS! The flowers know who's boss

may think twice before taking on her October 1994 project: "It occurred to us at MARTHA STEWART LIVING that we had never really focused on the pleasures of raising backyard livestock."

If Martha Stewart relied on people's actually doing what she suggests, as opposed to just watching her do it, she would be very poor indeed, instead of a multimillion-aire empress of elegance. The real secret to Martha is that the perfection she is pursuing is so out of reach of

So why is Martha, 55, so much more influential than, say Alice Waters, the Chez Panisse chef in California who transformed restaurant cooking? It's because Martha-land is a one-stop shop for everything from bed to kitchen to garden, where one thing stylishly builds on another. She pulls all this off with total earnestness (except when she is paid to be ironic by American Express, lining her swimming pool with a mosaic of cut-up credit cards). Otherwise, she stays in character: that of

a demanding schoolmistress who will be coming around to test for trace elements of bottled dressing in your *salade niçoise*. When Bryant Gumbel tries to poke a bit of fun at her during her segments on the *Today* show, she blithely ignores him. If she doesn't take cake decorating seriously, who will?

Dominique Browning, editor in chief of the relaunched "shelter magazine" *House & Garden*, which debuted in the fall, says Martha's dominance derives from the fact that "she's bossy, she knows what's good for us." What's more, Martha knows that good bossiness is good business. Martha Stewart Living is one of the great magazine success stories of the decade: circulation started at 250,000 in 1990 and has increased sixfold in six years. Her friend and neighbor in tony East Hampton, real-estate developer and media czar Mortimer Zuckerman, told the *Wall Street Journal:* "I would love to invest in her. She has a dazzling future going forward. She has no competitor." It has come to pass that in 1996 the universal zinger for a household shortfall is, "That's not how Martha would do it."

Which is another element of her success: rather than bring the subject matter down to the audience, the onetime Connecticut caterer is bringing the audience up to the subject matter, making it worthy of the effort it requires. Sure, it's easier for us ordinary mortals to identify with Gloria Steinem, who admits she once lived in an apartment for four years before

MARTHA COOKS! Better than you

realizing the oven didn't work. By making the impossible purchasable— at least in magazine and catalog form— Stewart is now simply Martha: cooking, sewing, gilding, planting, wallpapering and painting her way into every corner of your house. And as for Christmas? Well, you'd better watch out: Martha's making a list, and she's checking it twice. ∎

N THE BEGINNING, THERE WAS THE BOOK OF GENESIS. AND IT WAS GOOD. ONLY MUC later did different people begin to think of it in different ways. Steve Fintel, fc instance. It is 8:30 on a Sunday morning in Metairie, Louisiana, and Fintel, 49-year-old Eucharistic minister at St. Benilde Catholic Church, is playing a 198 hit song by Bette Midler, *Wind Beneath My Wings*, to his Sunday school class—thre

11-year-old boys and one girl. "Did I ever tell you you're my hero?" Midler sings. Fintel directs his four charges to chapter 12 of *Genesis*, in which God tells Abraham, follow me and I will bless you and "make of you a great nation." Says Fintel: "To me, Abraham is the person, and God is the wind." It is a lovely image and, as Fintel teaches it, *Genesis* seems a lovely book. Since he has followed God's instruction, Fintel explains, "Abraham is a hero" too.

Conservative rabbi Burton Visotzky used to share that simple, exalted view of Abraham and his immediate descendants. "I had always thought of these guys as saints," he says. Not many people in the country are as familiar with the workings of the Bible's first book as Visotzky, an expert in Midrash, the authoritative early rabbinical parsings of Scripture, or Torah. Yet in the late 1980s an impending divorce led to what he describes as "a bit of a religious crisis." Suddenly, when he read the Torah aloud in temple, the patriarchs of *Genesis* seemed all too familiar. Abraham and his wife Sarah bickering. Abraham appearing to endanger his marriage to get ahead in the world. Abraham and Sarah acting appallingly to their children. "The blinders fell off," he says. "This dysfunctional family was my family in every sense of the word. But why was it in Torah? I was holding onto my chair white-knuckled so I wouldn't run out of the room."

Both responses to the Bible's first book have their own validity. Both—in more sophisticated form—were on display in the autumn of 1996, when the Public Broadcasting System (PBS) launched the most ambitious Bible-study class ever to air on American television: a two-month series called *Genesis: A Living Conversation*, with Bill Moyers as host. Each of its 10 episodes featured a diverse panel grappling with the majestic, infuriating work, engaging both the stupendous acts of faith that inspired Fintel and the moral zig-zags that bedeviled Rabbi Visotzky. At the same time, a batch of new books, many written by *Living Conversation* panelists, amounted to a modest but unmistakable *Genesis* revival in American culture.

Could a text so old and so revered be subject to profitable re-examination? Did a work so central to Western culture need a spotlight? *Genesis* is widely regarded as

LET THERE

A TV series sparks a spirited new debate

humanity's first, revolutionary statement of the notion that there is but one God, and no day passes when we do not touch upon its stories. Glancingly, as when we note the bitten-apple logo on our computer. Or deeply, as when we heed the words of Jesus, Luther or Freud, all of whom took up the great truths and agonizing questions set out by Hebrew scribes, academics say, sometime between the 10th and 4th centuries before the advent of Christianity. Nobel laureate Isaac Bashevis

Singer once remarked to author David Rosenberg, "I am still learning the art of writing from the book of *Genesis*." The words could have been uttered by Shakespeare, Dostoyevsky or Mario Puzo. In the Mideast, the book of *Genesis* remains a matter of life and death: dozens died in Israel in September 1996 over boundaries first described in its pages centuries ago.

BE GENESIS

over the message of the Bible's first book

Even though Adam and Eve and Noah and the Ark constitute some of the earliest building blocks of a child's religious training, however, it is remarkable how thin most people's *Genesis* knowledge is. (A quick test: Was the mark of Cain good or bad? On the simplest level, at least, it was good: God laid it on him to protect him during his exile.) True, Bible literacy as a whole is woefully low in America. In this instance, however, it may be because the Sunday-school version of *Genesis* is a lot easi-

er to handle than the real thing. And for those who still understand the book as a series of heroic tableaux, a close encounter with the original text, its spiky narrative and decidedly imperfect heroes may prove an alarming yet exhilarating experience.

The first book of the Old Testament and of Jewish Scripture falls into two parts: primeval history (chapters 1-11); and patriarchal tales (12-50). The first part covers the Creation, Adam and Eve, Cain and Abel, the Flood and the Tower of Babel and establishes the basic premise of a God who intervenes in the history of his most problematic creation, the human race. The last three-quarters of *Genesis*, by contrast, is the wild and woolly saga of one family more widely perceived as historical. Exhorting Abraham to leave his father's house and country, God offers him incalculable descendants and property. Abraham accepts, and the rest of *Genesis* describes his triumphs and travails and those of his son Isaac, grandson Jacob and great grandson Joseph, as they and their extended families are tested by hostile neighbors, famines, recurrent infertility and sometimes by the Deity himself. Divine intent and human ambition blur as each generation, often through painful winnowing, produces a champion to advance Israel's destiny. The book ends with Abraham's tiny clan having blossomed into the foundations of the 12 Hebrew tribes and a brace of other nations; and with God's assurance that the people of the Covenant will survive and, with them, the Covenant itself.

Much of the popular controversy around *Genesis* has focused on the issue of whether the Creation should be understood literally. That debate has tended to obscure a further set of issues hinging on the character of both God and the patriarchs. More so than Jesus in the New Testament or even Jehovah in much of the rest of the Old, the *Genesis* God works in ways that many analysts, especially those willing to test the boundaries of conventional faith, find mysterious in the most profound and troubling sense.

Jack Miles, author of the arresting *God: A Biography*, has written, "Much that the Bible says about him is rarely preached from the pulpit because, examined too closely, it becomes a scandal." By way of proof Miles likes to cite the Flood in *Genesis* 8, wherein the Deity obliterates most of the creation he had termed "very good" only pages earlier, because of a trespass on rules that skeptics contend he has not yet stated. In chapter 22, in a passage that stands with the Book of Job as Scripture's most wrenching enigma, God demands that Abraham sacrifice his favorite son and long-awaited heir, relenting only as the knife is poised to strike.

Then there is the behavior of the patriarchs. Writes one analyst, with some understatement: "There is often a

disparity between these stories and the subsequent Judeo-Christian ethic that has been derived from them throughout the centuries." *Genesis* chapter 12, as Visotzky was disagreeably reminded, seems to find Abraham allowing his wife to be taken into Pharaoh's harem both to ensure the couple safe passage through Egypt and "so that all may go well with me." Sarah, barren, offers her slave, Hagar, to Abraham as a kind of surrogate mother, but when Hagar gets pregnant Sarah becomes jealous and beats her (16). Lot sleeps with his daughters (19). Jacob embezzles from his brother (27). Jacob's sons, angry at the rape of their sister, kill every man in a neighboring town (34). Much of this goes unpunished by God and, indeed, seems to fulfill his larger purposes.

The unruly story lines did not go unremarked upon by early ecclesiastics trying to create systems of faith based on Scripture. St. Jerome, who translated the Word from Hebrew into Latin, grumbled that many of the narratives were "rude and repellent." A medieval rabbi, borrowing an image from the story of Noah's drunken disarray after the Flood (9: 21), suggested that "as dutiful children, let us cover the nakedness of our fathers in the cloak of favorable interpretation."

Something of the sort eventually occurred. The Christian church developed a set of interpretations according to which the patriarchs prefigure Christians as heroes of faith. The Jewish Midrash, although more flexible and occasionally even playful, also strove to harmonize scriptural difficulties. Both approaches were developed as aids to the believer: they worked from the assumption that God's logic was impeccable; only man's understanding was wanting. But casual readers of Scripture may miss a chance to identify with the patriarchs' vibrant humanity and to sharpen their own faith against the peculiar abrasiveness of the Biblical characters.

Visotzky sought to settle his *Genesis* crisis in a way that came naturally to him: through Bible study. Some time before, when Visotzky, a professor at Manhattan's Jewish Theological Seminary, had first begun to muse about the work's peculiarities, he had initiated a monthly dinner discussion dedicated to making its way through

*C*hallenging God, the city of Babel began building a tower to reach heaven. But God defeated the effort by afflicting humankind with the confusion of many tongues.

the book a chapter at a time. Instead of the academics and rabbis who were his usual conversation partners, however, he stocked the group with an interfaith roster of fiction writers, hoping they might have insight into human character, if not into Midrash. The authors, who included Cynthia Ozick and screenwriter-director Robert Benton, proved fascinated by *Genesis* and fearlessly willing to connect it with their own life. Gradually they helped Visotzky come to his own satisfying, albeit unorthodox, understanding of the patriarchs. God meant them not as paragons but as a paradox: badly flawed yet nonetheless blessed. It was in the struggle to "mediate this dissonance," concluded Visotzky, that believers would achieve their own moral understanding. "It is not the narrative of *Genesis* that makes the work sacred," he later wrote. "Rather, it is in the process of studying *Genesis* that the transformation takes place."

Meanwhile, word of the seminar spread. One day a former Baptist preacher from Texas dropped by. Like Visotzky, Bill Moyers was not particularly nourished by the picture of the patriarchs he had encountered in Sunday school and seminary. "The figures were drawn for moral instruction and therefore had to be flawless individuals who ought to be in stained-glass windows," he says. Sometime after attending Visotzky's supper, Moyers found himself sitting in his apartment at 3 a.m., having just read *Genesis* straight through "as if I were discovering it for the first time." He became caught up in the saga of "heroes tinged with moral ambiguity and fallenness, yet through them some larger purposes unfolded of which they were not aware." Moyers decided that night that "I've got to do this." As television, he meant.

Yet Bill Moyers is a very different kind of believer from Steve Fintel or, for that matter, Burton Visotzky. For one thing, Moyers' belief has an extremely well-exercised civic aspect. "What I have sought for 25 years to put on television is the conversation of democracy," he says. Although that conversation has been eclectic, with shows ranging from the CIA to the black family, Moyers is convinced that "nonsectarian, nonseparationist" religious talk is an essential component of it. "We have to decide all

over again our identity as a people," he says. "Religion belongs in that discussion. We must learn how to write a new story including the deepest beliefs of people who are not like us." *Genesis*, he believes, provides Christians, Jews and Muslims with a unique common ground.

Moyers' belief may also be more tormented than Visotzky's. He has made a long personal journey from the Southern Baptist ministry into which he was ordained in 1954 to the far more liberal United Church of Christ. "I've had the experience of God," he says. "But there's a lot about God I don't understand and a lot about faith that I wrestle with. Faith is too hard. It creates too many conflicts. I think if I myself could do it over again I'd be a man of no faith." There were moments in his moderation of the telecasts when his ambivalence was expressed more clearly than his faith.

Moyers began each segment with a boiled-down version of the appropriate chapter and verse, narrated by an actor, either Alfre Woodard or Mandy Patinkin. He limited his fellow conversationalists to seven per episode: but since Visotzky was the only guest who appeared in more than two, the resulting cast came to 39. It included novelists like Bharati Mukherjee, John Barth and Mary Gordon; but also Bible experts, psychologists, preachers and a smattering of artists and poets. Among them were Catholics, Protestants, Jews, two Muslims, a Hindu, a Buddhist and several apparent agnostics. Yet Moyers decided not to include Christian Fundamentalists. "I called some" he says, "and they said, 'That's great. We're going to talk about Creation and abortion?' My guard went up. It would have struck people as the same discourse they've been hearing the last 15 years."

With nearly a dozen clerics on board, *A Living Conversation* was hardly an exercise in atheism, debunking or even agnosticism. Rather it was a fascinating collection of approaches, from traditional to avant-garde, jostling around those magnificent, infuriating tales. As one panelist, author Charles Johnson, commented early on: "The problem is not lack of meaning. It's too much meaning." Yet for millions of Americans, many of the issues raised in *Genesis: A Living Conversation* were not issues at all.

Pained by signs of man's corruption in the world he created, an angry God sent a flood that engulfed all life on earth—except for Noah, his family and the animals in the Ark.

Fundamentalists, Evangelicals and Orthodox Jews were well aware of the moral flaws of the book's human characters. But since they regarded the entire book as the saga of God putting humanity on trial rather than the reverse, these imperfections did not challenge their faith.

Nor would they have perturbed the work's original audience, maintains Southern Baptist professor Kenneth Mathews, an Old Testament scholar at Alabama's Samford University who has just published his own commentary, *Genesis 1-11*. "Moses' Israel would come to read the opening chapters through their eyes of faith and experience," he says. "Are we submitting to the picture of God in Scripture? Or are we putting ourselves over Scripture and rewriting it in terms of our own preferences?" Similar sentiments were expressed by Orthodox Rabbi Shalom Carmy of New York's Yeshiva University and Moyers panelist and Catholic priest/professor Alexander Di Lella.

And yet there are many in America who will accept only a God who speaks to them within the context of their own culture. And there are others of traditional faith who will forgive Moyers' lack of orthodoxy for the opportunity he provided to mine for Scriptural treasure. *A Living Conversation*, Moyers says, was "aimed at anyone who finds these subjects and this kind of conversation worth their time," and he thinks that number is growing in America. "I find in my own life and in the lives of other people a yearning for an authentic experience. This series may pass without notice, but there is something out there that it ratifies."

Visotzky would agree. The point of the series, he says, "isn't so much about belief as about whether you're willing to take the risk of study. Study leads to conversation, and conversation leads to community, and that's what we're desperate for." But he adds: "If people watch the series, at some point they're going to say, 'Is that really in there?' And they're going to look at a Bible. And they're going to be dumbfounded how it speaks to their own life." He feels no need to try to predict "whether this will make them march to the churches and the synagogues, or merely recognize that here is a classic of Western literature. That's almost incidental," Visotzky contends. "The Bible can pretty well speak for itself." ∎

BIG BAD BULLS

Forget Tinker to Evers to Chance. Rodman to Jordan to Pippen makes "da Bulls" Chicago's greatest team ever

WHAT DOES IT TAKE TO BECOME the greatest team in the history of professional basketball? Well, consider the recipe behind the unlikely unit that in 1996 earned the right to call itself the best ever, the world champion Chicago Bulls. The Bulls boasted the best rebounder in the world in the outrageously controversial Dennis Rodman, the most versatile forward in the N.B.A. in Scottie Pippen and the finest player who ever lived in Michael Jordan. Presiding benevolently over this three-ring circus was head coach/chief guru Phil Jackson, whose New Age philosophy, a mixture of American Indian and Zen Buddhism, kept the superstars and scrubs, the Croatian and the Australian, the young and the old, the sane and Rodman playing in harmony.

Under Jackson, the Bulls racked up an amazing 72 wins in the regular season—the most in N.B.A. history—against only 10 losses. They went on to dominate the Seattle Supersonics 4-2 in the championship series, recouping the title the Houston Rockets had borrowed for two years while Michael Jordan was off shagging fly balls.

What distinguished the Bulls from other teams, present and past, was not so much talent as intelligence. As Magic Johnson said, "They got guys that have that look." The Bulls knew that practice makes perfect; they knew not to burn the candle at both ends; they knew there is no *I* in team. They knew—and believed in—all the clichés. In basketball, such intelligence translates into power. New Jersey Nets forward Jayson Williams raved, "The Bulls are like Clint Eastwood in a western, Arnold Schwarzenegger in an action movie. You can shoot at them, you may even wound them. But guess who's gonna be standing there when the credits roll?"

The last man standing—and the unquestioned first man on the Bulls—would be Michael Jordan. Since his return to basketball in the '94-'95 season, Jordan had been intent on winning back the championship. In the '95-'96 season he averaged 30.4 points a game to earn his eighth N.B.A. scoring title. "He's not quite as explosive as he was five years ago," said Bulls guard Steve Kerr, "but he's stronger and a better shooter. His fadeaway jump shot is now his signature move, not the spectacular drive to the basket." That's not to say Jordan was getting old at 33. He could still put on a show: early in 1996, for instance, he lit up the Philadelphia 76ers for 48 points just to leave an impression on rookie and fellow North Carolina alum Jerry Stackhouse.

In fact, there were those who said the best player ever was even better this time around. Scottie Pippen, for one: "The game's

THREE BASKETEERS: The all-for-one, one-for-all play of Rodman, Jordan and Pippen lifted Chicago to a record 72 wins. Top left: Air Jordan outflies the Supersonics.

easier for him now," Pippen claimed. "He's a much smarter player. He's using his head a lot more." Jordan's leadership role had expanded as well, said Pippen: from setting an example to making sure his teammates followed it. Said the Nets' Williams: "Michael's second to God."

Second to the devil might be Dennis Rodman, a.k.a. "the Worm." His affectations were not restricted to the hue of his locks, his forays into cross-dressing or the Cinerama spectacle of his tattooed body. There were the 17 pierced areas above his neck and the one below his waist, for instance. In a better world, Rodman would be admired for his rebounding and passing skills, which are extraordinary, or for his work ethic, which was considerable when he chose to work. But those weren't the reasons kids came to arenas all across the land with magenta-colored hair. Still, in taking the risk of acquiring the flamboyant superstar from the San Antonio Spurs, the Bulls were smart enough to realize what Rodman the player could do for them, and that Jordan was a strong enough influence to keep him in line.

Second to Michael on the Bulls was Scottie Pippen. He was also first in assists, second in scoring and third in rebounds. While Jordan was gone, Pippen had become the team leader, and now they willingly played good captain/bad captain. "Scottie will do a lot of patting on the back," said Phil Jackson. "Michael, well, he's not afraid to rebuke and give a guy a hard look if he screwed up." Pippen and Jordan also went hard after one another in practice, and that, said Jackson, "brings the level of the team up."

The Bulls' supporting cast had a decidedly international flavor: Croatian guard/forward Toni Kukoc provided instant offense off the bench, Australian Luc Longley and Canadian Bill Wennington shared the pivot, and Kerr, born in Beirut, could spell Jordan and throw in a three-pointer. Coach Jackson kept the entire menagerie happy. "Phil choreographs the whole thing," said Kerr. "He knows how to blend personalities. A lot of teams would not be able to accept three guys getting all the attention, but we have no problem with that. Besides, we get a lot more recognition than we would on any other team. Every single guy is happy to be here." Dennis Rodman concurred—after his fashion. Asked to assess Jackson as a coach and as a man, he replied, "Great coach. As a man, well, I've never slept with him." ∎

The Stalled Revolution

Women confront the conflicting demands of work and the family

SOCIOLOGIST ARLIE HOCHSCHILD HAS A NAME FOR IT: "the stalled revolution." Since the '70s, so many women have poured into the workplace—compelled by economic necessity and personal ambition—that dual-wage-earner families are now the norm. Yet somehow neither the workplace nor the family has changed enough to compensate for this new reality. Day care is still catch as catch can. Employers still demand 110% from women, while spouses and children still need clean socks and a ride to the dentist. Add stagnating wages and layoff anxiety, and for millions of American women each week becomes a stressful triage between work and home that leaves them feeling guilty, exhausted and angry.

In a project called New Economic Equation, the Public Policy Institute at Radcliffe College, after conducting focus groups around the country, held a two-day conference to study the work-family conundrum and propose solutions. The more than three dozen business and labor leaders, economists and family experts agreed that the problem has taken on new urgency.

There is some evidence, in fact, that many people, women in particular, have "downshifted" in an effort to cope, trading money for time. Juliet Schor, author of *The Overworked American*, found in a national survey of 1,000 people that 28% had made a voluntary life-style change that involved a significant reduction in earnings: moving to a less stressful job, turning down a promotion or refusing a relocation. More and more mothers now work part time, even though they routinely make less an hour than full-time workers doing the same job.

Radcliffe's panels saw no deliberate villainy or single cause for blame; their recommendations were aimed at both government and business. Conferees proposed, for example, that the care of the young and the old should be made "critical elements of our economic structure." That means, among other things, preserving Medicare coverage for elder care, extending public education below kindergarten level and providing prorated benefits for part-time workers.

But the biggest changes, all agree, must come on the job, where family-friendly policies have too often been fringe benefits that anxious employees feel too insecure to exercise. One promising exception is General Motors' Saturn Co. in Spring Hill, Tennessee, where teams of up to 15 people decide how they will meet production goals set by management. Employees work 10-hour days, four days a week, with rotating day and night shifts. At the end of each three-week cycle, they get five consecutive days off. This adds up to far more family time per year and creates flexibility within the team for handling personal problems.

Some conferees proposed that the Federal government establish an award—like the coveted Malcolm Baldrige National Quality Award—for companies like Saturn that adopt family-friendly policies in the workplace. And they insisted that the issue be seen as affecting both men and women. Yet recognizing that the work-family dilemma has been felt most acutely by women, Martha Minow, a Harvard professor of family law, declared that "our best hope is CEOs with daughters"—who will presumably be made aware of the problem as these young women marry, have careers and struggle to be good mothers too. ■

Texaco's Dark Star

Racism tarnished the star of oil giant Texaco when tapes secretly recorded at an executive meeting in 1994 were played as evidence in a racial harassment case brought by black Texaco employees. Texaco execs were recorded as saying, "All the black jelly beans seem to be glued to the bottom of the bag," complaining about such ethnic-oriented holidays as Kawanzaa and Hanukkah, and, in one especially offensive passage, carping that "niggers" were causing too much trouble. Texaco President Peter I. Bijur deplored the incident, and the company quickly settled the lawsuit.

Too Young to ... Fly

Young Jessica Dubroff's sad death could be attributed to overzealous parents, to a media drawn to a natural human-interest story and to a willfully blind Federal Aviation Administration. The FAA gave its approval for a 4-ft. 2-in., 55-lb. seven-year-old whose feet did not reach the rudder pedals to fly an airplane across the country in a misbegotten publicity stunt—as long as a licensed pilot was beside her. Jessica, her father Lloyd and flight instructor Joe Reid died on April 11 when their single-engine plane plunged to earth shortly after taking off in a heavy rainstorm in Cheyenne, Wyoming. Said Jessica's mother: "I'd let her do it again in a second. You have no idea what this meant to Jess."

JESSICA: Her goal was "to fly till I die."

JUST SAY "YO": It's party time for kids at a pro-pot rally in Boston

Uncle Sam's Pot Party

Marijuana: is it a dangerous menace or a sort of benign and unfairly persecuted folk medicine? Once again the old question dominated discussions of America's drug habits, amid a soaring rise in pot use by the young. In August the U.S. Department of Health and Human Services released a study that surveyed almost 18,000 Americans and concluded that marijuana use among youths (ages 12 to 17) had roughly doubled in the past few years.

The Higher Costs of Higher Education

In today's America, a college degree and middle-class opportunity are much the same thing—and four of every five college degrees are delivered by a public university. Traditionally, public higher education was available at a nominal fee. But between 1991 and 1994, tuition at the average state university increased at least 10% a year, even as a 1992 government program raised interest rates on student loans. The average total cost for a year of public higher education in 1996: $9,285. Critics charged that the high costs of state college were subverting America's democratic ideals.

Battle over TV Ratings

At a February White House conclave, 30 top TV-industry executives vowed to devise a rating system for TV shows that would flag programs containing sex, violence and rough language. But the guidelines they unveiled in December were classified by age appropriateness: TV-7, TV-14, etc. Critics called for ratings that designated the specific content that might offend.

Charges of abusing women— and angry DENIALS from Mitsubishi— rocked an Illinois auto factory

WHAT HARASSMENT? This female employee supported Mitsubishi at a rally in Chicago

GUTS, GOLD

With more athletes competing than in any previous Olympics,

THE FACE OF VICTORY
Americans embraced sprinter Michael Johnson as a
new hero—and he appears ready to return the favor

STANDING ROOM ONLY
Some **83,000** spectators welcomed the Olympic
Games back to America in the opening ceremonies

& GLORY

the spirit of the Atlanta Games triumphed over terror

OLD FLAME
The surprise choice of Olympic great Muhammad Ali to light the torch thrilled the opening-night crowd

GREEK REVIVAL
In a highlight of the opening ceremonies, modern silhouettes evoked the Games' classical heritage

Shades of Ancient Splendor

"OUR LIFE," SAID PYTHAGORAS, "IS LIKE the great and crowded assembly at the Olympic Games," which is a roundabout, Olympian way of saying the Games are as full of terror and chaos as the lives they temporarily eclipse. The great and crowded assembly in Atlanta was tested by both terror and chaos: a deadly bomb exploded in a crowded park; transportation was snarled and computers snagged. But the Games became a triumph of perseverance, from the thousands who breathed new life into a haunted party at Centennial Park to the athletes who stayed focused amid bomb threats in a city that had waited forever to show off the New South (a phrase that was coined in 1886).

When the Centennial Games ended, it seemed as if a slim hope had gone 15 rounds with hard reality and emerged bloodied but just ahead on points. Atlanta had faced its share of biblical afflictions: rain and thunder, a plague of journalists and, everywhere, the smell of lucre. Yet the athletes raved about the crowds as much as the crowds raved about the athletes, the venues shone, the volunteers (mostly) smiled, and the events never failed the spectators. Simply put, the sports were thrilling.

In the age of "plausibly live" broadcasts and virtual-reality competitions, the highlights of the first interactive

Shadows of Modern Fear

CENTENNIAL OLYMPIC PARK WAS DESIGNED to be the spiritual heart of the Atlanta Games, a global village green where everyone could congregate without paying for tickets or passing through metal detectors. But security experts had privately been worried that the park was also the place that was most vulnerable to terrorist attack. Their fears were realized just after 1 a.m. Saturday morning, August 3, when a homemade pipe bomb exploded only 150 ft. from a stage where a band was playing rock music to a carefree crowd of thousands.

About 18 minutes before the explosion, a call came in to 911, and a "white male with an indistinguishable" American accent warned that a bomb would go off within 30 minutes. At about the same time, security officials found a suspicious green knapsack leaning against a sound tower. The bomb squad was called, but attempts to clear the park lagged. Moments later the knapsack exploded and the smell of gunpowder filled the air. When the smoke had cleared, Alice Hawthorne, 44, of Albany, Georgia, lay dead, and 111 people had been wounded.

Olympic officials quickly announced that the Games would continue after a memorial service. Despite an intensive manhunt—including a long, fruitless inquiry into the actions of a security guard, Richard Jewell, whom the FBI later cleared—investigators failed to apprehend a culprit. The bomb darkened the proceedings, but only temporarily. The Games resumed and gathered strength, Centennial Park was reopened with a rousing concert, and the spirit of the new South—and the ancient Greeks—triumphed over terror.

TERROR STALKS THE GAMES
Moments after a pipe bomb killed one and injured 111

Games were plain, old-fashioned human interactions. A Kiss beat a Deal in the hammer throw, and tiny Morris Brown College saw its largest crowd ever, waving rubber swords, when India and Pakistan played to a 0-0 tie in field hockey. Japanese said *"Muchas gracias"* to Cuban baseball players, and the Cubans responded, with typical charm, *"Domo arigato."* Basketball's tough Charles Barkley gave his practice jersey to the 14-year-old daughter of Alice Hawthorne, the woman killed in the bombing.

On the first day of the Games, David Robinson, the U.S. Dream Teamer, was asked if the rest of the world was growing less awestruck by the American pros. Yes, he said, "and our job is to re-create that awe." On a grander scale than Robinson was speaking of, that is what these Games achieved: Atlanta, no stranger to reconstruction, made the Olympic wonder feel young again.

GOLDEN FEAT
Not one to hide his light feet under a bushel, Johnson
flew to his two gold medals on specially gilded running shoes

RUBBERNECKING
Johnson knew he was running fast but claimed to be as
surprised as the crowd when he first saw his record time

THE LONELINESS OF THE SHORT-DISTANCE RUNNER
Sprint races often come down to four or five bodies lunging to
hit the tape first, but Johnson simply ran away from the field

Far from the Panting Crowd

IN AN OLYMPICS MARKED BY A HOST OF exhilarating track and field performances, the golden shoes of American sprinter Michael Johnson left the biggest imprint. Johnson not only became the first man in Olympic history to win both the 400-m and 200-m races; he shattered his own world record of 19.66 seconds in the 200 by more than a third of a second, skipping right over the .50s and .40s to alight at a stunning time of 19.32.

Only three days after Johnson handily won the 400, the gun went off for the 200 final. Johnson exploded from the blocks as the fireflies of thousands of flash cameras sparkled in the night. He momentarily stumbled, then shifted into a gear previously known only to Mercury. The fireflies followed him as he came slinging out of the turn, obliterating the staggered start and defying the laws of physics. According to Trinidad's Ato Boldon, who would

finish third, "I saw a big blur go by, *whoosh*, and thought, 'There goes first.'" Pity Namibia's Frankie Fredericks: he sprinted to the third-fastest 200 time in history, only to finish second, far behind Johnson (*above*).

They really are two different people, the Michael who runs the more strategic 400 and the Michael who runs the more aggressive 200. The 400 Michael listens to jazz on his headset in the days before a race; the 200 Michael listens to gangsta rap. The 400 Michael checks in on his Website to answer fan mail, and carries with him a letter from Ruth Owens in which she writes that she sees her late husband Jesse in him. "Greatest compliment I've ever

been paid," says Johnson, whose upright running style has often been compared to that of the '36 Olympics hero. On the other hand, the 200 Michael endorses a product line called "The Danger Zone" and heaped pressure on himself by coming to Atlanta with nine pairs of flashy gold shoes.

The double victory was a special vindication for Johnson, who was forced out of the Barcelona Games in 1992 by an untimely case of food poisoning. "You have to understand," said Johnson's coach, Clyde Hart: "Michael's been on a four-year mad ever since Barcelona." Now Johnson has plenty of reasons to smile: in Atlanta, he learned that revenge is a dish best served smoking hot.

Kerri Vaults into History

KERRI STRUG'S MOMENT OF OLYMPIC glory was the storybook climax to a brilliant team effort. A close second to the Russians after the compulsories, the U.S. women had moved into first during the finals. With only the vault remaining, the first U.S. team gymnastics gold medal ever was a lock—barring disaster. Then disaster happened. Dominique Moceanu, only 14, ingloriously landed on her rear end in both her vaults. That put the pressure on Strug, anchoring the team in her best event. But—incredibly—on Strug's first vault, she landed on her seat as well (*below*). Worse, she came up limping.

Strug's coach, Bela Karolyi, shouted encouragement as Strug tried to shake off the pain. Actually, her score on the first vault—9.162—was enough to ensure a U.S. victory without a second try. But no one knew that yet—least of all Strug, who saluted and ran down the runway. With the crowd transfixed, she ran, she jumped, and she landed—on her feet. Or foot. Instantly, she winced in pain and lifted her injured left ankle, hopping on one foot to face the judges before collapsing in pain. After her solid score of 9.712 was posted, Strug joined her teammates to receive the gold medal, cradled in the bearlike arms of Karolyi.

TRUE GRIT
After Kerri Strug injured her ankle on her first leap, above, she tried again. "We had no idea what the score was," said co-head coach Mary Lee Tracy. "What we saw was a kid who was shaking her leg but who saluted and ran down the runway." Said Strug: "I knew ... the gold was slipping away ... I let the adrenaline take over"

Two Lords a-Leaping

THE ATLANTA GAMES HELD MAGIC AND VINDICA-tion for two veteran Olympians, sprinter and long-jumper Carl Lewis and decathloner Dan O'Brien. Both had scores to settle. O'Brien had been relentlessly promoted as part of a Reebok marketing effort in the '92 Barcelona Games—but had missed qualifying for the U.S. team when he failed to complete a single pole vault in the trials. Lewis, who first soared to stardom in the 1984 Los Angeles Games, had become a controversial figure. Now 35—ancient by Olympic standards—Lewis was eager to compete in the Games, but was no longer a world-class sprinter, and his attempts to lobby a position for himself on a U.S. relay team struck many as grandstanding. But both O'Brien and Lewis rose to the Olympic occasion.

Lewis had struggled to qualify in the long jump; it was

the last event in which he was remotely a contender. Yet he refused to be beaten: on his best leap he clawed through the air to a distance of 27 ft. 10¾ in., well off his personal best, well off a record and against a less-than-stellar field. But it was good enough to earn Lewis his ninth gold medal, further embellishing his legendary status.

Dan O'Brien came to Atlanta still nursing a case of the Barcelona Blues. "Watching a competition you felt you could win," he said of the '92 Games, "was worse than getting picked last in gym class." This time around—

despite one dramatic miss (*below*)—O'Brien had no trouble with the pole vault. But he still had Frank Busemann of Germany on his tail as he headed across the infield to his ninth event, the javelin. Then O'Brien got some helpful advice from none other than Dave Johnson, his Reebok-created nemesis from '92. "Dave's the javelin expert," said Dan, "so I yelled at him, 'Which jav do I use, the 85 or 90 m?' He said 90, so that's what I threw." And O'Brien threw it for a personal best 69.96 m, putting him safely ahead with one event to go. Take that, Reebok!

AT LAST!
Above: Like sprinter Michael Johnson, Dan O'Brien
expelled the ghosts of 1992 by winning the decathlon

ONE MORE TIME
Left: The grand (and grandstanding) old man of U.S. track,
Carl Lewis soars into history with his ninth gold medal

MARIE-JOSE PEREC
France's speedy sprinter won gold in
both the 200-m and 400-m races

MONICA SELES
The veteran pro shed the trappings of
status to live with her U.S. teammates

MICHELE SMITH
The 26-year-old Dubliner, quickly dubbed
"the Irish Harpoon," took three golds and a bronze

DOT RICHARDSON
Perkiness personified, Dot led the U.S. softball
team to gold, then returned to her surgical rounds

The Girls of Summer

"GO, GIRL!" SISTERHOOD WAS POWERFUL at the Atlanta Games: U.S. women's teams soared to gold-medal performances in soccer, basketball, softball and gymnastics. France's Marie-José Pérec matched Michael Johnson's feat of taking first in both the 200-m and 400-m dashes, and American sprinter Gail Devers and Chinese diver Fu Mingxia turned in breathtaking individual performances. It was clear to all that women athletes had emerged from the shadows of the men's competition to take an equal—if not superior—place in the sun.

Early on, Olympic officials scheduled women's basketball at the tiny Morehouse College gym. By the second week, the U.S. women—who showed far more team spirit than the stars of the men's "Dream Team"—were drawing crowds of more than 30,000 at the Georgia Dome. The women's soccer finals drew 76,481 fans—the largest crowd ever for an Olympic soccer final. Said U.S. goalie Briana Scurry: "It's a great thing for women's sports."

MIA HAMM AND WANG LIPING
American star Hamm led her team to victory over a tough Chinese squad in a hair-raising 2-1 finale

MIKE POWELL
Biting the dust, the world record-holder in the long jump failed once again to win Olympic gold—and beat nemesis Carl Lewis

Faster, Higher, Stronger

ITIUS, ALTIUS, FORTIUS: FASTER, HIGHER, stronger. The Atlanta Games fulfilled the Greeks' Olympic motto with a bevy of stirring individual performances. *Faster:* Threatened thunderstorms never materialized on the first Saturday of the Games, but there was lightning on the Olympic Stadium track as Donovan Bailey of Canada won the 100 m in a world-record time of 9.84 seconds.

Higher: Charles Barkley and the other skyscraping stars of the U.S. men's basketball Dream Team prevailed for the second Games in a row. And as for crowd highs—

well, consider the scene as the fans cheered on Karch Kiraly and the other buffed and bronze beach volleyballers. Only 230 miles from the nearest real sand, the spectators grooved to the B-52s' "Love Shack" and sipped daiquiris in their bathing trunks while strangers sprayed them down with high-tech, fluorescent-green water pistols.

Stronger: They don't get much stronger than Turkey's "Pocket Hercules," 4-ft. 11-in. Naim Suleymanoglu, who won the 64-kg class for the third time, a record. Asked if he was the greatest weight lifter of all time, he said, "You can make your own decision." Faster, higher ... humbler?

CHARLES BARKLEY
Once again the U.S. Dream Team hung on to the gold

NAIM SULEYMANOGLU
Turkey's "Pocket Hercules" snatched the gold medal three Games in a row

KARCH KIRALY
America's grand old man of beach volleyball dug for gold—and got it

DONOVAN BAILEY
The Canadian sprinter ran a record 9.84 in the 100-m dash

Gold Medal Winners

INDIVIDUAL COMPETITION

SWIMMING AND DIVING

50-m freestyle	ALEKSANDER POPOV	Russia
	AMY VAN DYKEN	U.S.A.
100-m freestyle	ALEKSANDER POPOV	Russia
	LE JINGYI	China
200-m freestyle	DANYON LOADER	New Zealand
	CLAUDIA POLL	Costa Rica
400-m freestyle	DANYON LOADER	New Zealand
	MICHELLE SMITH	Ireland
800-m freestyle	BROOKE BENNETT	U.S.A.
1500-m freestyle	KIEREN PERKINS	Australia
100-m backstroke	JEFF ROUSE	U.S.A.
	BETH BOTSFORD	U.S.A.
200-m backstroke	BRAD BRIDGEWATER	U.S.A.
	KRISTINA EGERSZEGI	Hungary
100-m breaststroke	FRED DEBURGHGRAEVE	Belgium
	PENNY HEYNS	South Africa
200-m breaststroke	NORBERT ROZSA	Hungary
	PENNY HEYNS	South Africa
100-m butterfly	DENIS PANKRATOV	Russia
	AMY VAN DYKEN	U.S.A.
200-m butterfly	DENIS PANKRATOV	Russia
	SUSAN O'NEILL	Australia
200-m ind. medley	ATTILA CZENE	Hungary
	MICHELLE SMITH	Ireland
400-m ind. medley	TOM DOLAN	U.S.A.
	MICHELLE SMITH	Ireland
Platform diving	DMITRY SAUTIN	Russia
	FU MINGXIA	China
Springboard diving	XIONG NI	China
	FU MINGXIA	China

MEN'S GYMNASTICS

All-around	LI XIAOSHUANG	China
Floor	IOANNIS MELISSANIDIS	Greece
Horizontal bar	ANDREAS WECKER	Germany
Parallel bars	RUSTAM SHARIPOV	Ukraine
Pommel horse	LI DONGHUA	Switzerland
Rings	YURI CHECHI	Italy
Vault	ALEXEI NEMOV	Russia

WOMEN'S GYMNASTICS

All Around	LILIA PODKOPAYEVA	Ukraine
Balance beam	SHANNON MILLER	U.S.A.
Floor	LILIA PODKOPAYEVA	Ukraine
Uneven bars	SVETLANA CHORKINA	Russia
Vault	SIMONA AMANAR	Romania

TRACK AND FIELD

100 m	DONOVAN BAILEY	Canada
	GAIL DEVERS	U.S.A.
200 m	MICHAEL JOHNSON	U.S.A.
	MARIE-JOSÉ PÉREC	France
400 m	MICHAEL JOHNSON	U.S.A.
	MARIE-JOSÉ PÉREC	France
800 m	VEBJOERN RODAL	Norway
	SVETLANA MASTERKOVA	Russia
1,500 m	NOUREDDINE MORCELI	Algeria
	SVETLANA MASTERKOVA	Russia
5,000 m	VENUSTE NIYONGABO	Burundi
	WANG JUNXIA	China
10,000 m	HAILE GEBRSELASSIE	Ethiopia
	FERNANDA RIBEIRO	Portugal
Decathlon	DAN O'BRIEN	U.S.A.
Heptathlon	GHADA SHOUAA	Syria
High jump	CHARLES AUSTIN	U.S.A.
	STEFKA KOSTADINOVA	Bulgaria
Long jump	CARL LEWIS	U.S.A.
	CHIOMA AJUNWA	Nigeria
Marathon	JOSIA THUGWANE	South Africa
	FATUMA ROBA	Ethiopia

TEAM COMPETITION

	Men	Women
Beach volleyball	U.S.A.	Brazil
Baseball/Softball	Cuba	U.S.A.
Basketball	U.S.A.	U.S.A.
Soccer	Nigeria	U.S.A.
Team Handball	Croatia	Denmark
Volleyball	Netherlands	Cuba

AMY VAN DYKEN
America's most decorated Olympian in the Atlanta Games shows off her golden harvest

MODERNISM'S PATRIARCH

Philadelphia hosts a landmark exhibition that traces the epic journey of painter Paul Cézanne

THE GREATER THE ARTIST, THE greater the doubt; perfect confidence is granted to the less talented as a consolation prize. "As a painter, I become more lucid in front of Nature," Paul Cézanne wrote to his son in 1906, the last year of his life. "But that realization of my sensations is always very painful. I cannot attain the intensity which unfolds to my senses. I don't have that magnificent richness of coloration which animates nature."

As Picasso famously said, it's Cézanne's anxiety that is so interesting. But it's the achievement that counts. If Cézanne was not a heroic painter, the word means nothing. He compared himself to Moses: "I work doggedly, I glimpse the promised land ... Will I be able to enter it?"

Cézanne was the inspired, even enraged prophet who led the way to Modernism

WOMAN WITH A COFFEEPOT, CA. 1895

SELF PORTRAIT, 1875

ART

THE LARGE BATHERS, *1906*

*Not flesh but a kind of architecture: equilibrium achieved
at the end of a conflicted, inspired, heroic career*

Cézanne was indeed the Moses of late 19th century art, the conflicted, inspired, sometimes enraged patriarch who led painting toward Modernism. But just as Moses died before reaching Canaan, so Cézanne never lived to see Modernism take hold—and he might not have liked what he saw had he lived. Instead of theory he had "sensation," the experience of being up against the world—fugitive and yet painfully solid, imperious in its thereness and constantly, unrelentingly new. There was painting before Cézanne and painting after him, and they were not the same.

The Cézanne retrospective that opened at the Philadelphia Museum of Art in late May was one of the greatest shows that have ever been held in America. In size—112 oils and 75 drawings and watercolors—in scholarship, in the magnitude of its subject's achievement, it was a truly epic event. God help any fool who was not humbled by it.

There was no art in Cézanne's background in Aix-en-Provence, where he was born in 1839. Young Cezanne studied humanities at the College Bourbon in Aix, where he met the future writer who was to be his lifetime friend, Emile Zola. Under Zola's constant prodding, Cézanne began to paint. But he had no facility at all; the impression given off by his early *style couillarde*—his "ballsy style," as he called it—is of a thwarted, tumultuous, half-articulate imagination bashing against the limits of its own abilities.

CÉZANNE ADMIRED THE IMPRESSIONISTS, BUT the whole thrust of his work is about something other than the delight in the fleeting moment, the "effect" of light, color and atmosphere, to which Impressionism was dedicated. Underneath nature's delectable surface was structure, like reefs and rocks beneath a smiling sea, and that was what he sought and obsessively analyzed—the bones and masses of the world. Cézanne's famous remark about seeking in nature "the cylinder, the sphere, the cone" need not be taken literally, yet his greatest paintings often include abstract constructions of tremendous amplitude and sureness.

An example is *Woman with a Coffeepot*. One would need to go back some 400 years, to Piero della Francesca's *Madonna del Parto*, to find a painted human figure of such monumental gravity. All is volume, all is power, not only the large masses—the head that seems hewn from some skin-colored rock, the torso and the flaring blue pyramid of the skirt, the cylindrical coffeepot—but also the microforms, such as the knot tying the woman's apron at her waist, which has the finality of a turned lock. The poetry here isn't in expression—it is almost ineloquent—but in space, form and immense deliberation.

Early Cézanne the stumblebum turned into one of the finest manipulators of paint

Underneath the delectable surface is structure, like reefs beneath a smiling sea

who have ever lived. But "manipulator" suggests trickery, whereas in Cézanne the relation between the paint surface and the imagined surface of the object is astonishingly direct. Every trace left by the brush helps create the impression of solidity, so that you feel you could pick the apple—which is both a rosy sphere of light and a ball as heavy as plutonium—off the table. And yet the surface is never closed; that is part of the magic.

In the magisterial *Still Life with Curtain and Flowered Pitcher*, the heavy leaf-pattern curtain on the left and the folds of white cloth below it have the same sculptural density as the fruit and the jug. But there, on the right, Cézanne has another white cloth, its folds sharper and more geometrical, its surface unfinished, so that you see glimpses of table through it—and the balance is suddenly perfect, because of this shift of gear. Then there is

the play between mass and instability: how the fruit is so grandly solid, while the plates themselves tilt just enough to convey an underlying peril.

Cézanne is a universal artist, but he was a deeply local one as well—not just French but southern Mediterranean French, a Provençal; and the obsessive, enduring, reinforcing sense of the particular landscape of his cultural memory is wound into his work so far as to completely remove it from the domain of pure, unsymbolic form. You feel his love for the power embedded in the land, particularly in such landscapes as *Mont Sainte-Victoire Seen from Bellevue.* Here the tender, early springtime landscape, all new green, is traversed by a Roman aqueduct and crossed by a pale road whose kinks are tied to the branch forms of the pine that rises in the foreground to bisect the canvas.

But anxiety is never far away; it breaks through time and again, the Thanatos to the Eros of Cézanne's Provençalism. The summation of both is present at the end of his work in the unfinished masterpiece *The Large Bathers,* one of a series of peculiar arcadian scenes that are difficult to love even as they compel admiration, even awe.

This group of 14 stock nudes gathered around what must have been a picnic basket is as resolutely antisensuous as an assembly of naked women could possibly be. Some of them look like seals stranded on rocks. Others are lumpish giantesses. None were painted from actual models because, as his friend the painter Emile Bernard recalled, "he was the slave of an extreme sense of decorum."

Cézanne's sublimation produces not flesh but a kind of architecture. Yet this architecture is incontrovertible. Its scale is increased by the overarching trees, which supply a Gothic vault, and by the high, cloud-laden sky. And the final effect is one of exhilaration at the thought of the old man in his last year of life winning from his turmoil an equilibrium that was truly classical, and yet hiding so little of the inner compulsions that drove its making. ■

PICK A HOUSE, ANY AVERAGE AMERICAN HOUSE, AND CHANCES ARE THE folks inside will be fans of science fiction. This pretty house in Washington, for example. The family has just had the cable Sci-Fi Channel installed. Mom has been known to try to commune with a dead woman who once lived in the place. And Dad? He has just seen the new alien-invasion epic *Independence Day*—at home. Dean Devlin, the movie's co-writer and producer, watched Dad watch the film, and Devlin was impressed: "He was whipping off facts about history, talking about social and international issues. But when the movie started, he pulled out a big old bucket of popcorn, kicked back, and he was Bubba again."

Bubba, a.k.a. William Jefferson Clinton, lives in the White House, of course, the house that was zapped into flames by a flying saucer's death ray in *Independence Day*. The house that, around Christmastime, was invaded by uggy green creatures in Tim Burton's *Mars Attacks!* The house whose primary resident supposedly knows every secret of a secretive government—the hot dish

about alien sightings, alien abductees, alien autopsies. Except that, as viewers of TV shows like *The X-Files* are taught, the President doesn't know the half of it, because the information is kept from him by conspiratorial feds who may be, God help us, aliens themselves!

By summer's end, the only creatures on Earth who had the right to feel alien were those few who hadn't seen

INDEPENDENCE DAY In imitation-happy Hollywood, its smash success will breed replicants

Independence Day, or *ID4* as its studio called it. The most smartly hyped film of the summer, it was also the grandest: Devlin and Roland Emmerich, the director and co-author, dared to imagine the ultimate catastrophe as it kills off tens of millions of unseen victims and ennobles a dozen major characters, from the Commander in Chief to a stripper's pet dog. The season was a sweltering one for blockbusters: *Twister* earned $465 million at the U.S. and international box office, *Mission Impossible* $410 million. But *ID4*, with heroic humankind battling an army of soulless space lizards, was by far the biggest sensation: it earned a smashing $680 million worldwide to become the fourth-highest-grossing film in Hollywood history.

Independence Day was a vigorous, retro-'70s disaster movie, reminiscent of *Airport* or *The Towering Inferno.* Only this time the disaster was the end of the world. On July 2 in a near future year, humongous spaceships enter the Earth's atmosphere, hover over major cities around the globe, then send out a heat ray that pulverizes every urban center. Washington, New York, Los Angeles, Paris,

Moscow—all barbecued. On July 3 the U.S. President (Bill Pullman) plots his counterattack with the aid of a computer genius (Jeff Goldblum), a Marine pilot (Will Smith) and all their surviving relatives. By July 4, *ID4* has soared into flyboy heaven for the climactic dogfight between Us and the Evil Other.

Brisk and churning, *ID4* offered no grand vision, other than the fact that, in this post-cold war era, it looked to outer space to find new enemies worth hating and blasting into little squishy pieces. "The U.S. is desperately in search of an enemy," said Paul Verhoeven, a veteran sci-fi director *(RoboCop, Total Recall).* "Alien sci-fi films give us a terrifying enemy that's politically correct. They're bad. They're evil. And they're not even human."

Like most sci-fi movies, *ID4* was a sensation machine. You left saying "Wow!" instead of a speculative "Hmmm." The real head scratchers were on TV, where the genre's cool, metallic intellect was touched by the fever of despair. *The X-Files'* twin mantras—"The truth is out there" and "Trust no one"—were the ideal ingredients for a sci-fi

THE ALIENS HAVE LANDED!

And they're in complete control of the cultural mainstream

ALIENS ON THE AIRWAVES

H OLLYWOOD SCI-FI FILMS TEND TO BE EXPLOSIVELY picturesque. On TV the mood is more psychic and psychoanalytic. The benchmark in the genre is Fox's *The X-Files*, producer Chris Carter's haunting excursion into pop paranoia. NBC played copycat with the new *Dark Skies* and enjoyed a hit with the alien sitcom *3rd Rock from the Sun*, which debuted in 1995.

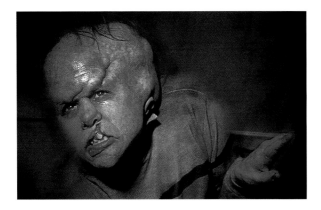

cocktail with a '90s twist. The paranormal and the paranoiac have joined hands through a pop-cultural wormhole; they meet and multiply. It was not so much science as psychic or psychoanalytic fiction. Psy-fi.

And the phenomenon was here to stay, for a while. Hollywood planned to launch more than a dozen science-fiction movies after the 1996 onslaught. Besides *Mars Attacks!* (a gleefully nihilistic vaudeville that played *Dr. Strangelove* to *ID4*'s relatively docudramatic *Fail-Safe*) and the inevitable sequels and remakes of *Alien*, *Star Trek: The Next Generation* and *Lost in Space*, moviegoers were promised big-budget versions of thoughtful sci-fi novels: Carl Sagan's *Contact* (director: Robert Zemeckis), Michael Crichton's *Sphere* (Barry Levinson) and Robert Heinlein's *Starship Troopers* (Paul Verhoeven).

The airwaves and cable wires were pulsing with a dozen TV series about the otherworldly, from the dizzy NBC hit *3rd Rock from the Sun* to the time-travel capering of *Sliders* on Fox, from Showtime's *The Outer Limits* to *Poltergeist: The Legacy* to the supposedly fact-based *Unsolved Mysteries* and *Sightings*. Two of the series, *The Sentinel* on UPN and Fox's new *Millennium*, from *The X-Files* creator Chris Carter, were psychic cop shows. The media sky was darker with eerie phenomena than a UFOlogist's nightscape.

In some of these shows, such as the proliferating *Star Trek* spin-offs, the aliens were benign and intellectually curious. The Zeitgeistiest programs, however, tapped into

a pop persecution mania. Consider this: in 1996 the U.S. stood unchallenged as a world power, was not at war, enjoyed a high standard of living and had relatively stable interest rates and unemployment; yet polls continued to show a profound malaise. People felt crushed by government, abused by corporate employers, baffled by computers. "Technology is moving fast-forward," says Carter, "and we rarely get a chance to understand the implications. Most of us can't program our VCR. We have the tools of science in our hands, and we're afraid of them."

T HE AMERICAN THEOLOGY OF THE '50S—THE MIDDLE class's belief in the government's bland benevolence—in 1996 seemed a dying creed. Rising expectations had given way to escalating suspicions about those in power. It wasn't only the Montana Freemen who believed that we have met the enemy and he is U.S. Moreover, as *ID4*'s Emmerich notes, "every generation creates its own mythology. Now the mythology centers on the government's hiding the dead alien bodies it discovered at Roswell."

Ah, Roswell. This New Mexico town is the Lourdes of psy-fi, just as Area 51, the purported supersecret facility in Nevada where alien bodies are studied, is its Vatican. Roswell and Area 51 have entered the pop lexicon: they were featured in the second episode of *The X-Files*, in *ID4*, in the Sean Connery summer action film *The Rock*, and in NBC's fall '96 rip-off of *The X-Files*, *Dark Skies*.

❝We are a superstitious species, and we need to look outside ourselves for

THE OUTER LIMITS TV sci-fi's old wave, this Showtime series is a revival of a '60s-era hit

THE X-FILES Agents Mulder (David Duchovny) and Scully (Gillian Anderson) parse the paranormal

DARK SKIES NBC's new series imagines that supposed alien landings in 1947 changed history

3RD ROCK FROM THE SUN John Lithgow plays a dignified Mork for the '90s on NBC's sitcom, a rare attempt at humor in the sci-fi genre

The notion that sci-fi is not so much a window to the stars as a mirror of our dark dreams is supported by David Hartwell, an editor at Tor Books. "The alien represents metaphorically what's in the real world. The aliens in '50s films often represented communists—faceless invaders who were going to take over our country. The mysterious beings of *2001: A Space Odyssey* in 1968 represented our transcendent future. *Independence Day* [is] the old form of sci-fi: the foreign invaders intend to wipe out our cultural heritage—ethnic cleansing. They don't want to come in and settle. They want to take over."

Why do we now paint the Other as bad guys in black spaceships? Clive Barker, the author *(Sacrament)* and filmmaker *(Hellraiser)*, thinks the attitude is dangerously, well, alienating. "It disconnects us from being able to operate in the real world," he says. "There's a sense we're unplugging from political activity, civic duties or even responsibility to our neighbors by saying there are … secrets hidden from us. We are a superstitious species, and we need to look outside ourselves for something larger that will bring either calamity or wisdom or maybe both. This is about belief, not just box office."

It may be about belief. It is certainly about box office. Peter Chernin, the 20th Century Fox chairman, didn't see a holy white light when he gave the green light to *ID4;* he was thinking grosses. Michael Sullivan of UPN didn't have religion in mind when he put four sci-fi shows on his network; he was thinking demographics. "Sci-fi has tradi-tionally been a cult item," he says, "and 20 years ago networks had to draw a mass audience. Now, with the networks' share of audience diminishing, that core audience becomes more significant."

But like that white house in Washington, Sullivan's notion of science fiction as a cult genre was zapped into oblivion by the enormous success of *Independence Day*, which demonstrated that science fiction could be a mainstream draw—especially if its special effects were truly special. In today's Hollywood, the movie director's job is to package an old idea with zippy effects so that the audience will think it's seeing something new—and be blown away. During the cold war, even the cheesiest sci-fi filmmaker, like the legendarily dyscompetent Ed Wood, had some moral admonition in mind ("He tampered in God's domain"). Now only size counts; sense and scruples don't.

ID4 was a doomsday fable told at warp speed. Minute by minute, though, things looked mighty familiar. If *Forrest Gump* was Everyman, *ID4* was Everymovie, a browse through the whole film catalog: *The Day the Earth Stood Still, Dr. Strangelove, Close Encounters, Alien, Top Gun, 2001, Apollo 13*. Though set in the future, it had the comforting feeling of an old friend. It was deja new. And if the picture gave us familiar thrills instead of the paranormal creeps, just wait. Ambitious writers and directors all over Hollywood spent the latter part of 1996 busily devising aliens whose evil was bounded only by their creators' imaginations. ∎

something larger that will bring either calamity or wisdom or maybe both."

CELINE DION Born in Quebec, the power balladeer lives in Montreal and Florida. Age: 28. Sales: 35 million albums

WHITNEY HOUSTON She led the way, creating the image of today's superthrush. Age: 33. Sales: 87 million albums

MARIAH CAREY She crams a song's worth of scat singing into a single note. Age: 27. Sales: 80 million albums

Viva the DIVAS

With lush ballads, vocal virtuosity and a savvy sense of style, women singers are forcing their way into pop music's "boys only" clubhouse

DIVA MEANS GODDESS IN LATIN. The dictionary definition is more modern: "an operatic prima donna." Let's fiddle a little with those words. "Operatic": note the strenuous, hyperemotional, aria-like feel to many pop ballads. "Prima donna": remove its suggestion of imperious temperament and translate it literally as first lady. Voila! Céline Dion or Gloria Estefan, Whitney Houston or Mariah Carey, Madonna or Enya, Toni Braxton or Alanis Morissette. The gilded songbirds of pop music come from the United States, of course, but also from French and English Canada, from Cuba, Ireland, Scotland, Australia, Japan and China. In every country, in any language: *la diva.*

There was no ignoring divadom in 1996. Alanis Morissette, an unknown from Canada, stunned the U.S. music business when her major-label debut album, *Jagged Little Pill*, released in June 1995, refused to stop selling—while new releases by such major boys-only acts as Pearl Jam and R.E.M. languished in the stores. Sales of *Jagged Little Pill* finally topped 16 million copies, making the album the biggest seller of the year and the biggest ever by a woman artist (including such decade-defining divas as Carole King, Joni Mitchell and Madonna.)

Those who didn't listen much to pop music heard the top thrushes at the movies. Céline Dion, another Canadian, chanted *Because You Loved Me* in the middle and at the end of the Robert Redford–Michelle Pfeiffer *Up Close and Personal.* Whitney Houston and a flock of divas made the CD of *Waiting to Exhale* as big a hit as the

ALANIS MORISSETTE The outlaw Canadian diva rocks hard and flaunts racy lyrics. Age: 22. Sales: 16 million albums

film. The insistence of the melodic lines in these songs, and the persistence of their air play, made them part of the sound track of modern life.

And those who avoided the movie theaters were ambushed by divas on their divans. Millions of TV viewers watched Céline Dion climax the Atlanta Games' opening ceremony with a hymn to the Olympic spirit, *The Power of the Dream,* backed by a 300-member gospel choir. Millions more tuned in to see Gloria Estefan close the Games with her anthemic *Reach.* Who but Estefan, brave survivor of a 1990 bus crash that broke her back, could give such autobiographical grit to her song of resilience? "So I'll go the distance this time," she intoned, "Seeing more the higher I climb." The huge audience soared with her.

This year, divas couldn't climb much higher. Around the world, they nestled at or near the top of their country's music charts. Some, like Dion, Houston and Mariah Carey—not to mention, for the moment, the raspy-voiced outlaw diva Morissette—were on the Top 10 lists in Europe, the Americas and the Pacific Rim simultaneously. More than pop creations, many of these women were fine singers. They were a link between the great voices of the past (think of Ella Fitzgerald, Ethel Merman, Edith Piaf) and the ears of people who couldn't get attuned to the howling self-pity of much contemporary rock but weren't ready to give up on pop music.

It's a small miracle—cynics would say a miracle of marketing by canny record executives—that the divas have flourished. For 40 years in Anglo-American pop, which sets music trends for the rest of the world, women have been an endangered species. Elvis, Stevie Wonder, Bruce Springsteen, Kurt Cobain—these were the ones who mattered. Rock's primal image was of a man and his guitar, the tortured satyr and his magic lute. "Chicks" were allowed to scream in the audience or sing harmonies. They were expected to play one role: backup.

All right, fine. Women would become vocal virtuosos with a comic touch, like Bette Midler. That women also became global pop superstars is thanks to Whitney Houston (and her mentor at Arista Records, Clive Davis). It was an old recipe—great chops, exotic looks and a clever choice of material—that had served Lena Horne, Eartha Kitt, Abbey Lincoln and Houston's cousin Dionne Warwick. But in the harsh prevailing winds of mid-'80s rap and heavy metal, Houston was a welcome spring breeze. Her delicacy of phrasing made songs like *Saving All My Love for You* and *The Greatest Love of All* easy listening in the best sense. Her prom-queen glamour made her an ideal star of the early video era, an antidote to Cyndi Lauper's ditzy ditties and Madonna's bad-girl sass.

Her first album, *Whitney Houston,* sold 10 million copies to become the all-time best-selling debut. The follow-up, *Whitney*, was the first by a female to enter the U.S. *Billboard* chart at No. 1. Her 1992 cover of Dolly Parton's *I Will Always Love You* reigned as the No. 1 single in *Billboard* for 14 weeks; its album, *The Bodyguard*, sold 33 million units.

Houston's huge success spurred a dozen divas-in-waiting. Many noted the structure of Houston's big hits—a slow-tempo devotional tune that escalates from the foreplay of whispers to the explosive orgasm of wails and whoops—and made the mistake of imitating it. Dion's early English-language albums are almost touching in their fidelity to the Whitney formula. It took her a while to realize she could relax on record.

Mariah Carey is the most successful Whitney wannabe. Like Houston, she'll mix ballads with synthesized dance music; she's a handsome woman with a video flair; she has a patron in Tommy Mottola, boss of her record company, who is also her husband. Carey has even outsold Houston in the '90s, partly because she releases albums at a busier pace. One big difference:

GLORIA ESTEFAN Havana-born, she is America's favorite Hispanic entertainer. Age: 39. Sales: 45 million albums

TONI BRAXTON The Aretha of the '90s? Braxton's first CD was a monster hit. Age: 29. Sales: 9 million albums

Houston sings straight soprano with some church inflection; Carey is a coloratura. She could even be called a cubist, for she appraises nearly every note in every song from a dozen or more angles. Her jazzy riffs suggest demon virtuosity, but it could also be musical browsing.

Thrushes like Carey, Houston, Estefan and Dion make music that is meant to be liked. Most of their music is not just middle of the road; it tiptoes on the white line in the middle of the middle of the road. And in social norms, the pop diva adheres to the proper side of the gender split in music. She is expected to be a sister before a lover; the operative slur word is "nice." Pop is the boarding school where the good girls live. Rock is the shooting gallery where the naughty boys hang out.

Somewhere between these polar opposites there should be a place for an outlaw diva. She can do some of the cool-guy things: write songs about malaise and disorientation, play a harmonica, take herself mighty seriously, sell 16 million copies of her first big CD. Why, she could

be Alanis Morissette—the mean Céline, the pariah Mariah, the anti-Whitney.

Anyway, that's how the 22-year-old comes across on a first hearing of the *Jagged Little Pill* CD. Morissette's songs sound aggressive, grudging, desperate. Her alto lurches among the octaves, from growl to shriek. A typical phrase will end in a gasp, as if one of the emotional inferiors in her songs had suddenly retaliated by pressing thumb and forefinger on her windpipe. The voice of Sinéad O'Connor, perhaps, in the mind of Patti Smith.

But Morissette is not that simple. A former teen star in her native Canada, she's smart enough to give her choruses sing-along melodies and overdubbed tight harmonies.

And that is Morissette's dirty little secret: inside her edgy plaints are craft and a yen to please. She's a mainstream diva in spite of herself. Her album is bubblegum music next to piano-princess Tori Amos' *Boys for Pele*, with its opaque lyrics, a voice that runs amuck over the octaves and the famous inside photo of Amos with a suckling piglet at her breast. Yet Morisette's album was the smash. Moral: You can be weird—but not too weird.

That is the message attended to by divas of every nation, creed and color. Like Enya, the Celtic lass whose ethereal soundscapes might have emanated from a very gentle UFO. She sings in Gaelic, English and Latin—the languages of family, school and church. Her melodies are so mellow as to seem downright shy, yet so popular that an entire genre of new music is known simply as Enya.

Or like the latest challenger for America's R. and B. diva crown, Toni Braxton, whose second CD, *Secrets*, sold 2 million copies in 1996. At 29, Braxton is an intriguing mix of strength and vulnerability, of pop-star outgoingness and old-school reserve. Her music has it both ways, too: she switches easily between dynamic, danceable rhythm tracks and more poignant, melodic songs delivered in a lush contralto. "Although they're sad love songs," she insists, "I always try to portray it like everything's going to be O.K.; I'm still strong." Spoken like a diva. ∎

The Perils of Anonymity

Whodunit? When a novel by "Anonymous" skewered the Clintons' 1992 run for the presidency, the mystery author lived to regret his grand deception

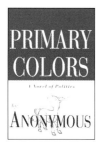

FOR MUCH OF 1996, IT SEEMED THAT everyone in Washington D.C.—a city where it is considered impossible to keep a secret—was obsessively grappling with one of the best-kept literary secrets of recent years: Who was "Anonymous," the reclusive author of the wildly successful book *Primary Colors*. The deftly drawn, acid-tongued political novel, a thinly veiled re-creation of the 1992 Democratic presidential primary race, was hailed by book reviewers and politicos alike as a dead-on snapshot of modern politics. The book scaled the best-seller lists and sold more than one millions copies. Its success was propelled by the brilliant publicity stunt of keeping the author's name a secret. But when the mystery was finally solved, the fun of the game gave way to serious questions of journalistic ethics.

Primary Colors was the best aide's-eye view of politics since Robert Penn Warren's *All the King's Men,* published exactly 50 years before. Narrated in the voice of Henry Burton, a George Stephanopoulos clone and the grandson of a Martin Luther King-like civil rights martyr, the novel painted a coruscating picture of immoral Governor Jack Stanton and his wife (generally assumed to be the Clintons) and included fictional sketches of an insider's *Who's Who* of the Clinton '92 campaign, from James Carville to Harold Ickes to Mario Cuomo. Yet the book transcended its gossipy tone in its moving account of how Henry Burton's youthful idealism is transformed into chilling cynicism in the pursuit of power.

Who was Anonymous? Leading candidates ranged from someone within the Clinton circle, like former Deputy Treasury Secretary Roger Altman, to journalists like *Newsweek* political columnist Joe Klein. But none of them took credit for the book.

Newsweek's Klein, who had traveled extensively with the '92 Clinton campaign, was a leading suspect. At first he was content to coyly deny authorship. But in February, after *New York* magazine offered a convincing argument that Klein was Anonymous—via a rigorous textual comparison of the novel against his columns—Klein was adamant, even abusive in his denials. He publicly berated the magazine and attacked its editor.

One of the few who knew the truth—that Klein was indeed Anonymous—was *Newsweek* editor Maynard Parker. In February he published an item guessing at Anonymous' identity (not Klein), thus dragging *Newsweek* into Klein's credibility gap. But in July, Klein was finally exposed by a handwriting analysis conducted by the Washington *Post*, which had acquired a copy of an early manuscript of the book that included the author's handwritten notes. A day later, Klein owned up.

The revelation that Klein, a practicing journalist, had gone on record with deliberate lies shocked fellow journalists. "The public looks at us as people who make judgments about character," said Tim Russert of NBC News, "When they see one of us lying, it hurts everyone." A blistering editorial in the New York *Times* called Klein's actions "corrupt."

Klein was put on temporary leave from *Newsweek* and quit his job at CBS, where he had been a commentator—and where he had failed to level with Dan Rather over his authorship of the book.

Yet like Governor Stanton himself, Klein survived and prospered: Hollywood bought the screen rights to his novel for $1.5 million, and he left *Newsweek* to write political columns for the *New Yorker*. For "Anonymous," there was no secret about the primary colors of 1996. They were pink—for shame—and green—for money. ■

All the Screen's a Stage

And all the men and women in Hollywood merely want to play Shakespeare, the hottest scriptwriter of the year

TABLOID-TV ANCHORS ANNOUNCE A BLOODY FEUD between two of Verona Beach's most notorious clans—thug royalty, whose young princes have the family name tattooed on their skulls. The streets of this resort town sizzle with ethnic enmity and the attitude clash of drag queens and skinheads. When the hormonal humidity is this high, only fools fall in love. So the daughter of one clan has eyes only for the son of her dad's hated rival. She searches for him in her dreams, by her swimming pool, beneath her balcony. She agonizes that he is a hated Montague. "Wherefore art thou Romeo?" she asks.

Oh, it's a Shakespeare movie! Well, there goes the youth market, out like the life in Claire Danes' and Leonardo DiCaprio's bodies at the end of the turbo-glam teen weepie, William Shakespeare's *Romeo and Juliet.*

But soft, what light through movie mogul's closed mind breaks? It is the glimmer of belief that there might be an audience for films based on the plays of Shakespeare. Since 1993, when Kenneth Branagh's rompish *Much Ado About Nothing* earned $23 million at the domestic box office on an $8 million budget, studios have begun to belly up to the Bard. After its romantic fling with Jane Austen, Hollywood besieged the multiplex with iambic pentameter in 1996. And when *Romeo and Juliet*, which cost just $16 million to make, showed real muscle at the box office, grossing $42 million in its first 6 weeks, it was a good bet that more movies based on the Bard would be coming soon to a theater near you.

The Bard boom actually began at Christmas 1995, which saw a stolid *Othello* (with Branagh and Laurence Fishburne) and a brutally enthralling, modern-dress *Richard III* (Ian McKellen). In late October 1996 three new Shakespeare films went on view: *Romeo and Juliet*, Al Pacino's *Looking for Richard* and *Twelfth Night*, directed by veteran British theater hand Trevor Nunn. Branagh released a four-hour, uncut *Hamlet* at Christmas. Filmmakers were trying every tactic—lavish spectacle, frenzied camerabatics and the casting of young stars—to put the masses in the seats.

In *Looking for Richard*, director-star Pacino placed himself front and center, performing scenes from *Richard III*, quizzing Brit theater luminaries and Manhattan street dwellers on the relevance of Shakespeare and whether Americans could act it. The result was naive, wildly self-indulgent and weirdly mesmerizing. Nunn's *Twelfth Night*, a comedy of Eros about loving brother/sister twins separated in a shipwreck and embroiled in a game of mistaken sexual identity, began as an upmarket *Blue Lagoon*, veered into farce, then darkened till it seemed a lost work of Chekhov's.

Twelfth Night was a play transferred to film. *Romeo and Juliet* was, defiantly, a movie. Director Baz Luhrmann enveloped Romeo and his goodfellas in portentous slo-mo for the shootouts, giddy fast-mo for comedy scenes. The camera literally ran circles around the lovers. When Romeo saw Juliet, his eye exploded in fireworks. The sound track pulsed with rap, rock and sound effects right out of a Hong Kong melodrama. The style was studiously kicky, MTV meets the Globe Theater.

Luhrmann, an Australian, made imaginative decisions that were, arguably, true to Shakespeare. "His stories are full of sex, violence, tragedy, comedy because he was, first of all, a great entertainer," Luhrmann said. "His audience was 3,000 drunken, fighting people, bear baiters and prostitutes." If that sounds like a Friday-night crowd at a big-city multiplex, well, sometimes it takes a radical like Baz Luhrmann to get to the root of a natural-born screenwriter like William Shakespeare. ∎

Broadway Brings in 'Da New

No falling chandeliers! No capering cats! No hovering helicopters! Two inventive shows bring new talent—and new audiences—to Broadway

THE MUSICAL THEATER, LONG ENTHRALLED BY PRO-
duction-heavy spectaculars of British origin, was
revived in 1996 by an injection of scruffy American
energy. The downtown musical *Rent* and the exhilarating dance show *Bring in 'Da Noise/Bring in 'Da Funk*
brought to Broadway the element it most needs if it is to
survive: new, diverse audiences. But this rebirth of the
musical was ushered in by the death of one of its creators.

The demise of a promising theatrical talent is always
tragic, but Jonathan Larson's legacy makes his all the
more painful. *Rent*, a rock opera based on Puccini's *La
Bohème*, opened to an ecstatic reception in New York City
just three weeks after Larson's sudden death at 35 from
an aortic aneurism. When critics hailed it as the breakthrough musical of the '90s, theatergoers began streaming
downtown, to the way-off-Broadway New York Theatre
Workshop. Within a week the show had sold out its entire
run, and it soon transferred to a Broadway house.

Rent is the most exuberant, original American musical to come along in this decade. Larson updated *La
Bohème* and set it among the artists, addicts, prostitutes
and street people of New York City's East Village. In the
place of Puccini's Mimi, dying of tuberculosis, is Larson's
Mimi (Daphne Rubin-Vega), a drug-addicted dancer in
an S&M club who is suffering from AIDS. The Rudolfo she
falls for is Roger (Adam Pascal), an HIV-positive rock
singer who longs for one great song to leave behind.

AIDS is the shadow hovering over all the people in
Rent, but the musical does not dwell on illness or turn
preachy; it is too busy celebrating life and chronicling its
characters' efforts to squeeze out every last drop of it. The
show is a bit overloaded with characters and subplots,

HEADING UPTOWN: *Rent,* above, featured a large cast of new
faces; *Noise's* Savion Glover, right, was a show-biz vet at 22

and the central love story, between Mimi and Roger, gets
all but lost in the bustle. But the energy and passion of
Larson's music makes up for it. A five-piece band on the
open, cluttered stage drives an insistent rock beat. The
lyrics (there is no spoken dialogue) are resonant but not
sanctimonious, with snatches of easy wit and clever,
rolling rhymes that never sound forced.

Rent was a surprising pick-me-up for another season
in which Broadway's musicals were mainly revivals *(The
King & I, A Funny Thing Happened on the Way to the
Forum, Chicago)*. *Rent* was Broadway's dream come true:
an audacious, really new musical with crossover appeal
and half a dozen starmaking roles. All that was missing
was its creative genius to take a bow—and promise more.

The creative genius of *Bring in 'Da Noise*, Savion
Glover, took a bow every night as chief choreographer and
virtuoso of his show. Produced and directed by George C.
Wolfe, head of the New York Shakespeare Festival, *'Da
Noise* tells the story of the black experience
in the U.S. in a series of vignettes, some
blazingly the-
atrical, some
only a set-up
for hoofing.

But what hoof-
ing! The nine gifted
dancers, all men, take
the stage with demon drive.
The sounds vary as strains of jazz,
hip-hop and gospel interweave.
This raucous show is about as far
removed from the classic buck-
and-wing as tap can get. The
dancers slap down the beat hard,
and, to further rattle the eardrums,
they are miked at the ankle. The
result: pure visceral excitement.

At 22, Savion Glover was
already a Broadway veteran.
He made his debut at 12 in
Tap Dance Kid, and later
starred in both *Black and
Blue* and *Jelly's Last Jam.*
Glover's silhouette—arms
raised but loose, hips and
legs stamping out the action
—was indelible. The show's
book may have been weak,
but in this revue the feet
brought in the news. ■

With a major retrospective of 225 paintings, drawings and sculptures at New York City's Museum of Modern Art, **JASPER JOHNS** was once again pop art's man of the hour. One quibble: critics feared that in recent years the quality of Johns' work ... flagged

ICON: Johns' flags were a head start for pop art

A Michelangelo in Manhattan?

For almost a century the small statue of Cupid stood quietly in the stately mansion on New York City's Fifth Avenue, near the Metropolitan Museum of Art, that became the French Embassy's Cultural Center in 1952. But in 1996 Cupid became one of the city's most famous residents: New York University art professor Kathleen Weil-Garris Brandt, who had spotted the statue through a window in 1995, claimed it was a lost work of Michelangelo. Art scholars scurried to take sides: Was Cupid the only Michelangelo on U.S. soil—or just a piece of bric-a-brac?

Julie to Tony: Take a Hike!

No one would have expected Mary Poppins to throw a hissy fit. But when she was the only one in her Broadway musical hit *Victor/Victoria* to be nominated for a Tony Award, theater legend Julie Andrews put her foot down. In front of an adoring matinee crowd, she announced that she was bowing out of the Tonys. "I have searched my conscience ... and I find that I cannot accept this nomination—and prefer to stand with the egregiously overlooked," said Andrews, still in costume. Perhaps most overlooked: director Blake Edwards, Andrews' husband.

Revenge: How Sweet It Is

Hell hath no fury—and Hollywood, it turns out, hath no better box-office—than a woman scorned. *The First Wives*

CUPID: Renaissance man?

Club, starring the terrific trio of Bette Midler, Goldie Hawn and Diane Keaton as discarded wives of a certain age who plot revenge on the husbands who turned them in for trophy wives, became a megahit, grossing more than $100 million. Like 1991's *Thelma & Louise*, the movie dipped into a well of shared female rage—in this case at the power imbalance that allows men to use up a woman's best years, then replace her with an ingenue with youth and looks. Movie theaters reported parties of as many as 60 women attending en masse to cheer the adaptation of Olivia Goldsmith's 1992 best seller.

Blame It on the Macarena

Let's see: there was the Bunny Hop, the Twist, the Frug—and in 1996 the Macarena, the novelty dance that swept America and wowed the Democratic Convention. First recorded in 1993 by the veteran Spanish duo Los del Rio, *Hey Macarena* and its *Hokey-Pokey*–style dance conquered the world before Americans surrendered to a bottom-heavy mix by Miami's Bayside Boys band. Ready? Put your right arm out in front of you, with the palm down. Now the left ...

HEY, MACARENA! This year's Electric Boogie

EXCELLENT EX-ES: For many, Hawn, Keaton and Midler were vendors of vicarious vengeance

CRITICS' CHOICE

Despite the takeover of pop culture by aliens, the arts thrived in 1996. The English Patient *brought David Lean-like scope back to the screen. Still laboring under a fatwa, Salman Rushdie produced one of his best novels. A rock update of* La Bohème *brought the Broadway musical resoundingly into the '90s. The Fugees sold millions of rap records free of gangsta's toxicity. And Jerry Seinfeld stayed funny, defying sitcom entropy.*

1 **THE ENGLISH PATIENT** For so many European wanderlusters who found an Eden in the Sahara, the desert was a woman—dazzling, enveloping, with a vastness that held all their dreams. In such a place, just before World War II, the Hungarian aristocrat Count Laszlo de Almasy finds his ideal desert woman and follows her to hell. He then lives, just barely, to tell the tale to a ministering angel (Juliette Binoche) who can give him what he needs: not absolution but understanding. The lovers are Ralph Fiennes—all coiled sexiness, threat shrouded in hauteur—and Kristin Scott Thomas, who has the gift of making intelligence erotic; they come together in a dance of doom that is abrasive, mysterious, powerful, inevitable. Anthony Minghella's beautiful film, based on the Michael Ondaatje novel, gets the rapture right.

2 **Big Night** Neither the time (the 1950s) nor the place (the Jersey Shore) is propitious for a gourmet Italian restaurant. But the struggles of the immigrant Pilaggi brothers to impose their delicate risottos on a red-sauce culture are perhaps the year's most unlike-

ly success. Primo, the chef (Tony Shalhoub), has the soul of an artist—watchful, uncompromising, mildly depressive. Secondo, the maître d' (Stanley Tucci, who, with Campbell Scott, wrote and direct-ed), is trying vainly to be an American entrepreneur. Stumbling toward bankruptcy, they also sail toward wisdom in this beautifully acted and utterly deli-cious comedy of table manners.

3 **Trainspotting** *A Hard Day's Night* on heroin, this gleefully amoral come-dy turned a quartet of Scot-tish drug addicts into transatlantic icons. The denizens of the Edinburgh

lower depths—blithe abusers of heroin, alcohol, nicotine and their best friends—are witty, cunning, brimming with the kind of sociopathic bravado that spells sexiness in the mid-'90s. Well, tsk-tsk and all that. But good movies make their own morals. And though grim death hangs like crepe over our antihero (star-in-the-making Ewan McGregor) and his mates, the John Hodge script and

Danny Boyle's direction couldn't be more vital.

4 **Lone Star** A skeleton, unearthed after a 30-year rest, leads sheriff Sam Deeds (Chris Cooper) on a deeply disturbing dig into his own past and that of a Texas border town that turns out to be a lot less somnolent than it looks. Sam manages to recover a lost love (shiningly por-trayed by Elizabeth Peña) but the countywide net-work of corruption eventu-ally snags them both. Writer-director John Sayles is a subtle, patient crafts-man who understands both fiction and history; he has a gift for showing the strangeness lurking be-neath the bland surfaces of American life—without a lot of bloody melodrama.

5 **Chungking Express** By the time Americans finally catch up with Hong Kong cinema—since the mid-'80s the world's most turbulent and entertaining—it may have been suffocated by the censorious new lords from the mainland. So Wong Kar-wai's kicky art movie (made in 23 days) about two cops on the night shift not only is as mod as tomorrow's couture, it also

serves as a nostalgia trip through what has been Asia's freest colony. Here are a cool killer–drug queen (Brigitte Lin) and an indefatigable ingenue (pop pixie Faye Wang) exercising their wiles on lovelorn guys—all caught in Wong's murky, slo-mo camera eye.

6 **Secrets & Lies** A white working-class London woman and her long-lost black daughter, unaware of each other's existence for almost 30 years, are reunited in this unexpectedly sunny drama from Britain's Mike Leigh, long known for his corrosive studies of family breakdowns. Leigh is an impresario of improv

who lets his actors find their own words. *Secrets & Lies* is a miniature epic, nearly 2½ hours of bruising tenderness and bravura acting, yet it sails along with the expectation that some families can end up with the happiness they have worked so hard to avoid. It features an Oscar-worthy performance by Brenda Blethyn, playing the mother as a teary, tempestuous tornado.

7 **Flirting with Disaster** Plunging into it, more like. Mel Coplin (Ben Stiller) assumes that somewhere in the neon wilderness of modern America his birth parents are alive, well and no nutsier than his adoptive ones. The conventional wisdom of mental health dictates that he seek them out. The unconventional sensibility of writer-director David O. Russell dictates that nothing and no one Mel encounters on his odyssey shall turn out to be what they at first seem to be. Mel's is a world where his social worker is terminally randy; his real mother and father are major drug traffickers; a pair of stern federal agents are revealed to be gently gay. Russell observes these and other folkways with an understated objectivity that renders his comic subversions all the more deadly.

8 **Everyone Says I Love You** All singing, all dancing, all talking, as they used to say. In Woody

Allen's lovely flight of fancy, the singing is often kind of croaky, the dancing sort of klutzy and the dialogue pure Woody—the noises that psychologically aware people make when they are at desperate sexual cross-purposes. But such folks are entitled to their romantic yearnings. This film's good-humored poignance—and high originality—lies in the contrast drawn between the characters' passionate desire to put a little music in their lives and their inability to carry a tune.

9 **Evita** It might have been an Oliver Stone political screed or a Ken Russell hallucinogen; the lead actress might have been Meryl Streep or Michelle Pfeiffer. But here it is—20 years after Tim Rice and Andrew Lloyd Webber first produced their gorgeously cynical opera about Eva Perón—reimagined through the eye of director Alan Parker and the flesh of Madonna. The take is dense and studious, an aptly conservative adaptation of a pop classic; it lets the score seduce and the star shine. Madonna, who is up to the vocal demands of the role, makes Eva—sexual predator, social climber, queen of the Argentine, would-be saint—an appealing character in a

cautionary fable. The moral: celebrity needs suffering and early death as its price and consummation.

10 **Jerry Maguire** In corporate America the assertion of principle is often the prelude to self-immolation. Case in point: Jerry Maguire (a superb Tom Cruise). Soon after he calls on his colleagues in a sports agency to consider human values as well as the bottom line, he gets fired. Spinning his wheels wildly, he seeks moral traction in an icy-slick world, aided by his one remaining client (a testy Cuba Gooding Jr.) and his sole employee (Renee Zellweger, fierce and mousy). Blending romance and realism, writer-director Cameron Crowe creates a fine, confident, endearing comedy ∎

1 EZ STREETS (CBS) Ken Olin's *thirtysomething* days are long gone. Here he's a desperate detective—the central figure in one of the more profound crime dramas ever to hit a television screen. Lyrically bleak in tone, *EZ Streets* is a haunting meditation on moral ambiguity, on city politics and—most effectively—on fate. Alas, the dismally rated series was abruptly canceled after two airings. Alone, perhaps, we anxiously await its scheduled return in the 1997 TV season.

8 The Essence of Emeril (The TV Food Network) Even with all those seasonings at their disposal, cooking shows have been notoriously bland offerings during the past few years—until the brash New Orleans chef Emeril Lagasse arrived to bring on the spice. Spirited, at home on the range, and prone to free-association, he is a kind of

Frank Sinatra of cooking-show hosts, a kitchen-bound swinger who likes to start off segments like this: "Lamb shanks, if you can find 'em—you get 'em, baby."

2 Seinfeld (NBC) Hard to believe—but the granddaddy of modern urban sitcoms is *still* hipper, *still* wittier than its off-spring. Now in its eighth season, the show has maintained its brilliant comic rhythms and dark undertones, and 1996 boasted some of the most original episodes ever. Kramer's stash of Japanese businessmen—need we say more?

3 Pride and Prejudice (A&E) Having arrived just when it seemed Austen-mania could be borne no longer, this lush production radiantly revived the rage for Jane. With perfectly observed sets and a keen grasp of the subversive social themes that underlie

Austen's comedy, this mini-series put competitors like PBS' *Moll Flanders* to shame.

4 Murder One (ABC) Watch one, get two free. Chronicling three consecutive trials rather than a single one all season, the revamped legal thriller returned more clearly focused and more energetically paced. The real bonus was the arrival of Anthony LaPaglia as the brash, ethically messy Wyler.

5 Politically Incorrect's Election Coverage (Comedy Central) It would be a challenge indeed to plumb recent TV history to find a funnier piece of sketch comedy than *PI's* Republican Party info-mercial spoof, which aired the week of the San Diego convention. As the networks lulled us to sleep, Bill Maher's wry, combative round-table show succeeded in covering the campaign with flair and bite.

6 Profit (Fox) A heinous antihero (named Jim Profit), who made J.R. Ewing look like Bob Saget on Prozac. A corporate empire shrouded in mystery. A wry subtext that attacked the evils of techno-culture. *Profit* had it all—except a decent-size audience. This mesmerizingly original thriller set in corporate America was canceled after just a few outings, and yet we will never forget the chill of star Adrian Pasdar's insidious whisper.

7 Ned and Stacey (Fox) Thankfully, this smart sitcom was not the victim of its network's scratch-happy spirit. Now in its second season, the show about

mismatched lovebirds in the making has given us a chance to feast on the prodigious comic gifts of Thomas Haden Church, who plays Ned, a voluble adman. Is there a more engagingly contemptuous character on TV? We don't think so.

9 Relativity (ABC) At first this new drama from Ed Zwick and Marshall Herskovitz seemed a tad too precious, a touch too eager to wrap up its conflicts with tidy bows. But the series, focused on a pair of new young lovers, quickly managed to ground itself more firmly in the rhythms of a real relationship. Poignant but never overwrought, *Relativity* has become one of television's finest hours.

10 Taking on the Kennedys (PBS) This documentary about the 1994 congressional race between young Patrick Kennedy and Kevin Vigilante, an accomplished physician, has all the populist wit of a Michael Moore piece without the contrivances. In a year when Jacqueline Kennedy's artifacts were sold for millions, we learn that Vigilante didn't stand a chance against an opponent who wooed voters with the musk of Camelot.■

2 **Esa-Pekka Salonen and the Los Angeles Philharmonic** *Bernard Herrmann: the Film Scores* (Sony Classical). Remember the shower in *Psycho*? The tower in *Vertigo*? Hitchcock was the director, but it was the gruff composer Herrmann who brought the scenes to vivid, shrieking life. Salonen eloquently states the case for this and seven more of Herrmann's best scores.

3 **The Fugees** *The Score* (Ruffhouse/Columbia). Tough but tuneful, ready to entertain but unwilling to compromise, this Haitian-American rap trio proved that positive, semi-political hip-hop could outsell gangsta rap—and alter-

native rock too. Drawing from reggae and soul, the Fugees created a fresh bicultural sound.

4 **Patty Loveless** *The Trouble with the Truth* (Epic). The title may imply emotional hesitancy, but this hardscrabble country diva has no trouble whatsoever singing about betrayal, abuse, loneliness—and the will to survive. Her spare versions of nifty dirges by Gary Nicholson, Richard Thompson and Matraca Berg are rites of downhome exorcism.

1 **CASSANDRA WILSON** *NEW MOON DAUGHTER* (Blue Note). With her knowing, nocturnal voice, Wilson is the queen of contemporary jazz vocalists and the true heir of Billie Holiday and Sarah Vaughn. Here she branches out with remakes of songs by the likes of U2, Hank Williams, even the Monkees. Wilson graces all of them—covers as well as spellbinding originals—with a classy Afrocentricity that shatters boundaries even as it breaks your heart.

5 **Nusrat Fateh Ali Khan & Michael Brook** *Night Song* (Real World/Caroline). Khan, a huge star in his native Pakistan, sings *qawwali*—Sufi religious music that, like gospel, seeks to bring listeners closer to God through ecstatic vocals and rhythms. Here, with Canadian producer-guitarist Michael Brook, Khan sings of earthly love; the spiraling, urgent songs are mostly in Urdu, but Khan's passion and purpose need no translation.

6 **Sublime** *Sublime* (Gasoline Alley/MCA). A good-hearted street riot of punk rock, avant-garde hip-hop and ska (a faster, jerkier reggae precursor), Sublime's music is hard to categorize and harder still to resist. The band is already defunct (the lead

singer and songwriter, the puckishly gifted Brad Nowell, died of a heroin overdose in May 1996), but no rock album this year sounds more alive.

7 **Ani DiFranco** *Dilate* (Righteous Babe Records). Tart, topical songs from this 25-year-old genre-bending singer-guitarist, who blends folk, punk, trip-hop and whatever else strikes her fancy into insurgent and often arrestingly beautiful music. DiFranco hitches these tunes to scathing lyrical takes on romance and gender issues, then releases her records through her own record company.

8 **Marcus Roberts** *Time and Circumstance* (Columbia). Since departing from Wynton Marsalis' band in 1991, Roberts has established himself as the most cerebral of jazz soloists, with a taste for sensuous, rich chords and intricately patterned melodies that resound with jazz's history yet push toward higher ground. Roberts polishes his work to a high gloss but never indulges in needless flash.

9 **Bobby McFerrin and Chick Corea** *The Mozart Sessions* (Sony Classical). The classical-music industry is suffering from a dearth of star performers—so along comes McFerrin, famed for his otherworldly vocalese and infectious charm. He and jazz pianist Corea turn in original, joyous performances of the familiar A major and D minor piano concertos with the St. Paul Chamber Orchestra.

10 **Maxwell** *Maxwell's Urban Hang Suite* (Columbia). Soulful, seductive and as smooth as lingerie, this charismatic R.-and-B. theme album follows a single love affair from the eyes-meeting-across-a-crowded-club start all the way to the marriage-proposal endgame. Think Marvin Gaye. Think Smokey Robinson. Think classic soul that recalls the '70s but knows all about the '90s. ■

FICTION AND POETRY

1 THE MOOR'S LAST SIGH (Pantheon). Salman Rushdie's first novel since *The Satanic Verses* exuberantly details its protagonist's fall from the grace of a wealthy Indian childhood into the hands of a madman who plans to kill him once the story ends. The hero survives, and Rushdie's bountiful comic narrative triumphs.

2 Infinite Jest (Little, Brown). The year's longest good novel, at 1,079 pages, is by turns enthralling and exasperating, with the emphasis on the former. David Foster Wallace brilliantly extrapolates cultural and commercial trends into a nightmarishly funny near future where years are named after products. One of the many subplots involves a movie, *Infinite Jest*, that can literally make its viewers die laughing.

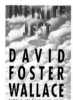

3 The Tailor of Panama (Knopf). The cold war may be history, but the master chronicler of its intrigues hasn't lost his touch: in his latest, John le Carré offers a typically stylish and subtle turn on the espionage game. Nothing is actually going on in Panama that demands being spied upon, but that doesn't stop a couple of itchy agents in British intelligence. In Panama City they blackmail a well-connected tailor, who obediently weaves a dire plot against British interests out of whole cloth. As with any good fiction,

imagined events lead to very real repercussions.

4 Ants on the Melon (Random House). Virginia Hamilton Adair's first book of poetry is one of the year's imaginative peaks. The 87 poems by this 83-year-old poet are short—the longest runs to 52 lines—and as richly terse as haiku. But the many themes Adair addresses in this collection—life and love and loss—are clear and capacious, a distillation of life into a perfect ordering of words.

5 The Odyssey (Viking). In thrilling fashion, Princeton Literature professor Robert Fagles' verse translation retells an epic tale 2,700 years old that some would argue is the mother of all novels. In recounting Odysseus' long journey home from the Trojan War, Fagles finds a contemporary English style that beckons to the ear as well as the eye. His straightforward new version starts off speedily and connects with its economical, concrete descriptions. ■

NONFICTION

1 ANGELA'S ASHES (Scribner). When it comes to sad tales of childhood hardships, "nothing can compare with the Irish version." So writes former schoolteacher Frank McCourt, who quickly proves his point. His memoir of growing up poor in the slums of Limerick radiates misery, humor and the cheerful humanity that got him through.

2 Hitler's Willing Executioners (Knopf). In the year's most talked-about book, Harvard historian Daniel Jonah Goldhagen argues that the Holocaust should be blamed not just on Nazi faithful but also on ordinary anti-Semitic Germans. His evidence of widespread cruelty toward Jews by rank-and-file German soldiers seems irrefutable; his explanation for it has produced spirited debate on the source of human inhumanity.

3 Red China Blues (Anchor Books). Jan Wong, born the privileged daughter of Chinese-Canadian parents in Montreal, became a true-believing Maoist and decided in 1972 to return to the land of her ancestors. The journey led to disillusionment—and also to this lively and shrewd reminiscence. Wong still loves China, but she can laugh at it and her youthful follies.

4 A Life of Picasso: 1907-1917 (Random House). In the second volume of his biography, John Richardson applies his

skills as storyteller and art historian to a prodigious decade in Picasso's life. At the beginning a still struggling Spanish artist in Paris, he was by the end truly Picasso, a co-founder (with Georges Braque) of Cubism and the paradigmatic figure of modern art. From *Les Demoiselles d'Avignon* to Cubism, Richardson presents a behind-the-scenes look at the apotheosis of an artist.

5 My Dark Places (Knopf). James Ellroy's mother was murdered in 1958, when her only child was 10. The crime was never solved, and the son affected to be glad he was no longer under her strict spell. But now that Ellroy has grown famous as a writer of crime fiction—by no coincidence—he has decided to reopen the case and his own wounds. Ellroy's search for his mother's killer is part memoir, part detective story, part meditation on the kind of men who kill and the women who die at their hands. It displays a reality more chilling than fiction. ■

NOBEL PRIZES

Peace
Bishop Carlos Filepe Ximenes Belo and Jose Ramos Horta
For their efforts to end abuses by Indonesian forces in East Timor

Literature
Wislawa Szymborska
Polish poet

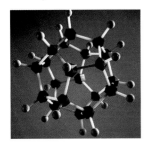

Medicine
Peter C. Doherty and Rolf M. Zinkernagel
For discovering how the immune system identifies cells infected with viruses

Economics
William S. Vickrey and James A. Mirrlees
For contributions to the theory of incentives under asymmetric information

Physics
David M. Lee, Robert C. Richardson and Douglas D. Osheroff
For their discovery of superfluidity in helium-3

Chemistry
Richard E. Smalley, Robert F. Curl Jr. and Sir Harold W. Kroto
For their discovery of a previously unknown class of carbon molecule

TONY AWARDS

Best Play
Master Class
Best Musical
Rent
Best Actress, Play
Zoe Caldwell
Master Class

Best Actor, Play
George Grizzard
A Delicate Balance
Best Actress, Musical
Donna Murphy
The King & I
Best Actor, Musical
Nathan Lane
A Funny Thing Happened on the Way to the Forum

BOOKS

Best-Selling Fiction
1. *The Celestine Prophecy*, Redfield
2. *Falling Up*, Silverstein
3. *Primary Colors*, Anonymous
4. *The Tenth Insight*, Redfield
5. *The Horse Whisperer*, Evans
6. *The Runaway Jury*, Grisham
7. *How Stella Got Her Groove Back*, McMillan
8. *Executive Orders*, Clancy
9. *Absolute Power*, Baldacci
10. *Moonlight Becomes You*, Clark

Non-Fiction
1. *Midnight in the Garden of Good and Evil*, Berendt
2. *Emotional Intelligence*, Goleman
3. *Undaunted Courage*, Ambrose
4. *The Dilbert Principal*, Adams
5. *How Could You Do That?* Schlessinger
6. *Rush Limbaugh Is A Big, Fat Idiot*, Franken
7. *In Contempt*, Darden with Walter
8. *Bad As I Wanna Be*, Rodman
9. *It Takes A Village*, Rodham Clinton
10. *Unlimited Access*, Aldrich

HOLLYWOOD FILMS

Domestic box-office leaders
1. *Independence Day*
2. *Twister*
3. *Mission: Impossible*
4. *The Rock*
5. *The Nutty Professor*
6. *The Birdcage*
7. *Ransom*
8. *A Time to Kill*
9. *Phenomenon*
10. *The First Wives Club*

TELEVISION

Fall season favorites
1. *ER*
2. *Seinfeld*
3. *Suddenly Susan*
4. *Friends*
5. *NFL Monday Night Football*
6. *Home Improvement*
7. *Single Guy*
8. *Spin City*
9. *NYPD Blue*
10. *Touched by an Angel*

ACADEMY AWARDS

Best Picture
Braveheart
Best Director
Mel Gibson
Braveheart
Best Actor
Nicolas Cage
Leaving Las Vegas
Best Actress
Susan Sarandon
Dead Man Walking
Best Supporting Actor
Kevin Spacey
The Usual Suspects
Best Supporting Actress
Mira Sorvino
Mighty Aphrodite

SPORTS

Baseball
• World Series
New York Yankees
• College World Series
Louisiana State Tigers

Basketball
• N.B.A. finals
Chicago Bulls

• NCAA Men
Kentucky Wildcats
• NCAA Women
Tennessee Lady Vols

Football
• Superbowl XXX
Dallas Cowboys
• Collegiate consensus
Florida Gators

Hockey
• Stanley Cup
Colorado Avalanche

Horse Racing
• Kentucky Derby
Grindstone
• Preakness Stakes
Louis Quatorze
• Belmont Stakes
Editor's Note
• Breeder's Cup Classic
Alphabet Soup

Golf
• Masters
Nick Faldo
• U.S. Open
Steve Jones
• U.S. Women's Open
Annika Sorenstam
• British Open
Tom Lehman
• P.G.A.
Mark Brooks
• L.P.G.A.
Laura Davies

Tennis
• Australian Open
*Boris Becker
Monica Seles*
• French Open
*Yevgeny Kafelnikov
Steffi Graf*
• Wimbledon
*Richard Krajicek
Steffi Graf*
• U.S. Open
*Pete Sampras
Steffi Graf*
• Olympic singles
*Andre Agassi
Lindsay Davenport*

Sources: Facts on File (Nobels, Tonys, Oscars, Sports), Cowles/Simba Information (Books), Baseline (Films), Electronic Media (Television)

FRACTURED

FAIRY TALE

As the royal marriage ends, young Prince William may be the monarchy's last, best hope

THE DREAM DIES hard. The Prince and Princess of Wales are two people who stumbled into a fantasy fervently embraced by millions.

AFTER THE FALL
How has the divorce affected Prince William?

She embodied it; he was swept up in it, much against his will. When the fairy tale began, all Charles wished for was more of what he had: a comfortable life of conscientious royal duty, playing polo, painting his pictures—and a nice, quiet double standard. People may never forgive him for puncturing the dream.

The divorce settlement announced in mid-July reopened the scrapbooks of memory,

A good deal is riding on the Eton schoolboy who one day will be called King William V.

reminding people of the dream that was too good to be true. The shy teenager in the diaphanous skirt. The wedding shot: he in his dashing uniform, she in her silly, billowing gown. He looking every inch Prince Charming, she gazing at him in rapture.

The Crown sent them forth to conquer the world, and they did. In just a year or so, they rejuvenated the royal family. Nights on television, mornings in the papers, there were pictures of them that made the rest of the news look meager and soiled: whirling around the dance floor in Australia with Diana's emerald necklace subbing as a headband, kicking up their heels at a White House ball and, back home, kissing at a polo match.

Now the marriage—and the fairy tale—are dead. Under the terms of the divorce agreement, Diana received a generous financial deal estimated at $23 million, and will keep her 30-odd-room apartment at Kensington Palace, but not the right to style herself as Her Royal Highness. Charles rid himself of the difficult, crowd-pleasing woman he married in what seems another age. But while Charles and Diana's legal ties were being severed, they are still joined by their children and, whatever their failures as husband and wife, they seem to have made a suc-

PRINCE CHARLES

Free at last of Diana, he is constrained by public opinion from marrying longtime mistress Camilla Parker Bowles

cess of their roles as father and mother. If the Waleses have damaged the monarchy terribly, they may also have provided its salvation in William, the bright, likable prince just emerging into young manhood and just beginning to capture the public's imagination. As the divorce brings one act of the royal drama to an end, another one begins, with a fresh and appealing star.

A GOOD DEAL IS RIDING ON THE BOY EXPECTED to become King William V. The current generation of royals has been catastrophic. At the time of his wedding in 1981, Charles was expected to update the traditional role of constitutional monarch, while Diana would be the charismatic popular symbol. But largely because of the rancor between the heir to the throne and his wife—fueled by Charles' affair with Camilla Parker Bowles—public acceptance of the monarchy is much weaker today than it was even five years ago. While the institution is not in mortal peril, discussion of a republic has become vigorous and respectable. The best scenario now is a three-act drama: long, long life to Her Majesty Queen Elizabeth II, who is exemplary; a brief reign for Charles, who might be as old as 70 when he ascends the throne; and then the reign of William, the Crown's last, best hope.

What kind of King might William make? At 14, he is at an age when many boys are trying to decide whether to dye their hair orange or green. But some judgments can be made even of one so young. He is an intelligent youngster—he passed the test for Eton, a tough prep school—and he has poise beyond his years. But it will be impossible to know for some time how the Waleses' shenanigans have strengthened or warped his character.

Life started well for William. His birth was an occasion of national rejoicing; the succession was secure and the perfect family established. Charles was crazy about him. Back then Charles and Diana were at their best as parents. They were determined not to replicate the clois-

tered childhood that left Charles forever wary socially and emotionally. When William was five and brother Harry three, they were sent to ordinary playgrounds around London. They went to fast-food joints and amusement parks and attended real schools, albeit exclusive ones. Charles had been tutored at home until age eight.

As a lad, Wills could be obstreperous, and photographers fed on his misbehavior. But by the time the future sovereign was eight or so, he had calmed down and was generally more reflective than Harry. He also showed precocious self-possession. With his ancient great-grandmother, the Queen Mum, he is a model little gentleman, helping to guide her down church steps and holding the umbrella over her head.

Life in a fishbowl is hard on anyone; for a child it is also very confusing. William has had to put up with volley after volley of mortifying revelations shouted from the headlines: Dad wants to be a tampon, the better to be close to his mistress; Mum was having an affair with that young riding instructor, who also taught William.

Yet, however irresponsible his parents became, they at least gave William options; he will have plenty to say about what university he attends and what he does after that. Meanwhile, there is one person close at hand who is ready and willing to instruct the prince in what is expected of him. Eton, where William matriculated in 1995, is close to Windsor Castle, where the Queen often weekends—and William frequently has tea with his grandmother by himself on Sundays at 4 p.m. A car is sent for him, and they spend a couple of hours together. What do they talk about? Duties.

Eton is a good preparation for those duties. It is famous for its blue bloods and for the statesmen and men of letters it has turned out. Eton students acquire an elegance and gloss, thanks to its strict drill. Up at 8, compulsory chapel after breakfast, classes all morning. A lengthy sports session follows, and afternoon classes start at 4. The traditional university prep subjects are required, but some outré electives such as Swahili and cooking are offered. There are rules for everything, and punishment is automatic. In Eton's self-contained world, titles confer no privileges, and the prince is probably not the only boy with a bodyguard. Eton has upgraded itself academically in the past 10 years and is now considered not just a training ground for the titled but one of the best schools in the country.

In the next few years, William's life will become more public and more complicated, and his personality will be more sharply defined. He is already going to dances, and is rated by his female contemporaries as "snoggable," Britspeak for sexy. That attribute has made him a pinup in teenage fanzines. But it won't help him rule.

William will have a powerful role in shaping the monarchy in the coming century, and Buckingham Palace is beginning to make use of him. He cannot afford to stumble. The burdens are enormous, but at least he is surrounded by billowing gusts of goodwill. He may be that stable leader who is so badly needed to strengthen a besieged but valuable institution. Long live the prince! ∎

PRINCESS DIANA
She's no longer "Her Royal Highness," but retains her dazzle, as displayed on a September visit to Washington, D.C.

A Simple Country Wedding

AVOIDING A HELI-copter assault by zealous photographers that might have outdone the ones onscreen in *Apocalypse Now*, **JOHN F. KENNEDY JR.**, 35, and **CAROLYN BESSETTE**, 30, managed to keep their marriage on Saturday, September 21, a secret from the press. Of course, the shy newlyweds couldn't hide forever; the tabloids later found them honeymooning in Turkey.

But the couple accomplished more than simply the news blackout. They managed to orchestrate a wedding that had dignity, style, mystery and joy, in the manner of the groom's mother. The occasion may have been the most important of Kennedy's adult life so far, publicly as well as privately, and he carried it off with an imagination and delicacy that not everyone assumed he possessed.

The setting was Cumberland Island, one of the wild, unspoiled Sea Islands just off the coast of Georgia, home to armadillos, wild boar and wild horses. There, in a simple wooden chapel, as crickets sang in the grass outside, the candlelight ceremony was performed by a Jesuit deacon.

On Friday night, about 40 close friends and relatives had gathered for the rehearsal dinner. Senator Edward Kennedy gave a humorous toast recalling John's childhood and quoting some poetry that sister Caroline had written about John when she was 10 or 12 years old. Caroline gave a toast that left many of the guests in tears. Then John toasted his bride, saying, "I am the happiest man alive."

The next day Bessette, a onetime publicist for Calvin Klein, walked down the aisle wearing a fluid, bias-cut dress of pearl-white crepe with a panel floating from the waist in the back that gave a suggestion of a train. In her hands, covered by long white gloves, the bride carried a small bouquet of lilies of the valley. The groom's boutonniere was made of cornflowers, the favorite flower of his father, and he wore a watch that had belonged to his father.

The groom's sister, Caroline Kennedy Schlossberg, was the matron of honor; Anthony Radziwill, the son of Jackie's sister Lee, served as best man. After the ceremony the couple walked over to a nearby fence to receive their guests' congratulations, when Bessette felt a tug on her bouquet. A wild horse had stretched its neck over the fence and was nibbling at the flowers.

The Unbearable Lightness of Shannon

Talk about coming down to Earth ... On September 26, spacewoman extraordinaire **SHANNON LUCID** finally returned to the home planet after six long months aloft. The 53-year-old shuttle veteran had amassed 223 days in orbit since 1985, making her America's most experienced astronaut. When hurricanes and technical glitches delayed shuttle flights that should have picked her up almost seven weeks earlier, Lucid's 188-day mission bested Russian cosmonaut Elena Kondakova, who had held the women's record for consecutive days in orbit. Lucid, who took the delays sportingly, joined her "two Yuris"—Russian cosmonauts Yuri Onufrienko and Yuri Usachev—on Mir in March. The trio got along well on the cramped Russian station, a cluster of six camper-size pods, where a "hot shower" was a tepid sponge bath. Lucid's landing brought a gift from President Clinton of the thing she confessed to most missing in space—candy—and Congress honored her with a Congressional Space Medal of Honor.

Surprise! Mr. Nice Beats the Beast

Heavyweight Mike Tyson could only complain, "I got caught in something strange." Or something quite wonderful, depending on your viewpoint. On November 9 **EVANDER HOLYFIELD**, 34 and thought to be on the ropes of his career, vanquished the supposedly invincible W.B.A. champion Tyson with an 11th-round TKO in Las Vegas to become only the second heavyweight champion—besides Muhammad Ali—to win the title on three separate occa-

sions. One of the sweetest men ever to practice the sweet science, Holyfield had won only two of his past four fights, and the Nevada state athletic commission was so worried about a heart irregularity that it would not sanction the fight without clearance from the Mayo Clinic. The new champ, a strongly religious man, credited his victory to his belief in Jesus and to the support of his new wife, Dr. Janice Itson, an internist whom he had met at a revival meeting several years ago.

Coming Up Rosie

Move over, Oprah—there's a new contender for your crown as queen of daytime talk TV. The newcomer is actress and comic **ROSIE O'DONNELL**, and you wouldn't believe her gimmick: no squabbling families, no trash talk, no unkempt yokels flaunting their unseemly moral transgressions ("She stripped at uncle's bachelor party"). O'Donnell, 34, is part brassy New Yorker, part perky den mother. She modeled her syndicated show, which quickly scored winning ratings, after those of cozy entertainers Dinah Shore, Merv Griffin and Mike Douglas. Rosie was so darn nice she even provided milk and Drake's Cakes for everyone in the studio audience.

A Revolutionary Meeting in Rome

Maybe religion is an opiate for masters *and* the masses. Supreme socialist **FIDEL CASTRO** certainly seemed dazzled by his visit to **POPE JOHN PAUL II** in late

November. Who knows what the noted atheist and the noted anti-Marxist talked about in their private Vatican meeting? The Catholic teachers who schooled each of them back in the '30s? Why Castro expelled so many priests? How the Pope helped bring about the demise of Marxist Europe? They did agree on one thing: a papal trip scheduled for 1998 to Castro's island, the only Latin American country the Pontiff has not visited.

A Chip off the Old Lip

In the 1990s, ingenuedom has become interminable: Lauren Bacall was a woman at 19; Sandra Bullock and Sarah Jessica Parker are girls at 31. But then many young actresses today work harder at charming us with their boppy neuroses than luring us with their sensuality. Of this sin Hollywood's Girl of the Year, **LIV TYLER**, is not guilty. A card-carrying adolescent who turned 19 in 1996, Tyler is an ingenue unflustered by her sexuality, one who has lately been busy cultivating her inner grownup. This year she starred in three big films: Tom Hanks' *That Thing You Do*, Bernardo Bertolucci's *Stealing Beauty* and James Mangold's *Heavy.* Pretty good company for a model-actress who first came to the world's attention wearing a silver bra in an unseemly Aerosmith video featuring her father, the band's lead singer Steven Tyler. Liv's mother is a famed '70s model and groupie, Bebe Buell, and young Liv grew up thinking her father was a rocker of a different sort, Todd Rundgren. She claims she realized Tyler was her father immediately upon seeing him at an Aerosmith concert. The giveaway: the Mick Jaggeresque lips shared by father and daughter.

Golf Takes a Ride on the Tiger

From the time when **TIGER WOODS**, 21, was a toddler, his father Earl and mother Kultida encouraged his golf talent. At five he appeared on *That's Incredible*, and the kid has been living up to the title ever since. After coming from behind to capture an unprecedented third U.S. Amateur in a row in spectacular style in August, Woods turned pro and promptly won two tourneys and $790,594. Woods' father is an American black, his mother a Thai. His dark skin, pan-Pacific background and incandescent, winning personality mark him as a potential global marketing superstar in an almost all-white game. He cleaned up in the first week he turned pro, as Nike and the golf-ball maker Titleist combined to guarantee him a reported $43 million during the next five years for product endorse-ments. Even though golf lacks basketball's mass popularity, Woods could be the sport's Michael Jordan. To be Jordanesque, however, a player in any sport has to be like Mike: the best ever. Woods, whose mighty 330-yard drives are among the longest balls ever hit in pro competition, just may be.

You Gotta Have Joe

As the song from Broadway's *Damn Yankees* insists, you gotta have heart. New York Yankee manager **JOE TORRE**, a 32-year baseball veteran, has heart—and now so does Joe's brother Frank, who underwent a successful heart transplant in a New York City hospital the day before the sixth game of a thrilling World Series, in which an emotional Joe led his team to a come-from-behind victory over the tough Atlanta Braves. The secret? Torre's Yanks weren't damned; they were blessed—for Joe's sister Marguerite, a Roman Catholic nun, was praying for them.

Poland's Poetic Prizewinner

The judges of the Nobel Prize for Literature wield a spotlight that can illuminate the work of little-known writers for a worldwide audience. Such was the fate of the obscure Polish poet and critic Wislawa Szymborska, 73, who in 1996 was named the ninth woman writer to win the Prize. The Nobel judges particularly praised her ability to combine lyricism with simplicity of expression, citing the concluding image in the last stanza of her 1980 poem *Nothing Twice:*

> *With smiles and kisses, we prefer*
> *To seek accord beneath our star*
> *Although we're different*
> *(we concur)*
> *Just as two drops of water are.*

Szymborska passed through a long evolution as a poet, repudiating her early poems, written in the '50s in the state-approved Social Realism style, to turn to the luminous, sometimes mordant verse for which she received the Nobel.

Love Among the Coloring Books

You must remember this: a kiss is not a kiss—no, it's sexual harassment. Or at least it was when six-year-old Lothario **JOHNATHAN PREVETTE** of Lexington, North Carolina (pop. 16,583), laid a smacker on the cheek of a fellow first grader. The reason: partly because Johnathan liked her and partly because (he says) she asked for it. But a teacher saw the romantic deed, the girl complained, and the boy was barred from his classes for a day, causing him to miss not only color-

ing, but playtime and an ice-cream party. Initially, school officials said the boy had broken written rules against sexual harassment. Later, in the face of national derision, they backed down.

And Now—Jacko Junior?

Which would be worse: Having a dad who wears mascara or having LaToya as your aunt? Soon someone may have to deal with this very unusual dilemma. **MICHAEL JACKSON**, whose life must be considered one of the most bizarre of the 20th century, got married for the second time in early November, only a week after startling the world by declaring he was going to be a father. Exactly how the pregnancy happened was unclear. Bride **DEBBIE ROWE, 37**, a longtime friend of Jackson's who is a nurse for his dermatologist, was reported by a British tabloid as saying she had been artificially inseminated, but Jackson denied this. He also insisted she isn't being paid for carrying Jacko Jr., though there's speculation that she's getting as much as $500,000. The wedding took place in a secret midnight ceremony in Sydney, Australia. "I am thrilled that I will soon be a father and am looking forward with great anticipation to having this child," the onetime boy singing sensation said in a statement. "This is my dream come true." Ah, if only one could buy psychotherapy futures.

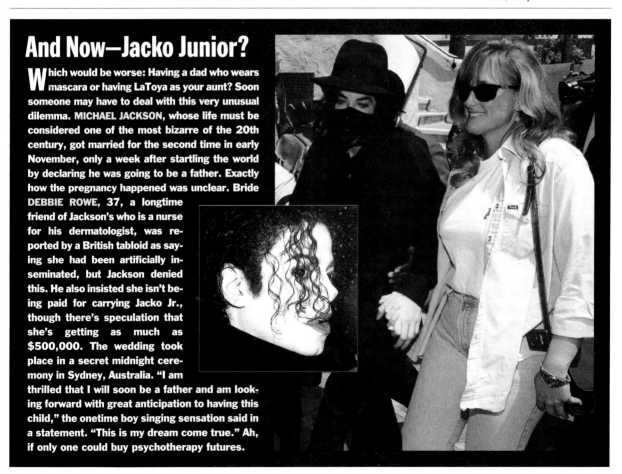

Say Goodnight, George

In his century, George Burns conquered vaudeville, Hollywood, radio and TV

Burns used a stogie as his straight man

"RETIRE?" GEORGE BURNS POSED the rhetorical question to himself during a tribute on his 90th birthday. "I'm going to stay in show business until I'm the only one left." He lasted another decade, but by the time Burns died in March at 100 his prophecy had in a sense come true. He was the last of a generation of comics who grew up in vaudeville, helped inaugurate the era of sound films and radio, and embodied during the television age a style of comedy that has been celebrated or satirized—often both—by virtually every comedian since.

His raspy voice, wryly unflappable manner and ever present cigar were trademarks as familiar as Chaplin's cane or Lucy's red hair. Burns was not a particularly influential or groundbreaking comic, like Groucho Marx or Jack Benny. But no one commanded the stage with more easygoing—and, as the years went on, inspiring—authority. He was 62 when his wife and longtime partner Gracie Allen retired, but his career was barely past its midpoint. He went on to even greater success in nightclubs, television and movies. His longevity became fodder for his comedy. "It's nice to be here," he would announce. "At my age, it's nice to be anywhere." Years in advance, he scheduled a 100th birthday appearance, first at the London Palladium, then in Las Vegas. But after a bathtub fall in 1994, his condition deteriorated, and he spent the occasion at home.

He was born Nathan Birnbaum on New York City's Lower East Side, one of 12 children. By his teens he was doing anything he could to break into vaudeville, from trick roller-skating to performing with a trained seal. He did comedy routines with a series of partners, changing his name with each new act—because, he claimed, the booker would never have rehired him if he knew who he was. In 1923 he teamed with Gracie, a young Irish-American actress

and dancer, whom he married three years later. At first Burns did the jokes and Allen played it straight, but that was soon corrected. George's indulgent prodding of Gracie's flighty non sequiturs and malapropisms helped make them the most popular male-female comedy act of the century. He always credited Allen with being the "genius" and deprecated his own sizable contribution.

In 1929 Burns and Allen appeared in their first movie short, and went on to make a string of successful films. But radio was their real metier: beginning in 1932 their CBS show was among the most popular in the country. Switching to TV in 1950, *The George Burns and Gracie Allen Show* ran for eight years as a quaint mixture of vaudeville and sitcom: Burns would speak directly to the camera, narrating the story, and each program ended with a stand-up routine, topped off with George's inevitable "Say good night, Gracie." The series ended in 1959 when Allen retired; in 1964 she died of heart disease.

GEORGE BURNS 1896-1996 (WITH GRACIE ALLEN)

George was wryly impervious to Gracie's flighty non sequiters

Forced to reinvent himself as a solo performer, Burns tried a couple of TV sitcoms, which failed to catch on, but soon found new life as a performer in nightclubs and on TV variety shows. Wielding his cigar as a silent straight man—a puff between punch lines—he regaled audiences with show-biz anecdotes and obscure songs. He launched an improbable third career in 1975, with his turn as an aging vaudevillian in Neil Simon's *The Sunshine Boys.* Burns' droll performance opposite Walter Matthau won him an Oscar for Best Supporting Actor and led to other roles, most notably the wisecracking deity in *Oh, God!* and its two sequels.

As he outlived most of his contemporaries, Burns' age became a surefire running gag. On his dating life: "I would go out with women my age. But there are no women my age." Near the end, he admitted that "things haven't been the same" since his bathtub accident. "I'm still an optimist," he added. "But I'm not stupid. That nurse isn't watching me all day to see if my toupee is on straight." ∎

Farewell to "Mama Jazz"

With her songs—and her songbooks—Ella Fitzgerald left a timeless legacy

I SING LIKE I FEEL," ELLA FITZGERALD WOULD SAY. By that casual standard, it was a wonderful life. She sang some of the best music ever written in America, and, feeling it, she sang it wonderfully. For many, indeed, she sang it definitively. "I never knew how good our songs were," Ira Gershwin once remarked, "until I heard Ella Fitzgerald sing them."

By the time she died at home in Beverly Hills at 78, she had spread the treasure of her voice over thousands of songs and half a dozen generations, cutting all of us in on the wonder. There was something in her voice that glistened, that refracted off an up-tempo number like a sudden shot of sun or shone off a ballad like a sidling beam of moonlight.

She started singing with Chick Webb's Big Band in the mid-'30s, when she was still a teenager, and later did a lot of swinging and scatting with Dizzy Gillespie. But it was her collaboration in the '50s with producer-manager Norman Granz on a benchmark series of "songbook" albums that gave Fitzgerald the musical regentship that never passed from her. "The Cole Porter Songbook," she claimed, "was a turning point in my life."

Together—and often working with the brilliant arranging skills of Nelson Riddle—Fitzgerald and Granz then went on to songbooks for the likes of Jerome Kern, George and Ira Gershwin, Harold Arlen, Duke Ellington, Richard Rodgers and Lorenz Hart, Irving Berlin and Johnny Mercer—the great composers of the great era of American popular music. Those songbooks became the foundation of a legacy, the single source for a musical standard that Fitzgerald, as much as anyone, helped make

ELLA FITZGERALD 1918-1996

A voice like a sudden shot of sun or a sidling beam of moonlight

timeless. "Some kids in Italy call me 'Mama Jazz,'" she recalled. "I thought that was so cute. As long as they don't call me 'Grandma Jazz.'"

Born in Newport News, Virginia, Ella Fitzgerald never knew her biological father. According to a biographer, she was raised in Yonkers, New York, and fled her abusive stepfather after her mother died, making money by singing and dancing on the sidewalks of Harlem and warning prostitutes of the arrival of the police. At 16, dressed in cast-off clothes and wearing men's boots, she won an amateur-night contest at the Apollo Theater. When she was brought to Chick Webb's attention, he complained, "I don't want that old ugly thing!" But he took her.

She married and divorced twice. Her first husband was Benny Kornegay, a shipyard worker; her second the jazz bassist Ray Brown. In the past decade, her many illnesses had seemed incompatible with the bell-like clarity of her voice. She was performing as late as 1992, but the physical debilitation was crushing, aggravated mostly by the diabetes that led to the amputation of her legs below the knees in 1993.

Shy onstage, ill at ease in interviews, Fitzgerald let her songs do all the talking. As a performer, even to someone hearing her for the first time, she was an old friend. Talk about Ella and no further I.D. was required. "It used to bother me when people I didn't know came up and called me Ella," she admitted once. "It seemed to me they should say Miss Fitzgerald, but somehow they never do." She had, simply, become a part of the life of everyone who listens to music, part of a shared tradition that will never pass. ∎

Eternally, Singin' in the Rain

Gene Kelly took America by storm with robust athletic exuberance

Showers of joy

FRED ASTAIRE WAS WHITE TIE and tails; Gene Kelly was white socks and loafers—often enough with his cuffs casually rolled up so we could better appreciate the flash of his footwork. If the sinuous elegance of his great (and friendly) rival shone most brilliantly on the polished surface of a ballroom floor, Kelly's robust athleticism seemed to rise most exuberantly from a gritty city sidewalk. Astaire put us in touch with our romantic ideals and with that perfection of manner the rest of us attain only in blissful daydreams. At his best, Kelly reminded us that, in reality, we are obliged to improvise our happiness with such rough materials as fall to hand.

One of his most memorable partnerships was with his shadow self (in *Cover Girl*); another was with a cartoon mouse (in *Anchors Aweigh*). He danced on roller skates and garbage-can lids (*It's Always Fair Weather*). And then, of course, there was that umbrella, that downpour, that bepuddled street and that befuddled cop, out of which he and Stanley Donen, his creative partner in all these enterprises, created *Singin' in the Rain's* signature sequence—and one of the movies' most privileged moments.

There is no Ginger Rogers linked immortally to Kelly's name, and that's no accident. For he was a solipsist who did not share the screen easily with anyone. Suspiciously good at playing hammy, self-serving show folks, he sometimes made you wonder: Is he exercising egocentricity or satirizing it?

Maybe a little of both. But, sooner rather than later, his "irresistible Irish-American charm" and his "overwhelming, unstoppable energy" (Donen's phrases) blew away your reser-

vations. For there was always something disarming in the forthright way that Kelly, who was born in Pittsburgh, Pennsylvania, the third of five children, and worked his way up out of the chorus line to Broadway stardom with his tough, taut performance in 1940's *Pal Joey,* stated his needs and his aspirations. While Rodgers and Hammerstein were reimagining the stage musical, he sought to reinvent the movie musical. Like them, he saw no reason why song and dance should not reflect the realities of everyday life—and at the same time illuminate our everynight dream life.

When Kelly and Donen, co-directing for the first time, took a company to New York City in 1949 to film some of the musical numbers for *On the Town*—the story of three horny sailors on shore leave—on actual locations ranging from the Brooklyn Navy Yard to Rockefeller Center, it was a first. When toward the end of the picture they inserted a jazzy, muscular but definitely balletic dream sequence, it was an equally significant innovation. No longer did filmmakers have to invent implausible backstage stories or silly never-never lands in order to provide a plausible environment for performers to sing and dance in.

GENE KELLY 1912-1996

"Irresistible Irish charm ... [and] overwhelming, unstoppable energy."

When Gene Kelly died at 83, he left us to contemplate certain ironies. Despite his long life, he was granted only the few years of the movie musical revival in which to assert his genius as a dancer. And for all the effort he and directors like Vincente Minnelli put into balletomanic spectaculars like the 20 minutes that conclude *An American in Paris*, it is the sweet simple things like *I Got Rhythm*—just Kelly, some cute kids, a cobblestone street in Montmartre, a catchy little Gershwin tune—that lived most affectingly in memory. But this, too, is true: we could not have had the one without the other.

Together, the complexity of Kelly's ambitions and the underlying innocence of his spirit constitute the inextricable weave of this dear man's singularity. ∎

Dr. Tim's Last Trip

Psychedelic prophet Timothy Leary "de-animated" in his usual high style

TUNE IN. IT'S SUNDAY AFTERNOON, ST. PATRICK'S Day, 1996, and traditional Celtic music is wafting through the air outside a Benedict Canyon ranch home high above Beverly Hills, California. Inside, musicians are serenading an Irish philosopher as he lies dying in bed among linens that depict cartoon rocket ships zooming over planets. Throughout the afternoon and well into the night, visitors come to pay their respects: a grandchild, filmmaker Oliver Stone, Rastas, slackers, alternative rocker Perry Farrell, Webheads. "I run a salon," says Timothy Leary. "Throughout human history, the salon has always been a fermenting place where creative people meet."

Indeed, Leary's recent guest list is both eclectic and electric: Yoko Ono, goddaughter Winona Ryder, former Mama Michelle Phillips, dolphin researcher John Lilly, onetime Dodger catcher Johnny Roseboro, the widow of Aldous Huxley, and Ram Dass, who used to be Leary's old Harvard bud Richard Alpert.

While the concept of a salon may be traditional, this particular one can only be described as "late-century cyberpunk frat." The garage is less a garage than a World Wide Web command post. In the living room are a video-game power glove, the latest issue of *Rolling Stone* and a Yoda mask. The dining room is dominated by a psychedelic poster from an old Don Knotts movie. But the master bedroom, which Leary refers to as his "de-animation room," is the strangest place of all. Amid the clutter of bills, floral bouquets, newspaper clippings, medical journals and stash boxes is Leary's deathbed, and on either side of it are a huge tank of laughing gas and an Apple computer. Bathing the Mac in red light is that hippie relic, the lava lamp.

Turn on. In this instance, one of Leary's friends adjusts the valve of the nitrous-oxide tank, and a balloon inflates. Leary takes a hit off the balloon, and his eyes roll back into his skull. The laughing gas eases the

TIMOTHY LEARY, 1920-1996

"All my life I've hated legal drugs and loved illegal ones."

intense pain he feels in his hip. "All my life, I've hated the legal drugs and loved illegal ones," he says when he comes back to earth. Of course, laughing gas isn't his only remedy. There are injections of Dilaudid, doses of hallucinogens, various vials of white powder, a pack of Benson & Hedges and a daily highball. "I'm an Irishman," he declares. "I can handle my liquor!"

Some may have dismissed the gaunt and frail-looking 75-year-old suffering from prostate cancer as just another artifact from the psychedelic era. But there was a time when Leary's "Tune in, turn on, drop out" was the mantra of a generation. People have forgotten how influential the onetime Harvard lecturer was and how dangerous the government considered him. It wasn't just the kids who fell under the spell of Leary and LSD but Establishment figures as well: Cary Grant and Steve Allen, not to mention the co-founder of TIME magazine, Henry Luce.

The beginning of the end, though, came in 1966 when a Dutchess County (New York) assistant D.A. named G. Gordon Liddy raided Leary's Millbrook mansion, which the doctor used courtesy of an Andrew Mellon heir. Two minor-possession arrests eventually landed Leary in a California prison in 1970, but he escaped with the help of the radical Weather Underground, then materialized among the Black Panthers in Algeria. Betrayed and recaptured in 1973, Leary spent most of the next three years in prison. When he was released, he turned his attention to vaudeville—a debate circuit with Watergate figure and old nemesis Liddy. His final years were spent trading on nostalgia for lava lamps, dealing with cancer doctors, hosting salons—and staging his very public death in cyberspace.

Leary's last lucid conversation was apparently with author William Burroughs, to whom he said, "I hope someday I'm as funny as you." Two months after St. Patrick's Day, Timothy Leary dropped out for good. ■

SPIRO AGNEW, 77, former Vice President. A moderate Republican Governor of Maryland, Agnew was chosen by Richard Nixon as the G.O.P. vice-presidential candidate in 1968. In Nixon's calculus, Agnew was a safe bet, a border-state novice with no heavy baggage and a Greek-immigrant father, which would help with the ethnic vote. As Vice President, Agnew played a menacing though semisatirical rabble-rouser of the much maligned love-it-or-leave-it Silent Majority. With the help of White House speechwriters Pat Buchanan and William Safire, Agnew developed a distinctive, jeering speech style that mixed some heavy fun into the contempt, lampooning the "effete corps of impudent snobs," the "nattering nabobs of negativism," and "hopeless, hysterical hypochondriacs of history." A month after the second Nixon-Agnew Inaugural, it came out that a grand jury in Baltimore was investigating Agnew on charges of bribery and tax evasion dating from his earlier career in Maryland. In October 1973 he pleaded no contest to one count of income-tax evasion and resigned his office—the only Vice President ever to be forced from office for legal reasons. A Maryland civil court found in 1981 that Agnew had solicited $147,500 in bribes as Baltimore county executive and as Governor—and that he had accepted the final $17,500 in cash when he was Vice President. Agnew vanished from public life, re-emerging briefly to attend Nixon's funeral in 1994.

MEL ALLEN, 83, sportscaster whose tenor-toned Alabama drawl became the voice of the New York Yankees.

MARTIN BALSAM, 76, actor. Born in the Bronx in New York City, Balsam went from the career-minting Actors Studio to live '50s TV to the movies, where he became a star portraying men who would never be stars. He was an uncertain juror in *Twelve Angry Men* (1957); a doomed detective in *Psycho* (1960); and a hardworking family man at odds with his unreliable brother in *A Thousand Clowns* (1965), the role that earned Balsam an Oscar for Best Supporting Actor.

MELVIN BELLI, 88, flamboyant personal-injury and defense attorney dubbed

the King of Torts. Belli pioneered the use of "demonstrative evidence" (unveiling an artificial limb, baring a client's disfigurement) to win over juries, and represented televangelist Jim Bakker and Jack Ruby, the killer of Lee Harvey Oswald.

JEAN-BEDEL BOKASSA, 75, ex–Central African President and self-proclaimed Emperor who ruled for 13 years as one of Africa's most brutal despots. His lavish, bizarre and murderous ways embarrassed his chief patron, France, which finally helped depose him in 1979.

JOSEPH CARDINAL BERNARDIN

The Archbishop of Chicago and a major influence in shaping modern American Catholicism, Bernardin was a skilled yet humble conciliator, steering a course between social progressivism and traditional church doctrine. When a former seminarian accused him of sexual abuse, Bernardin calmly denied the charges until his accuser recanted—and then the Cardinal said a Mass for his accuser when he died. After he learned in June 1995 that he had terminal pancreatic cancer, Bernardin, 68, faced death with a courage and grace that attracted admirers of all faiths; 250,000 attended his visitation.

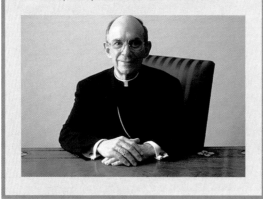

ERMA BOMBECK, 69, humorist. The titles of her books spoke volumes about her view of motherhood, housewifery and life: *I Lost Everything in the Post-Natal Depression; The Grass Is Always Greener over the Septic Tank.* Starting at $3 a column in 1964, she eventually appeared in 600 papers, but still lived the unpretentious life she wrote of, laughing through travail.

HAROLD BRODKEY, 65, famously self-absorbed *New Yorker* writer whose first novel took 27 years to deliver. His massive work was finally published in 1991 as *The Runaway Soul,* to mixed reviews.

JOSEPH BRODSKY, 55, exiled Russian poet, 1987 Nobel prizewinner and poet laureate of his adopted U.S. Brodsky's 1964 Soviet trial for "parasitism," prompted by the underground distribution of his works, made him a cause célèbre in the West and led to his expulsion in 1972. His intense verses, filled with images of loss and wandering, won him wide acclaim and America's highest honor for poetry in 1991.

MARCEL CARNE, 90, French film director. Cárne's *Les Enfants du Paradis* (1945), made in collaboration with poet and screenwriter Jacques Prévert, is widely considered one of the best films ever made.

JOHN CHANCELLOR, 68, for four decades an NBC *News* reporter, anchor and commentator. During a wide-ranging career, Chancellor covered the 1957 Little Rock, Arkansas, school-integration crisis, served as Moscow correspondent and interviewed every U.S. President since Harry Truman. He also served briefly as Voice of America director.

CLAUDETTE COLBERT, 92, effervescent star of an earlier Hollywood. In films that included such classic comedies as *It Happened One Night* (for which she won an Oscar) and *The Palm Beach Story,* she became the epitome of couture elegance and city-girl pluck. The Colbert heroine walked the earth in sensible shoes and met each adversity with a throaty, musical laugh. Sophisticated but not stuffy, a superior creature who never condescended, she flummoxed leading men into stammering or spouting purple prose by wielding the comeback, the put-down, the come-on, all in one sprightly barrage. "I can say immodestly that I'm a very good comedienne," Colbert told TIME in 1981. "But I was always fighting that image too. I just never had the luck to play bitches."

SEYMOUR CRAY, 71. A brilliant and legendarily eccentric electronics engineer who put together an automatic telegraph machine when he was 10 years old, Cray built in the 1960s what many consider the world's first supercomputers.

MARGUERITE DURAS, 81, writer. The author of 35 novels, she frequently used the land of her birth, colonial French Indochina, for her spare but expressive portraits of the redemptive and destructive power of love, like 1984's autobiographical *L'Amant (The Lover)*.

VINCE EDWARDS, 67, actor. As Dr. Ben Casey, he was surly, sarcastic, short-tempered—and that's just how he treated his co-stars. Yet TV viewers in the 1960s couldn't get enough of the neuro-surgeon, or of Edwards, who portrayed the combative Casey as the polar opposite of his ratings rival, the saintly Doctor Kildare (played by Richard Chamberlain).

SHUSAKU ENDO, 73, widely acclaimed Japanese novelist who was popular in the West and often ranked with his fellow Catholic, Graham Greene. Author of *Deep River* and *Scandal and Silence*, Endo focused on faith and the clash of cultures.

PAUL ERDOS, 83, quirky Hungarian-American mathematician with more than 1,500 papers to his name. Erdos died of a heart attack while living homeless, by choice, in Warsaw.

MAX FACTOR, 92, the Hollywood cosmetics genius who invented, named and marketed many of the most basic elements of modern makeup, including lipstick, waterproof mascara, body paint, pancake, stick and liquid foundation. Born Frank Factor, the fourth child of the original Max Factor, he took the name when his father, also a pioneer of cosmetics, died in 1938.

CHARLIE FINLEY, 77, over-the-top owner of baseball's Kansas City and Oakland A's. He became known for his innovations, such as the designated hitter, nighttime World Series games and colored uniforms.

GREER GARSON, 92, Oscar-winning actress. Once described by TIME as "a goddess sculpted in butterscotch," the Irish-born Garson specialized in playing noble, tender, poised women—"walking cathedrals," she called them—like Mrs. Chips in *Goodbye, Mr. Chips* and the title role in *Mrs. Miniver*, for which she won her Oscar.

MARGAUX HEMINGWAY, 41, model and actress. Defined by her beauty and her family's celebrity, (she was Ernest's granddaughter), Hemingway burst onto the modeling scene in the mid '70s as a fresh-faced, 6-ft. 19-year-old from Ketchum, Idaho. In 1975 she appeared on the cover of TIME to illustrate a story on new beauties. But after failing to establish herself as a movie star, she struggled with bulimia and alcoholism, and declared bankruptcy in 1991. Her death was ruled suicide by a Los Angeles County coroner.

BARBARA JORDAN, 59, ground-breaking Congresswoman. The first African-American woman from the South to

ALGER HISS

Despite the thousands of words written by and about him, Alger Hiss, who died in November at 92, remains one of the most tantalizing figures of the cold war. The 1949 trial and retrial of the former Supreme Court clerk, Wall Street lawyer and government bureaucrat in a Soviet-espionage case personified the explosive political conflicts of the red-baiting era. And the case gave national prominence to one of its investigators, Congressman Richard Nixon. Hiss's first trial for perjury ended in a hung jury; he was found guilty at a second trial, and eventually served 44 months in a federal prison. To a dwindling band of zealous believers, Hiss was one of the first victims of anticommunist hysteria. Yet the weight of historical evidence indicates that Hiss was what he steadfastly denied ever being: a member of the communist underground and a Soviet spy.

serve in the House since Reconstruction, Jordan sat on the Judiciary Committee that weighed the impeachment of President Richard Nixon. Her voice and eloquent reverence for the law lent an Old Testament *gravitas* to the proceedings—and made her a Democratic star. She left Congress after 1978 to devote the rest of her career to teaching.

LINCOLN KIRSTEIN, 88, author and arts patron. If George Balanchine made American dance possible, it was Kirstein who made Balanchine possible, bringing the Russian choreographer to the U.S. in the '30s and co-creating the School of American Ballet and New York City Ballet.

RENE LACOSTE, 92, French 1920s tennis champion and founder of the sports-wear firm that bears his name. Called "le Crocodile" for his tenacity on the court, he turned the reptilian nickname into a yuppie icon.

DOROTHY LAMOUR, 81, actress who took to the road—sometimes sporting only her signature sarong—with Bing Crosby and Bob Hope. Though she starred in more than 50 movies, Lamour won over audiences—especially World War II G.I.s—with the seven *Road* films she made with Crosby and Hope.

MARY LEAKEY, 83, archaeologist. She was an unschooled, 20-year-old part-time illustrator and amateur archaeologist in 1933 when she met Louis Leakey, already a famous scientist, 10 years her senior, who was married with two children. They fell in love, created a scandal, got married and moved to Africa. By the time of her death Mary Leakey's scientific reputation had surpassed that of her husband. In 1948 she discovered part of the jaw and skull fragments of a creature called *Proconsul africanus*, then widely thought to be a human ancestor (though now considered more closely related to the apes). In 1959 at a favorite digging spot, Olduvai Gorge in Tanzania, she found two brown fossilized molars, which turned out to be from the skull of a 1.75 million-year-old human ancestor the Leakeys called *Zinjanthropus* ("Man from East Africa"). In 1978 at a different site in Tanzania Mary found the unmistakable footprints of a human ancestor, possibly *Australopithecus afarensis*, in the region's 3.6 million-year-old volcanic ash. The cigar-smoking, whiskey-drinking Leakey was revered as the "grande dame of archaeology."

FRANCES LEAR, 73, outspoken feminist and magazine editor. Married for 28 years to TV producer Norman Lear (and believed to be the model for the title character of his sitcom *Maude*), she used part of her splashy $100 million 1985 divorce settlement to found the short-lived *Lear's*, a magazine "for the woman who wasn't born yesterday."

MARCELLO MASTROIANNI, 72, film actor. The postheroic hero, Mastroianni defined the European male in all his charm, complexity, failure. Husband and lover, deft comedian and suavest delineator of atomic-age anomie—there was a Marcello for every sexual taste, every moral mood. For half a century he starred in more than 120 pictures, including star turns in the Fellini classics *La Dolce Vita* and 8½. Born in Fontana Liri, 50 miles outside Rome, Mastroianni did time in a German labor camp during World War II, then escaped to Venice and later to Luchino Visconti's famed Milan theater troupe. He was the greatest Latin lover on the screen since Rudolph Valentino.

RAY McINTIRE, 77, Dow chemist who inadvertently invented Styrofoam in a 1944 experiment.

BROWNIE McGHEE, 80, guitarist-singer. McGhee and harmonica player Sonny Terry brought the folk-flavored blues of the Carolina Piedmont to the world, influencing generations of rockers, folkies and bluesmen.

AUDREY MEADOWS, 71, actress. She began her career as a soprano on Broadway. Then in 1952 she became Alice on *The Honeymooners.* Meadows and co-star Jackie Gleason (who died in 1987) made that sitcom a peak experience of American pop culture. Meadows as Alice Kramden was slight, cool, drolly down-to-earth. She imbued Alice with prefeminist feistiness that rendered ridiculous Ralph's boisterous threats of domestic violence.

CHRISTOPHER ROBIN MILNE, 75, model for the Christopher Robin character in his father A.A.'s books about the adventures of Christopher's teddy bear, Winnie-the-Pooh. He grew up to resent his notoriety.

JOSEPH MITCHELL, 87, writer and journalist. In prose both vivid and wry, Mitchell, a *New Yorker* regular for most of his career, chronicled the city's more unconventional citizens, from workers at the Fulton Fish Market to the Mohawk Indians who toiled as high-altitude construction crews.

JESSICA MITFORD, 78, muckraking journalist and best-selling author. In her quest to "embarrass the guilty," Mitford wrote such devastating satires as *The American Way of Death,* 1969. She was disinherited from her aristocratic and eccentric British family after eloping with a second cousin in 1936. Her eldest sister was the novelist Nancy Mitford.

FRANCOIS MITTERRAND, 79, former President of France. The son of a railroad employee turned vinegar producer, Mitterrand went to Paris to study law in 1934. Drafted at the outbreak of World War II, he was imprisoned by the Germans in 1940. He escaped, then co-

ROGER TORY PETERSON

The world's most famous birder and the man who single-handedly opened up ornithology to the masses, Peterson provided a visual vocabulary so useful that it is difficult to imagine how people ever looked at the natural world without it. His breakthrough occurred with 1934's *A Field Guide to the Birds,* which combined the two passions of his childhood: looking at birds and painting. The revolutionary pocket-size guide grouped the birds by look rather than species and included brief, no-nonsense avian descriptions. Peterson, 87, opened up the natural world to millions who might otherwise have gone through life seeing only fluttering shapes and colors.

founded a Resistance group with a network of ex-prisoners in 1943. After the liberation, he was elected to the National Assembly, and between 1947 and 1957 held 11 Cabinet positions. During a quarter-century in opposition, he forged the French Socialist Party from the fragments of the non-Communist left. In 1981 he finally captured the presidency and launched a veritable revolution, nationalizing banks, raising the minimum wage and installing a wealth tax. In foreign policy, though instinctively hostile to U.S. domination, he nonetheless proved a staunch ally at critical moments like the 1991 Gulf War. He threw his weight behind the cause of European integration, with the Franco-German axis as its motor. Mitterrand also launched some $6 billion worth of instant landmarks, firmly placing his imprint on the Paris skyline. The disastrous defeat of the Socialists in 1993 tarnished the closing moments of his career.

BILL MONROE, 84, singer, mandolin virtuoso and father of bluegrass music. His chiseled demeanor gave him the aura of a patriarch, and indeed Monroe was one of those rare artists who sired a musical genre. In 1938 he formed his first band, calling it the Blue Grass Boys after his home state, Kentucky. The group soon took on the bluegrass configuration of mandolin, fiddle, guitar, bass and banjo, paired with the near-falsetto harmonies that Monroe called his "high, lonesome sound."

GERRY MULLIGAN, 69, the premier baritone saxophonist and a leading composer-arranger of the past four decades, who oversaw the birth of "cool" jazz with Miles Davis in 1947. Mulligan defied classification, playing and writing with a distinctive pulse, wit and imagination.

EDMUND MUSKIE, 81, erstwhile Democratic Governor, Senator and Secretary of State. His rangy physique and reputation for plain dealing bestowed upon the son of a Polish immigrant the life-long label "Lincolnesque." The image propelled Muskie to two terms in the Maine statehouse and 21 years in the U.S. Senate. There, his environmental concerns earned Muskie the nickname "Mr. Clean," part of a low-key liberalism that landed him the V.P. slot on the Democrats' failed 1968 ticket. But the presidential nomination eluded Muskie four years later. He left the Senate in 1980 to serve as Secretary of State in the final months of the Carter Administration.

HAING S. NGOR, 55, doctor-actor. Ngor was shot to death outside his home in Los Angeles. No one missed the irony: he had survived four years in the slaughterhouse of Khmer Rouge Cambodia during the '70s, only to be struck down in the violence of an American city. In between he won an Oscar for his portrayal of fellow survivor and photojournalist Dith Pran in the 1984 movie *The Killing Fields.*

DAVID PACKARD, 83, electronics and computer pioneer. Packard and his Stanford University classmate William Hewlett opened a workshop in a garage in 1939. Today Hewlett-Packard is the nation's second largest computer maker (behind IBM). Packard eschewed corporate pomposity; his personable style and civic activism inspired a generation of hackers. His entire fortune of some $4.3 billion was placed in a charitable trust.

VANCE PACKARD, 82, critic of American consumerism whose 1957 best seller *The Hidden Persuaders* exposed the advertising technique of using subliminal messages to sell products.

ANDREAS PAPANDREOU, 77, the first Socialist Prime Minister of Greece. He was democrat and demagogue, a man whose doctrinaire ideology and fist-in-the-air oratory could just as often inflame an audience as inform it. He parlayed a virulent anti-Americanism to power, delayed only by a military coup that imprisoned, then exiled, him. He became Prime Minister in 1981 and, despite resigning in January because of illness, was the central political figure of Greece until his death.

MINNIE PEARL, 83, comedian. Offstage she was Sarah Ophelia Colley Cannon, the elegant, sophisticated neighbor of Governors. But onstage she was the country cutup whose raucous "Howww-dee!," price-tag-bedecked hat ($1.98) and 50-year search for a "feller" made her an institution at Nashville's Grand Ole Opry.

JULIET PROWSE, 59, leggy redheaded dancer who achieved fame in the 1960 movie musical *Can-Can.* Raised in South Africa and trained as a ballerina, Prowse made worldwide headlines when Soviet leader Nikita Khrushchev visited the Hollywood set of *Can-Can* and denounced the dancing as indecent. After her film career petered out, she went on to star in a series of TV specials.

PAUL RAND, 82, innovative graphic designer and creator of instantly recognizable corporate logos for IBM, ABC and UPS, among others. A devotee of

functionalism, Rand was one of the first to bring modern design's simplicity to commercial art.

MARIO SAVIO, 53, fiery, eloquent leader of the Free Speech Movement at the University of California, Berkeley, in the 1960s whose success inspired similar protests nationwide.

TUPAC SHAKUR, 25, rap star. Shakur was born in New York City into a nobility of violence: his mother, a Black Panther, was jailed on a bombing charge while she was pregnant with

CARL SAGAN

Though he was a widely respected planetary astronomer, Sagan, 62, was best known as a popularizer whose lectures, books and TV appearances brought the majesty of the universe to ordinary earthlings. His 1980 PBS series *Cosmos* attracted a global audience of more than 500 million people in 60 countries. A prolific writer, Sagan won a Pulitzer Prize in 1978 for *The Dragons of Eden,* a book on the evolution of human intelligence. He believed in the existence of extraterrestrial life and in humankind's need to colonize the universe. Said he: "We make our world significant by the courage of our questions and by the depth of our answers."

him, although she was later acquitted. His father was shot and killed when Tupac was a child. Their son, meanwhile, wrote sensitive poetry while attending the High School of Performing Arts in Baltimore, Maryland. Shakur became a gangsta rap star who sold more than 10 million albums. His life—and then his death—came to imitate his art. Shakur's songs were laced with sneers at "bitches" and the cop-killing taunts of gangstaism; he carried a gun and shot at people. He escaped conviction on a series of assault charges, but a 1993 sexual-abuse complaint stuck. He arrived for sentencing in a wheelchair;

days earlier, he had been shot five times in a Manhattan "robbery" he regarded as a failed hit. Shakur was cut down in a hail of bullets in Las Vegas while riding in a car driven by Marion ("Suge") Knight, the notorious president of Shakur's record label, Death Row. No arrests were made in the murder.

JERRY SIEGEL, 81, co-creator of *Superman.* In a single fateful bound in 1938, Siegel and his artist partner Joe Shuster sold their *Superman* rights to Detective Comics for a mere $130.

McLEAN STEVENSON, 66, actor. Stevenson starred in the first three seasons of the '70s television hit *M*A*S*H* as Lieut. Colonel Henry Blake, a fumbling fisherman-out-of-water who ruled over the blood and irony of an Army hospital during the Korean War.

CARL STOKES, 68, former big-city mayor. In 1967, when only 37% of Cleveland's electorate was black, Stokes was elected mayor with 50.5% of the vote. His distinction as the first African-American mayor of a major U.S. city would eclipse the subsequent highs of his life: stints as a TV anchorman in New York City and as ambassador to the Seychelles.

P.L. TRAVERS, 96, author. The real name of the writer of the *Mary Poppins* children's classics was Helen Lyndon Goff. She had been variously a dancer, a poet, a journalist, a theater critic and a Shakespearean actress before gaining fame with her invention of an authority figure who was acerbic, magical and wise.

DIANA TRILLING, 91, social and cultural critic who wrote of literary figures, the trial of Jean Harris and her marriage to writer-professor Lionel Trilling. She belonged to a Manhattan-based intellectual circle that thrived in the '30s, '40s and '50s and included Irving Howe, Saul Bellow, Mary McCarthy and Irving Kristol.

LAURENS VAN DER POST, 90, South African–born conservationist acclaimed for his books on Africa. Best-selling author of *The Lost World of the Kalahari* (1958), Van der Post was Prince Charles' guide to alternative lifestyles and non-Christian religions. ∎

INDEX

INDEX

CREDITS

Clockwise from top left, except as noted.

The Year in Review iv-v Porter Binks—AP/Wide World **1** Walter Weissman—Globe, Chris Bjornberg—Photo Researchers, Michael Gallacher—*Missoulian/Gamma* Liaison, J. Conrad Williams—*Newsday* **2-3** Ron Haviv—Saba, Mike Hewitt—AllSport **4-5** Robert Sagliocca—Photo Unit/FBI, N.Y., Jon Levy—Gamma Liaison **6-7** (left to right) Alexander Zemlianichenko—AP/Wide World, Victor Korotayev—Reuters/Archive Photos, Gamma Liaison, SIPA **8-9** Robert King—Sygma **10-11** Robert Allison—Contact Press Images, Christopher Morris—Black Star for TIME, Jean Marc Giboux—Gamma Liaison **12-13** James Nachtwey—Magnum for TIME **14-15** Illustrations, from left to right: Tim Bower, Daniel Adel, Drew Friedman, Glynis Sweeny (3), Mike Benny, Joseph Salina, Anita Kunz, Tim O'Brien, Scott Gurdley, David O'Keefe, James McMullen, Matt Mahurin, James Bennett, Theo Rudnak, Owen Smith **16-17** The Stock Market, Porter Gifford—Gamma Liaison, Robert Nicklesberg for TIME, Cynthia Johnson for TIME.

The Elections **18-19** Diana Walker for TIME **20-21** Ken Jarecki—Contact Press Images for TIME, Brooks Kraft—Sygma **22-23** Dirck Halstead for TIME, Diana Walker for TIME **24** Ted Soqui—Sygma, Porter Gifford—Gamma Liaison, Steve Lehman—Saba, Steve Liss for TIME, Dan Habib—Impact Visuals **24-25** Steve Liss for TIME **25** Alex Koester **26** Wally Santana—AP/Wide World, Wesley Hill for TIME **26-27** Dirck Halstead for TIME **28-29** P.F. Bentley for TIME, Diana Walker for TIME (2) **30-31** Diana Walker for TIME (3), P.F. Bentley for TIME

Nation **34** Michael Gallacher—*Missoulian/*Gamma Liaison **35** FBI/Saba **36** Evergreen Park H.S. Yearbook/AP/Worldwide, Carter Smith—Sygma, AP Wide World/family, AP/Wide World, Lewis and Clark County Assessor **37** AP/Wide World (2), SIPA (2) **38-39** J. Conrad Williams—*Newsday* **40** John Paraskevas—*Newsday* **42** R. Ellis—Sygma **43** Charles Rex Arbogast—AP/Wide World. **44-45** Les Stone—Sygma, Lynn Reese/Saba. **46** G. Castilla—Globe **47** Insurance Institute for Highway Safety (2) **48** Martin Simon—Saba, ABC News, Scott Peterson—Gamma Liaison for TIME **49** Terry Ashe for TIME, Jeffrey Lowe for TIME, Cynthia Johnson for TIME, Jane Beckman—Retna

World **50-51** Brodner—SIPA, Sergei Karpukhin—AP/Wide World **52** Vladimir Sichov—SIPA **53** Vladimir Sichov—SIPA, Sergei Guneyev for TIME, Shone—SIPA, Christopher Morris—Black Star for TIME **54-55** Greg Girard—Contact Press Images, Anat—AP/Wide World **56** Wayne W. Edwards- U.S. Navy/AP/Wide World, Kareem Sahib—AFP **57** Reuters, Saeed Khan—AP/Wide World **58** Alfred—SIPA

for TIME **59** Nati Shoat—Hash 90 **60** Srdjan Llic—AP/Wide World **61** Christopher Morris—Black Star for TIME **62** Murdo McLeod, Pascal Rossignol, Newsflash, Uimonen—Sygma **62-63** Verdienst—Sud Deutchen Verlag **63** Sherlyn Bjorkgren—Gamma Liaison, Thomas James Hurst

Business **64** Claudio Edinger—Saba **65** Ray Bartkus (art) **66** Ray Bartkus (art) **67** Marty Lederhandler—AP/World Wide **68-69** no credit **70** United Features Syndicate **71** Peter Charlesworth—Saba, no credit, Tim O'Brien (art), Courtesy Seagrams

Technology **72-73** C.F. Payne (art) **74** David Strick—Outline **75** Karen Moscowitz—Outline **76-77** Marc Rosenthal (art) **78** Shawn Mortenson—Outline **79** Adam Nadel, Brian Cronin (art), no credit (2)

Science **80** NASA **80-81** Chris Bjornberg—Photo Researchers **82-83** NASA **84** Ann States—Saba, Kelly Jordan—Sygma, David Strick—Outline **85** Hadj/Jobard, Farnood—SIPA, Eric Heinilla—Shooting Star **88-89** NASA Goddard Space Flight Center Laboratory for Atmosphere **90** David Strick for TIME **90-91** From the Smithsonian Traveling Exhibition *Yesterday's Tomorrows* **92** Lockheed Martin, *The Gold of Troy*—Abrams, Blake Little, Barray Iverson for TIME **93** David M. Phillips—Photo Researchers, Paul Dimas, Institute of Human Origins, John Meyer

Man of the Year **94-95** Gregory Heisler for TIME **96-97** Gregory Heisler for TIME **98** Institut Pasteur—CNR/SPL/Photo Researchers **100** Jeffrey D. Scott—Impact Visuals **101** Greg Girard—Contact Press Images for TIME **104-105** Anita Kunz (art)

Society **106-107** John F. Kennedy Library, The Mark Shaw Collection—Photo Researchers **108-109** Lisa Larsen—LIFE, no credit (7), **110-111** Neal Beidleman—Woodfin Camp & Assoc. **112** Photo: Ed Viesturs **113** AP/Wide World, Scott Fischer—Woodfin Camp & Assoc., Formasia, Scott Fischer—Woodfin Camp & Assoc. **114-115** Nicole Bengiveno—Matrix **116-117** John Chiasson—Gamma Liaison, Richard Pierce (2) **118** William Abranowicz, Bruce Wolf **118-119** Jessie Frohman—Outline **119** Christopher Baker—MARTHA STEWART LIVING **120-121** William Blake **122** William Brueghel **123** Hans Baldung **124** Andy Hayt/N.B.A./AllSport **124-125** Bill Smith **126** Polly Becker (art) **127** AP/Wide World, Brooks Kraft—Sygma, Scott Olson—Reuters, John Green—San Mateo County *Times*/Sygma

Olympics **128-29** Gerard Vandystadt—AllSport for TIME **129** Nathan Bilow—Allsport for Time **130** Michael Cooper—AllSport for TIME **130-131** David

Taylor—AllSport for TIME **131** AFP/DPA **132** Jose Azel—Aurora/Contact, Heinz Kluetmeier—SPORTS ILLUSTRATED **132-133** Heinz Kluetmeier—SPORTS ILLUSTRATED **134** Mike Powell—AllSport for TIME **135** Mike Powell—AllSport for TIME **136-137** Mike Powell—AllSport for TIME **137** David Burnett—Contact Press Images for TIME **138** Bruno Bade—Vandystadt/AllSport for TIME, Gary Prior—AllSport for TIME, V.J. Lovero—SPORTS ILLUSTRATED, Mike Hewitt—AllSport for TIME **139** Robert Beck—SPORTS ILLUSTRATED **140** Gary Prior—AllSport for TIME **141** Manny Millan—SPORTS ILLUSTRATED, Simon Bruty—AllSport for TIME, Mike Hewitt—AllSport for TIME, Jim Gund—SPORTS ILLUSTRATED **143** Ross Kinnaird—AllSport for TIME

Arts & Media **144** Private Collection—Paris **145** Erich Lessing—Art Resource **146-147** Philadelphia Museum of Art **147** Metropolitan Museum of Art, N.Y.C., H.O. Havemeyer Collection, Hermitage Museum, **148** Photofest **148-149** no credit **150** Curran—Showtime, Photofest **151** Drinkwater—NBC, Haston—NBC **152** Frank Micellota for TIME, Neil Calendra—LGI, Capital Pictures—LGI **153** Frank Micellota—Outline **154** Walter Weissman—Globe, Andrea Renault—Globe **155** Michael Witte (art) **156** Merrick Marton—20th Century Fox **157** Joan Marcus, Michael Daniel **158** Najlah Feanny—Saba, Matt Mendelsohn—Gamma Liaison, Andy Schwartz—Paramount

The Best of 1996 **159** David Cowles (art) **160** Phil Bray—Miramax (2), Miramax, J. Clifford—Rysher **61** Miramax, Appleby—Cinergi, Cooper—Tristar, October Films **162** Chuck Hodes, Patrick D. Pagano, Doug Hyun, no credit, Stephen Danelian —Outline, Ron Tom **163** Jack Vartoogian, Martyn Jones Gallena—LGI, Ken Franckeling—LGI, Chris Buck—Outline, CBS **164** T. Horan—Sygma, Everke—Gamma Liaison **165** Henry Groskinsky(2), Al Freni

People **166-167** Patrick Lichfield—Camera Press **167** LCPL—SIPA **168** Steve Finn—Globe **168-169** Jim Bennett—Rex **169** Cherrault—SIPA **170** Arnaud—Sygma, ©1996 Dennis Reggie **171** NASA—SIPA, *L'Osservatore Romano/*SIPA, Vince Bucci—AP/Wide World **172** Firooz Zahedi—Botaish Group, H. Miller—Zuma, James Keyser for Time, Michael Lloyd—*The Oregonian/*Sygma **173** Pressens Bild—SIPA, J. Wolford—Sygma, Chris Pizzello—AP/Wide World, News Ltd., Austra—Sygma

Milestones **174** Eddie Adams, AP/Wide World **175** Eliot Elisofon—LIFE **176** Memory Shop **177** Mojgan B. Azimi for TIME **178** James Schnepf—Gamma Liaison **179** UPI **180** Alfred Eisenstadt—LIFE **181** Peter Serling